IMAGES
of America

LEVITTOWN

VOLUME II

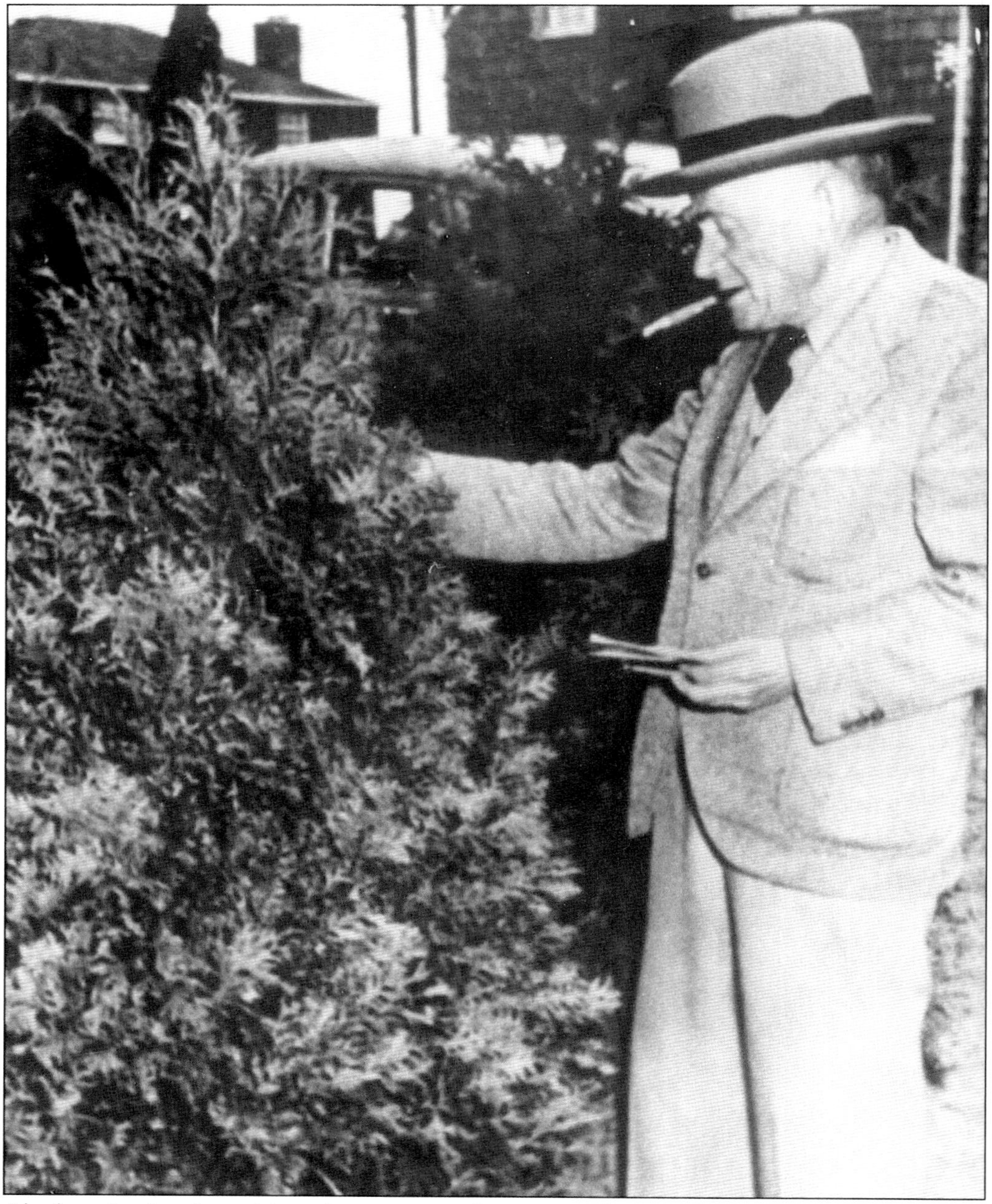

Abraham Levitt, dressed in a dapper suit with a cigar in his mouth, inspects an evergreen. A successful real estate lawyer and businessman, Levitt's true love seems to have been horticulture. His expertise was such that he supervised the selection and planting of shrubs throughout Levittown, and he later contributed articles to horticultural magazines. This attention to landscaping was somewhat unusual in new housing developments. Within a few years, Levittown had lost its barren look. A familiar sight to many of the "pioneers" was Abraham as he drove through Levittown in a white Cadillac to keep an eye on the plantings. Many early Levittowners recall that he would make note of trees or shrubs that had died and would dispatch a crew to plant a replacement. (Collection of the Levittown Library.)

IMAGES
of America

LEVITTOWN
VOLUME II

Margaret Lundrigan and Tova Navarra

ARCADIA
PUBLISHING

ISBN 978-0-7385-6229-2

Published by Arcadia Publishing
Charleston, South Carolina

Printed in the United States of America

Library of Congress Catalog Card Number: 2008933187

For all general information contact Arcadia Publishing at:
Telephone 843-853-2070
Fax 843-853-0044
E-mail sales@arcadiapublishing.com
For customer service and orders:
Toll-Free 1-888-313-2665

Visit us on the Internet at www.arcadiapublishing.com

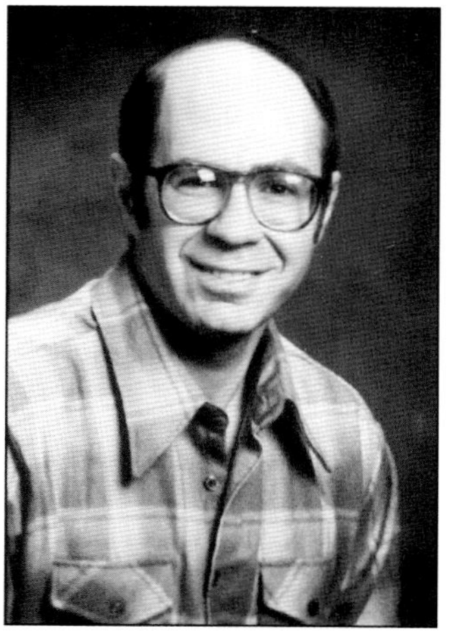

We dedicate this volume to our dear friend and colleague, Randall Gabrielan. Randall personifies love and devotion to local history, and has in fact referred to the pursuit of local history as "an inalienable right." He has written 18 volumes on the history of Monmouth County. He is presently engaged in writing several other volumes, including one that deals with local history in postcards, one on Brooklyn, and another on Wall Street and the financial district surrounding it. Randall is an avid collector of vintage postcards and old books, president of the Middletown Historical Society, and president of the Board of Trustees of the Middletown Library. We are personally indebted to Randall for his professional support, generous use of his collection, and his outstanding contributions toward greater awareness and appreciation of local history. He is a mentor and spiritual thinker who believes giving and receiving are the same, and touts the "psychic remuneration" for doing these books. In commemoration of his achievements, the Board of Chosen Freeholders of Monmouth County recently named September 10 "Randall Gabrielan Day," a rare and well-deserved accolade.

We would also like to dedicate this volume to our grandfathers, Daniel Farren and Albert Leslie, who believed their library cards were among their most valuable possessions.

—M.L. and T.N.

Contents

ACKNOWLEDGMENTS

As always, the authors would like to express sincere gratitude to the Levittown Library, not only for the generous use of their local history collection, but for their expert assistance in researching this volume. Special thanks go to Library Director P.W. Martin, Carol Price for the use of her private collection, and our friends Janet Spar and Ann Glorioso, who has recently taken the reins of the library's remarkable local history archive. We would also like to thank the general library and media room staff; the professionalism and courtesy of the staff sets a high standard of excellence. We were overjoyed to find pioneers Meta Smith, Dr. and Mrs. Cytryn, Sybil Rosenblum, and Lillian Weiss, whose assistance proved most worthwhile. Many thanks to Mary Ann Nuzzi, CPA, for sharing her heartwarming collection that spans the life of Levittown and for reproducing photographs (saving us so much valuable time for writing!). Many blessings to her for her deft annotation, which gives a "pioneer's view" of Levittown. Once again, we would like to thank our friends and original Levittowners Clare and Jerry Worthing for their continued support and generous use of their collection. We also thank newlywed Jane Arginteanu, who made singer/songwriter/composer Billy Joel's photograph contributions possible and to whom we extend all the best wishes. Thank you also to the following: television star Chris Burke; Arcadia staff members Rebecca Heflin, Amy Sutton, Heather Roy, Mark Berry, Katie White, Michael Guillory, and Kirsty Sutton; and, may they rest in peace, Abraham, William, and Alfred Levitt.

INTRODUCTION

Nearly a decade before the Levitts fought city hall and won the opportunity to build affordable homes, which was initially unacceptable in the region's housing industry because the Levitt homes had no basements, Americans experienced many dramatic transitions. Of the following changes, the last had the greatest impact on the young men and women who joined the armed forces: the 40-hour work week was established in America; popular songs included "Flat Foot Floogie with a Floy Floy" and "September Song," 1938; Nylon stockings became popular, and polyethylene was invented, 1939; Anna M. Robertson, known as "Grandma Moses," rose to fame, and John Steinbeck wrote Pulitzer Prize-winning novel *The Grapes of Wrath*, 1939; "Father of Psychiatry" Dr. Sigmund Freud, Irish poet William Butler Yeats Jr., and American actor Douglas Fairbanks died, 1939; Germany invaded Poland, which triggered World War II, 1939.

The 20th century also brought cataclysmic changes to the entire world. The advent of the automobile revolutionized travel and made possible the growth of the American suburb. But few places showed a transformation as complete—or as massive—as the one that occurred in Levittown. Everything about Levittown was different, from its name and appearance to its way of life. If time travel were possible, a time-traveler would have to be a keen observer to find any identifying landmark left from the blight-affected potato fields in the thousand lanes of small but expandable homes. Social critic and author Lewis Mumford and many other skeptics damned them immediately as "the slums of the future."

But just as Alfred Eisenstaedt snapped the famous photograph of the young sailor kissing a nurse on V-E Day 1945, the Levitts "kissed" their new charges and taught them what a turning point in history really means. Now many people could feel they were the luckiest people on Earth to leave overcrowded city apartments and have their own homes! Levittown was an American dream come true, and Levittowners proceeded dutifully to create a good environment for their families and their neighbors. "Anywhere, USA?" The critics were dead wrong. Instead, Levittown stepped into the role New Hampshire is known for politically: "As New Hampshire goes, so goes the country." The prototype suburban development was destined to become part of everyday knowledge. A strange and formidable set of circumstances put the former Long Island communities of Island Trees and Jerusalem on a course to become the first Levittown in the world.

Conceived as a plan to meet one of the most basic human needs, shelter, Levittown would go on to be one of the grand social experiments of the 20th century. Unlike the Utopian communities of the 19th century that hoped to create a better person, Levittown sought to put roofs over the heads of returning GIs. Paradoxically, Levittown asked some of the preeminent philosophical questions of all time: given an opportunity, what will the average person do with it? Was the "country mouse" better than the "city mouse?" Did owning a home make people better citizens like those in the movie *It's A Wonderful Life?* The sociological oddsmakers cast it as a dark horse. Mumford, called "the last of the great humanists" by Malcolm Cowley, was unbridled in his condemnation of Levittown. Mumford and his allies prophesied a sociological "Armageddon" for Levittown.

The future of Levittown is as interesting as its past. Upon its 50th birthday in October 1997, Levittown could proudly say it had done what it set out to do, which, in the words of William Levitt, was to "provide housing." As the celebrations continued, many of the major players during Levittown's inception were not there to see the outcome. A time capsule was signed by Levittown children to be opened at the community's 100th anniversary. Our book *Levittown: The First Fifty Years*, published by Arcadia in time for the prototype suburb's 50th anniversary, will indeed be a tough act to follow. The distinction of being arguably the best-known suburban community in the world does not come without its trials.

The recent movie *Wonderland*, which depicted Levittown as a 50-year replay of Mumford's criticism with a good deal of sex thrown in, was enough to set Levittown lovers' teeth on edge. Now it seemed even the ability to refute the early critics was being robbed. It is our hope as authors to pay tribute to a very special generation that faced enormous challenges from the Depression of 1929 to World War II, and whose efforts made possible the world that many enjoyed growing up in. Because Levittown was so intimately connected with global events, we offer brief timelines for certain decades.

Wherever possible we have used Levittowners' own words to describe their experiences. As singer and songwriter Billy Joel said in a recent interview, "It's not as easy as saying, well, it was a cultural wasteland or that it was a boon to GIs. There were a lot of things in the middle . . . . There were a lot of different lives being lived. And there were a lot of hopes in that place—a lot of dreams fulfilled and a lot of dreams dashed." Undeniably, the following common threads between Levittowners made a strong but ever workable "cat's cradle" of Levittown: residents' fascination with home renovation, their efforts to develop an emotional as well as a physical sense of community, and their desire for an altogether better life. All three aspects are still alive and well, a living monument to the Levitt foresight, persistence, and incredible talent.

One

SUBURBAN PIONEERS

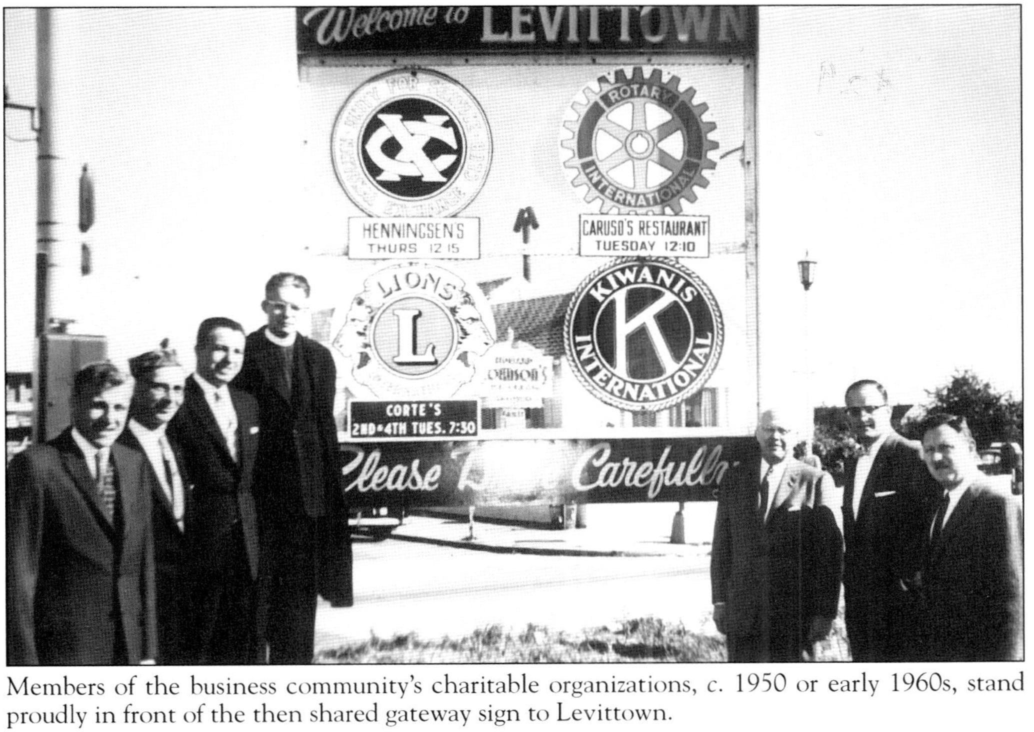

Members of the business community's charitable organizations, *c.* 1950 or early 1960s, stand proudly in front of the then shared gateway sign to Levittown.

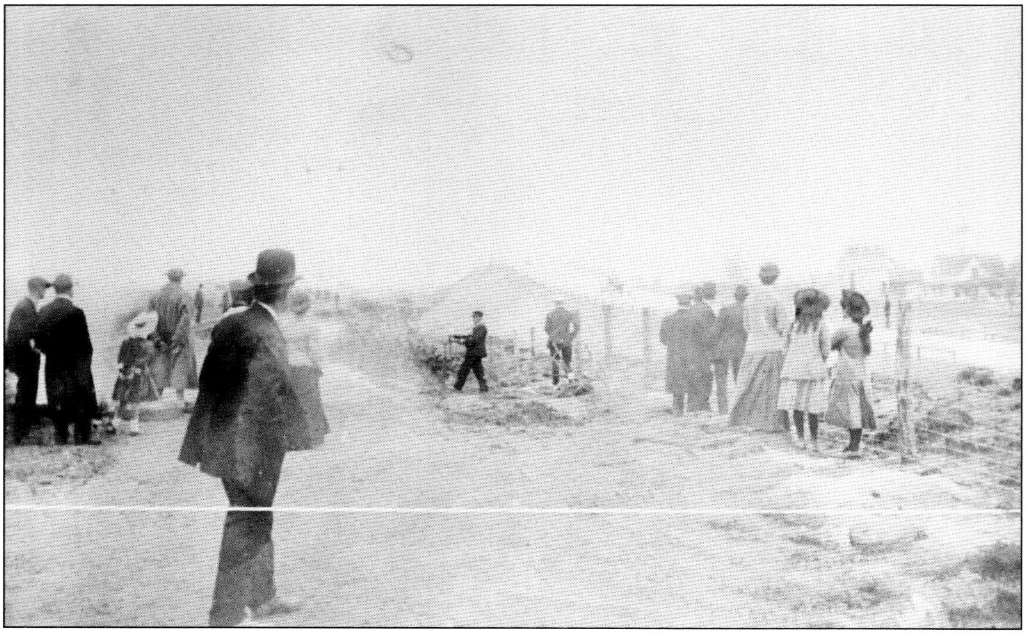

The excitement of the races attracted many high-class spectators such as the Vanderbilts, Whitneys, Guggenheims, and Fords. In this photograph, we see some spectators craning their torsos toward the roadway. In 1910, the crowd leaned so far attempting to get a better view that 22 people were injured and three people died. The following year, the races were relocated to Savannah, Georgia. (Collection of the Levittown Library.)

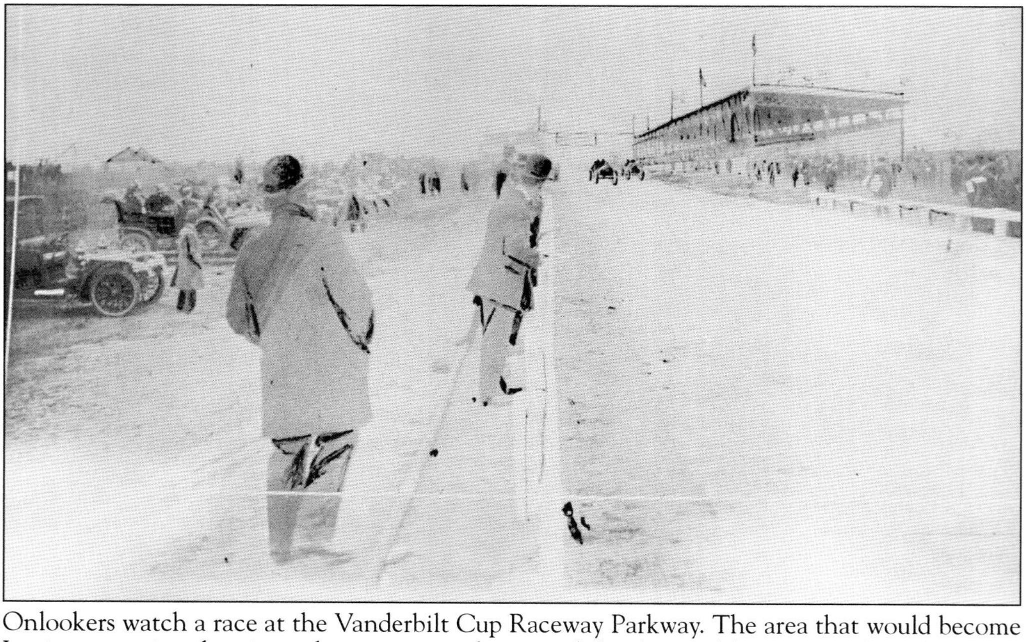

Onlookers watch a race at the Vanderbilt Cup Raceway Parkway. The area that would become Levittown enjoyed a time when it was a playground for the wealthy. It served as the site of motorcar races, replete with a grandstand and reviewing stand. The 23.3-mile parkway was the first road of its kind built exclusively for motorcars. (Collection of the Levittown Library.)

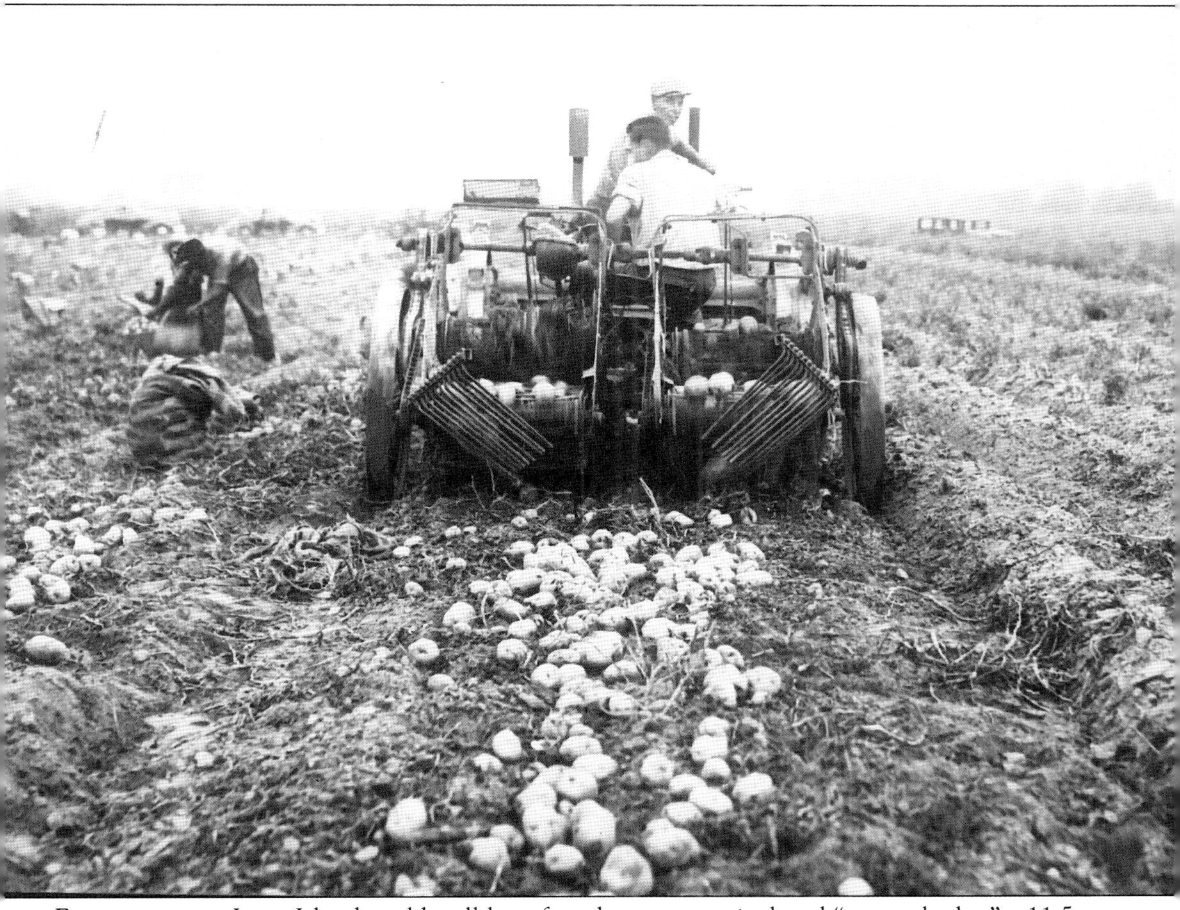

For many years, Long Island could well be referred to as an agricultural "potato basket"—11.5 million bushels were produced annually. In 1919, the community of Island Trees enjoyed a production of two million bushels. (Collection of the Nassau County Museum.)

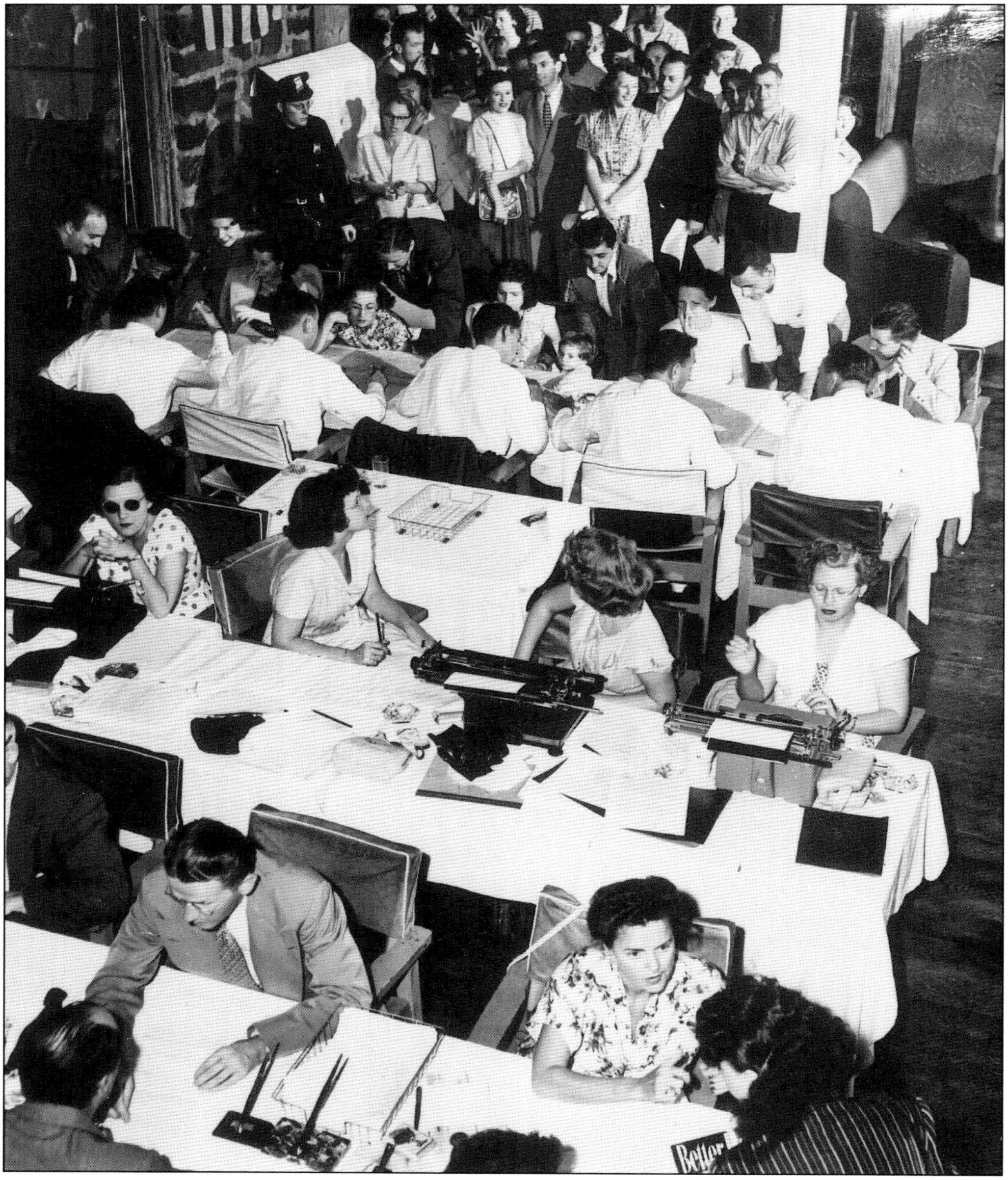

One of the authors' favorite photographs shows prospective homeowners standing in line to purchase a Levitt home. On August 15, 1949, sales representatives sold 650 homes in five hours. In a process reminiscent of Levitt's assembly line building techniques, buyers were organized into five separate lines and then went through a three-step process. At the first table were sales representatives, at the next clerks and typists, and at the last table FHA and Veterans Administration representatives. William Levitt, who sat at the first table, expressed his astonishment by saying, "It's even bigger than we thought." (Collection of the Nassau County Museum.)

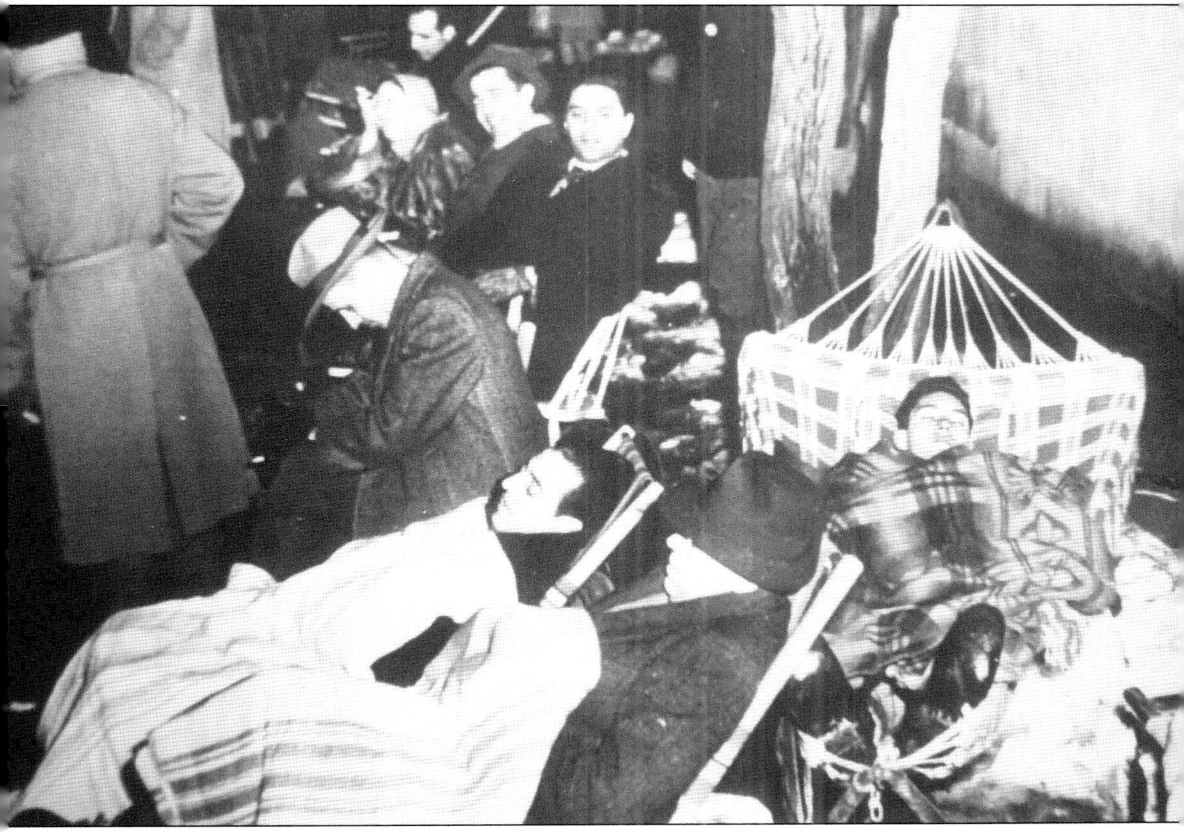

The lure of Levittown is evidenced in the determination of these veterans in this famous photograph, who "camped out" the way people today unravel their sleeping bags while waiting in line for special-event tickets. In the hope of gaining a home in Levittown, some slept in hammocks and deck chairs, while others seemed eager to smile for the camera. (Collection of the Levittown Library.)

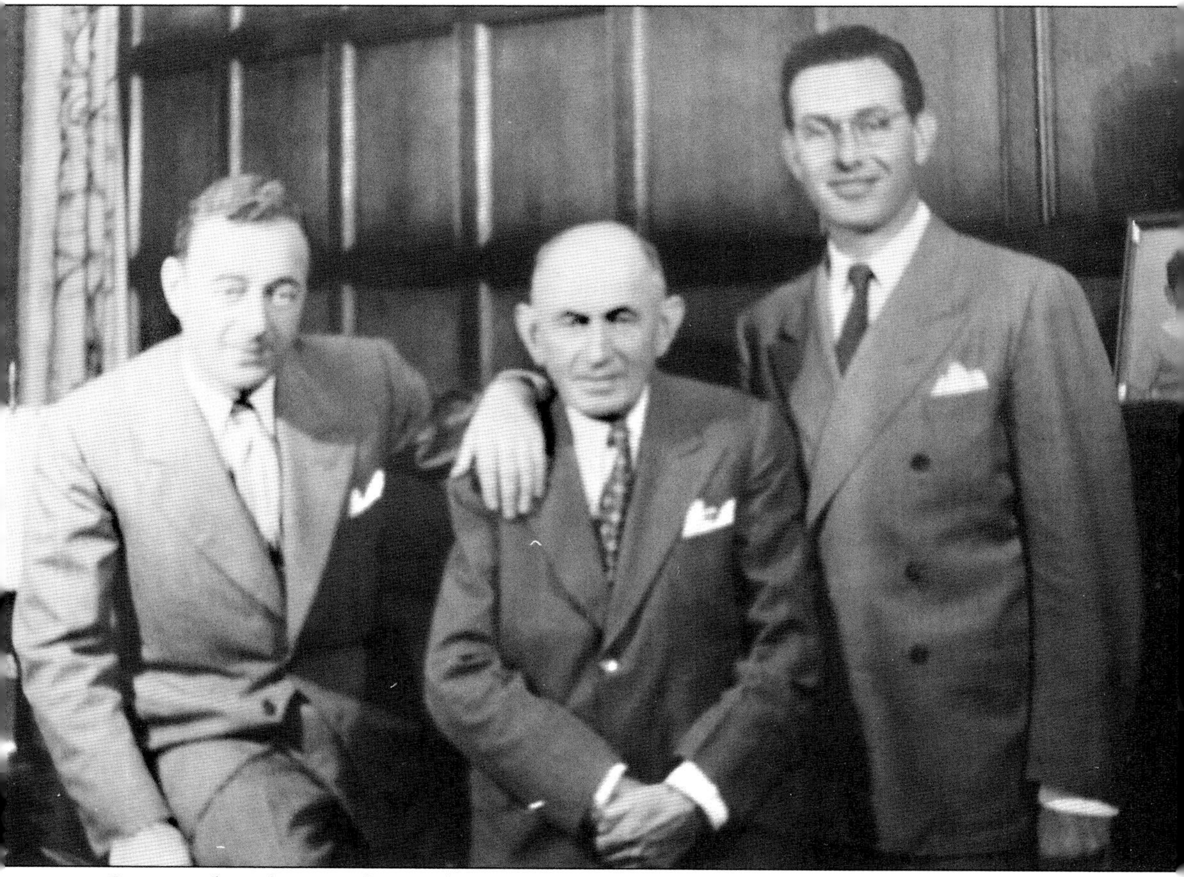

Seen in this photograph are, from left to right, William Jaird Levitt, Abraham Levitt, and Alfred Stuart Levitt, of Levitt & Sons. The trio that founded Levittown brought a unique blend of talents to what would become the best-known suburb in the world. The best known of the three, William, was a superb showman who took Ford's assembly line technique to the housing industry in what is called "the factory in the field." Abraham Levitt, who established Levitt & Sons building firm in 1929, had many years of experience as a real estate lawyer. Although he did not have a formal degree in architecture, Alfred is responsible for the flexible, expandable design of the Levitt homes. Years later, the design was especially praised by the homeowners themselves. (Collection of the Levittown Library.)

Mr. and Mrs. Abraham Levitt stand on the deck of a ship. Abraham Levitt was born in Brooklyn on July 1, 1880. He was the son of a Russian-born rabbi, Louis Levitt, and an Austrian-German mother, Nelli. Although he left school at an early age, Abraham was able to go to New York University Law School. He practiced real estate law for many years before creating the Levitt & Sons builders the year of the stock market crash. The firm's early building ventures were in the pricey custom-home market on Long Island. Abraham married Pauline Biederman in 1906. The couple had two children, William Jaird and Alfred Stuart Levitt. (Collection of the Levittown Library.)

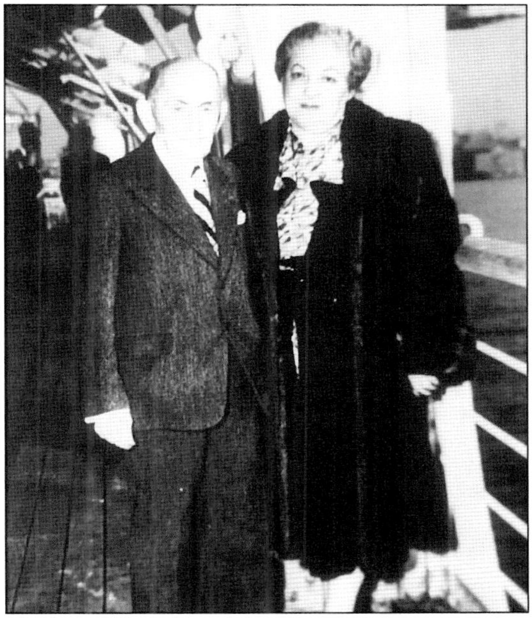

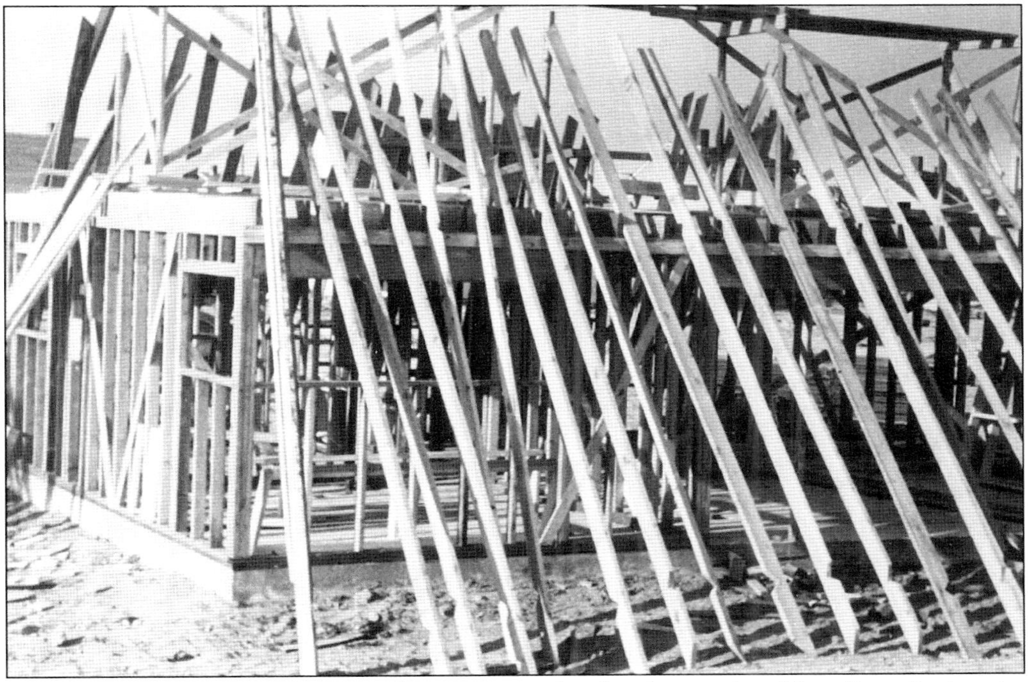

Piles of precut lumber for framing a home rest on the already completed first floor. During the building process, which was often compared to Henry Ford's assembly-line procedures, trucks would deposit at each homesite the materials needed for construction, such as the lumber, copper piping for the radiant-heating system, and shingles for the roof. Separate crews would move from homesite to homesite completing one of the 27 operations that went into building the homes. These streamlined techniques allowed the Levitts at the height of construction to complete more than 30 homes a day. (Collection of the Levittown Library.)

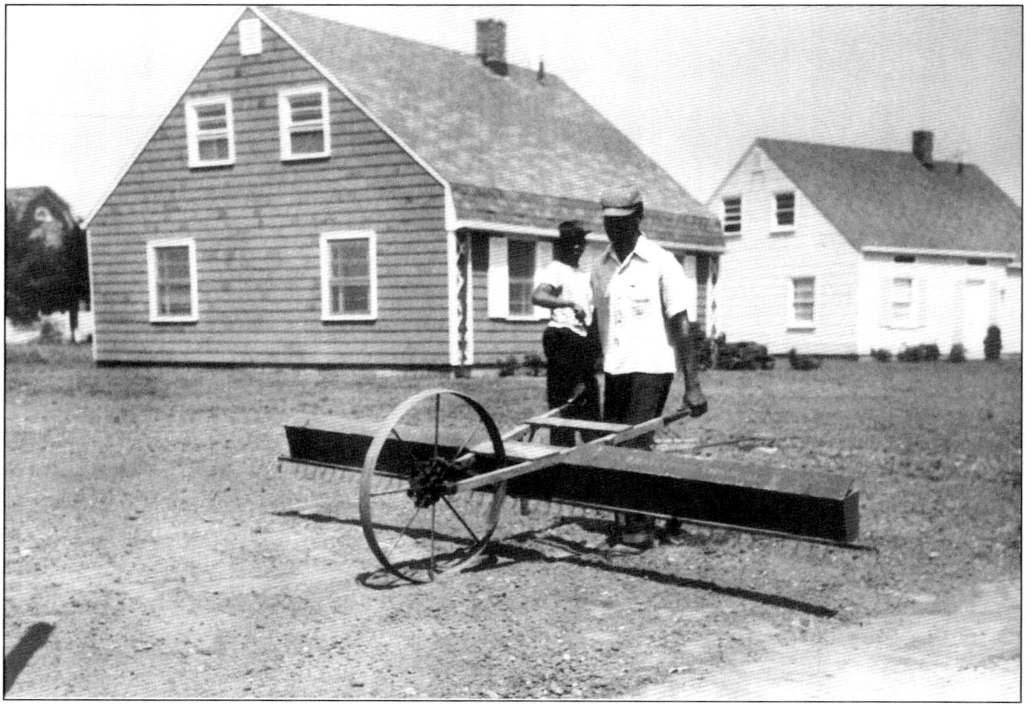

Workers also seeded the lawns of the Levittown homes. Levitt was often criticized for not using union labor. He felt incentives based on an individual's productivity were more beneficial to the employer and, ultimately, the worker himself. (Collection of the Levittown Library.)

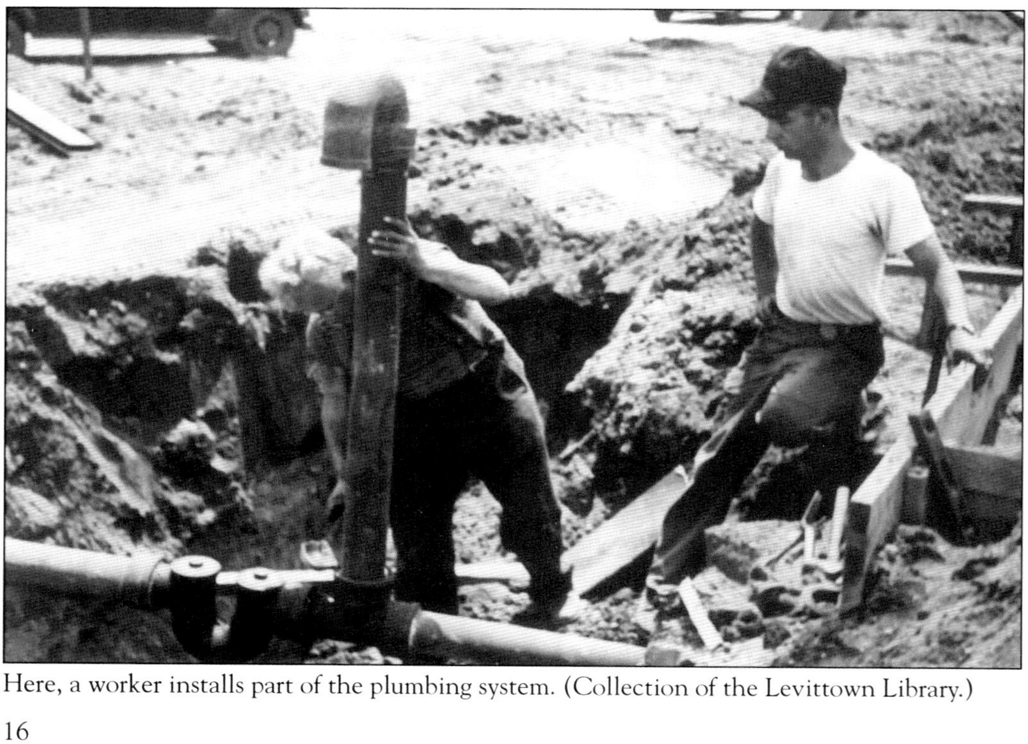

Here, a worker installs part of the plumbing system. (Collection of the Levittown Library.)

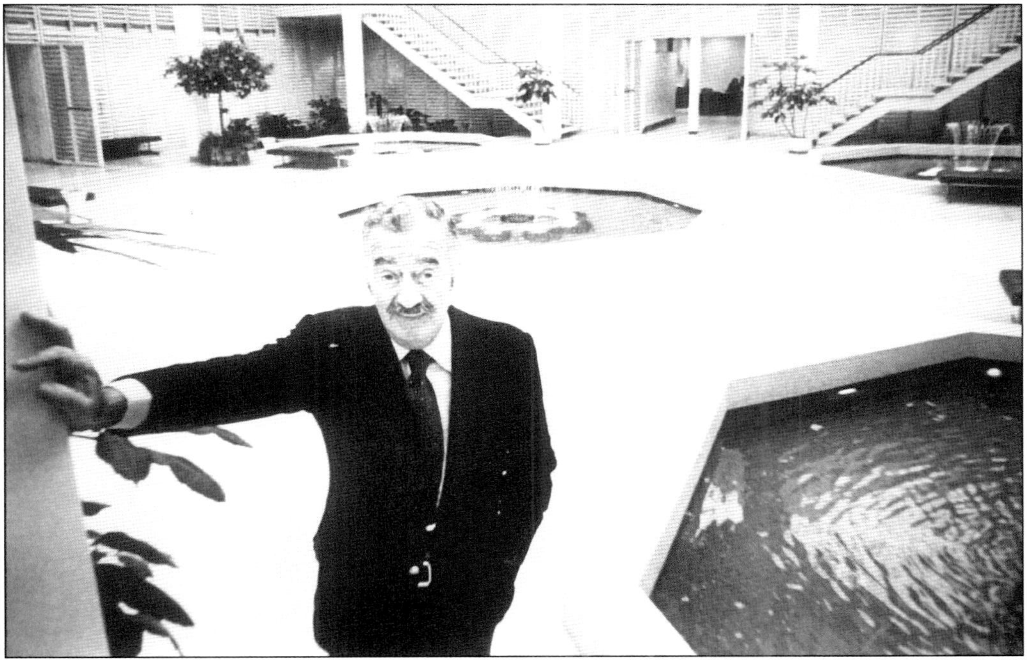

William Levitt is shown at the Lake Success headquarters. (Collection of the Levittown Library.)

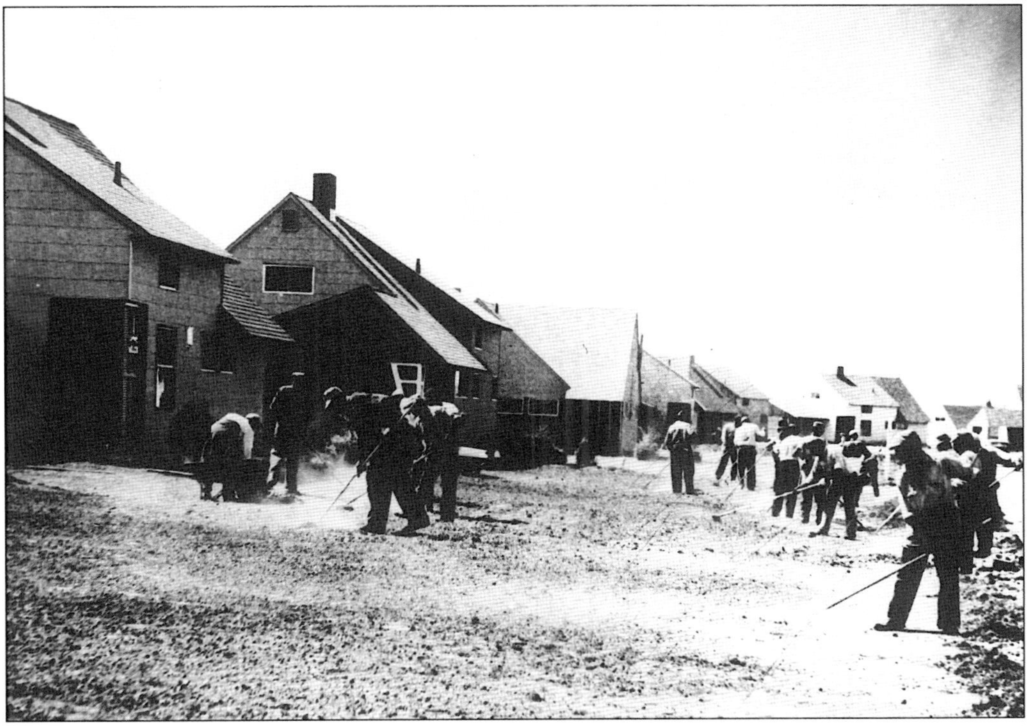

Crews with hoes are getting the lawns of the new ranch homes ready for seeding. (Collection of the Levittown Library.)

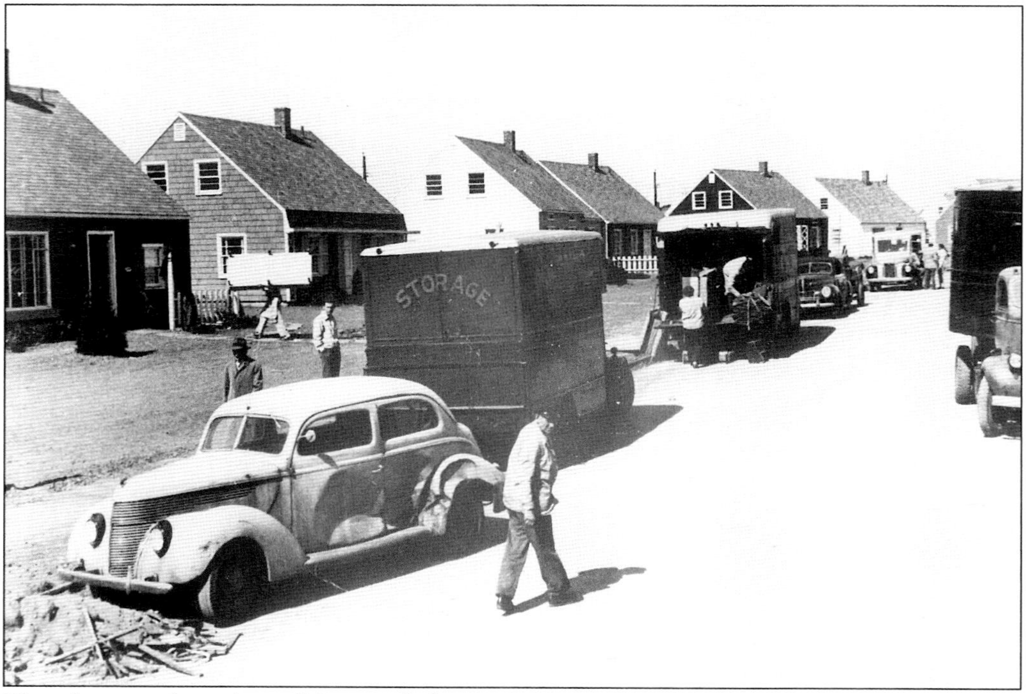

This photograph might well be entitled "Moving In." It captures the spirit of the pioneers as they started their new lives "en masse." On October 1, 1947, 300 families moved into the first Cape Cod-style homes. Mr. and Mrs. Theodore Blaydas moved into "Job # 1" at 67 Bellmore Road. (Collection of the Levittown Library.)

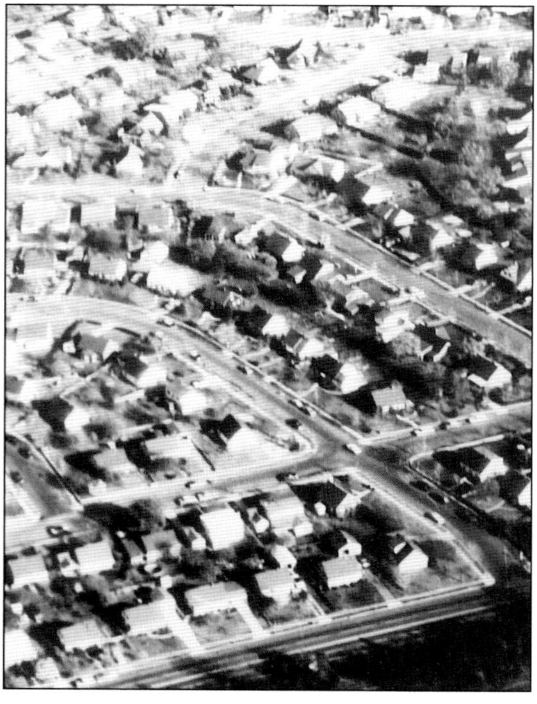

This early aerial view of Levittown shows the streets, curved to discourage speeding, and the thoughtful ordering of the homes referred to derogatorily in a 1960s protest song called "Little Boxes."

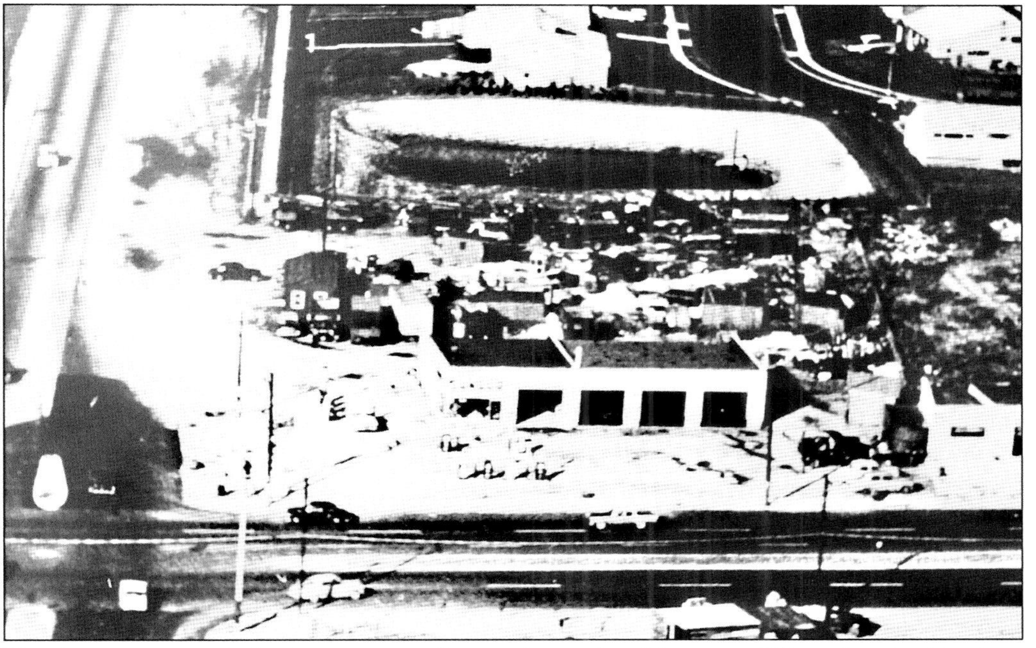

The first gas station in Levittown was a Sunoco located on Hempstead Turnpike. At this time, Hempstead Turnpike was a two-lane road. (Collection of the Levittown Library.)

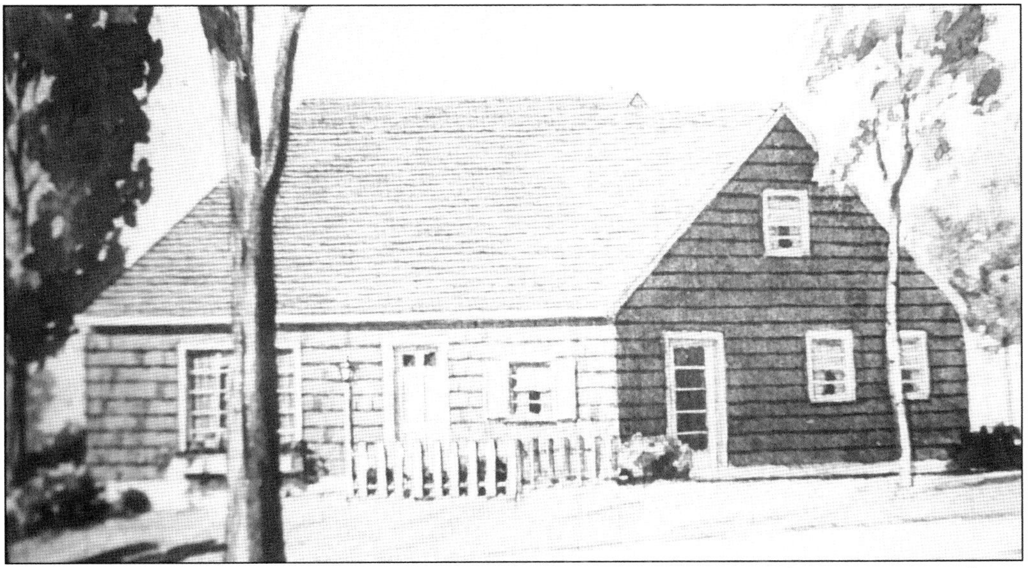

This artist's rendering shows a 1947–48 Type 4 Cape Cod. Because of government policies at the time, the Capes were initially rented to veterans for $60 per month. There were five different types of Capes, which differed only in small ways, such as variations in the roofline or placement of windows. The Capes were four-and-one-half-room homes that were built on concrete slabs and placed on 60-by-100-foot plots of land with no garage or driveway. A big draw of the homes was the unfinished attic because of the additional space it offered growing families. The Type 2 and Type 4 also sported a small birdhouse. (Collection of the Levittown Library.)

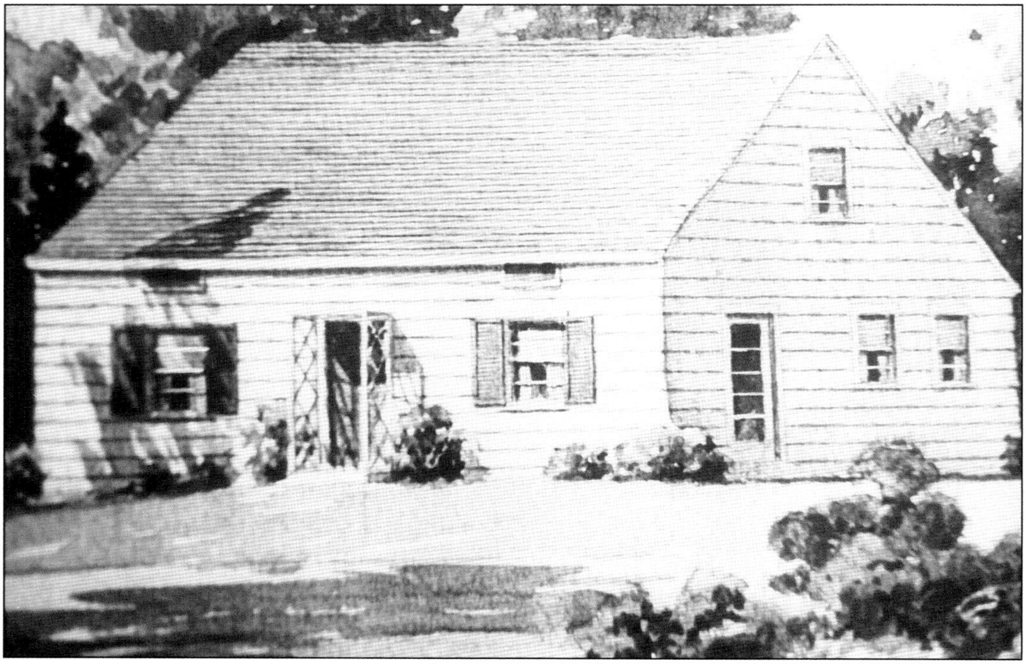

This is a Type 5 Cape Cod. A stumbling block that almost prevented Levittown from coming into being was the issue of the concrete-slab floor construction. At the time, a Hempstead building ordinance prohibited the building of homes without a basement. Would-be homeowners inundated the local newspapers and zoning boards with letters demanding the ordinance be rescinded. On May 27, 1947, the Hempstead Town Board repealed the section of the building code to allow the Levitt homes to be built. (Collection of the Levittown Library.)

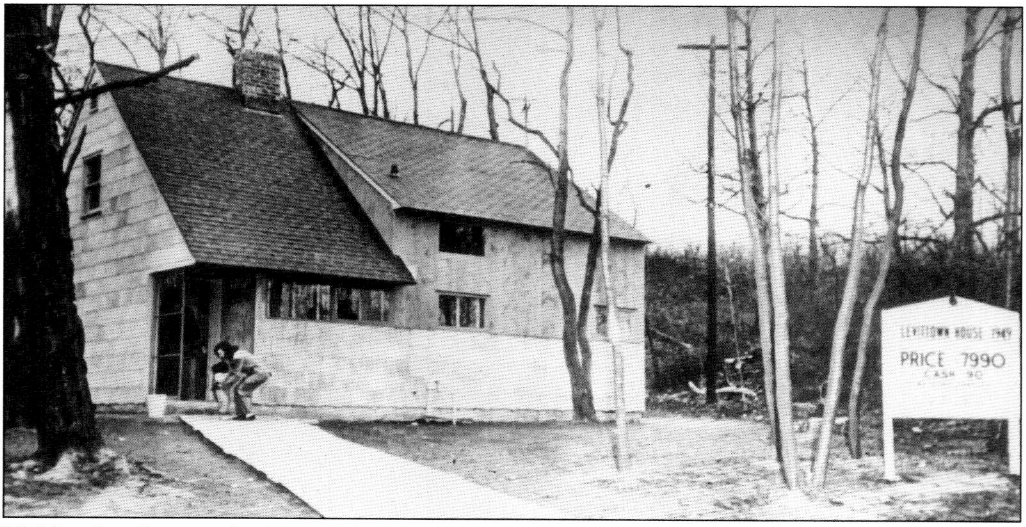

Unlike the Capes, which were first rented, the upscale ranch model introduced by Levitt in 1949 sold for $7,990. Renting turned into selling the homes because increased funding made purchasing advantageous to both builders and homebuyers. Like the Capes, there were five models, which were also the same except for differences in rooflines and window placement. (Collection of the Levittown Library.)

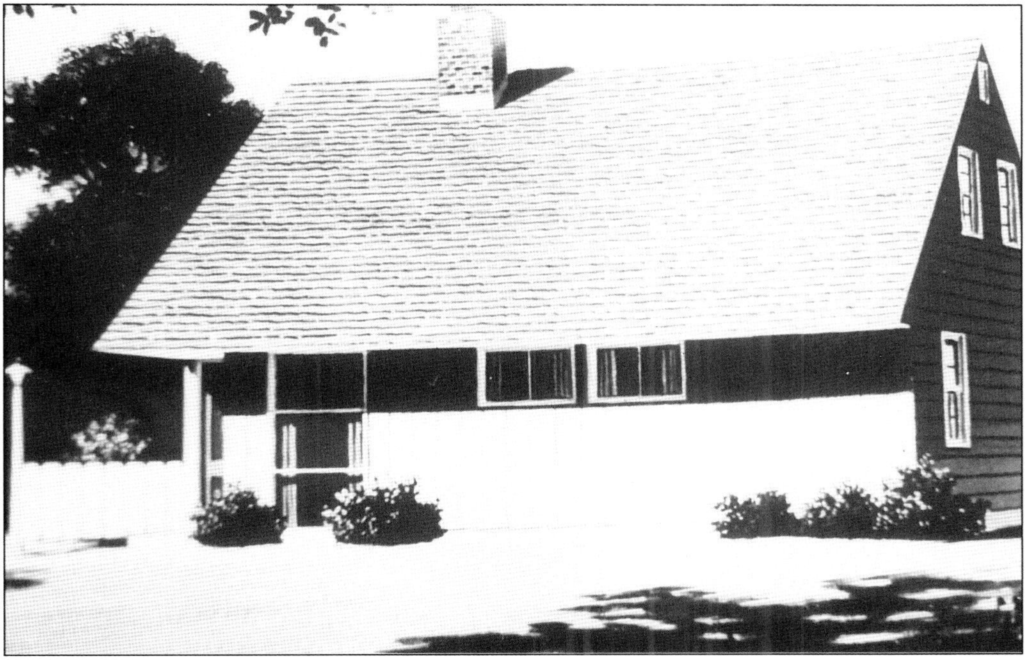

Here we have an artist's rendering of a 1949 Type 1 ranch. In the ranch, the homeowner gained another 50 square feet of living space over the 750 square feet of the Cape Cod. (Collection of the Levittown Library.)

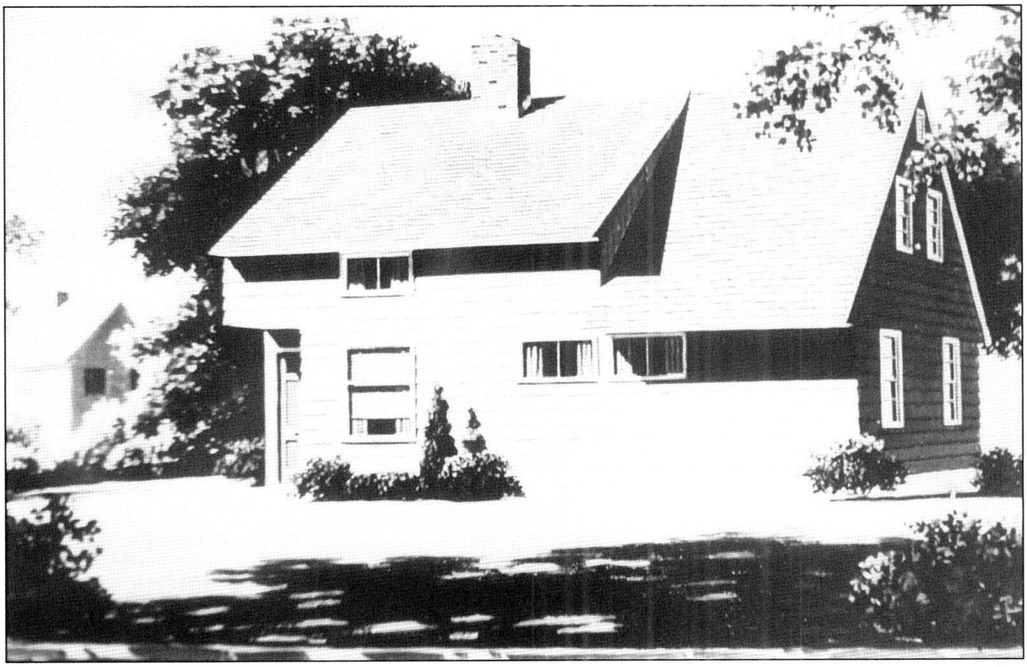

Changes in rooflines and window placement made a substantial difference in the appearance of the houses. The model shown here is a 1949 Type 2 ranch. (Collection of the Levittown Library.)

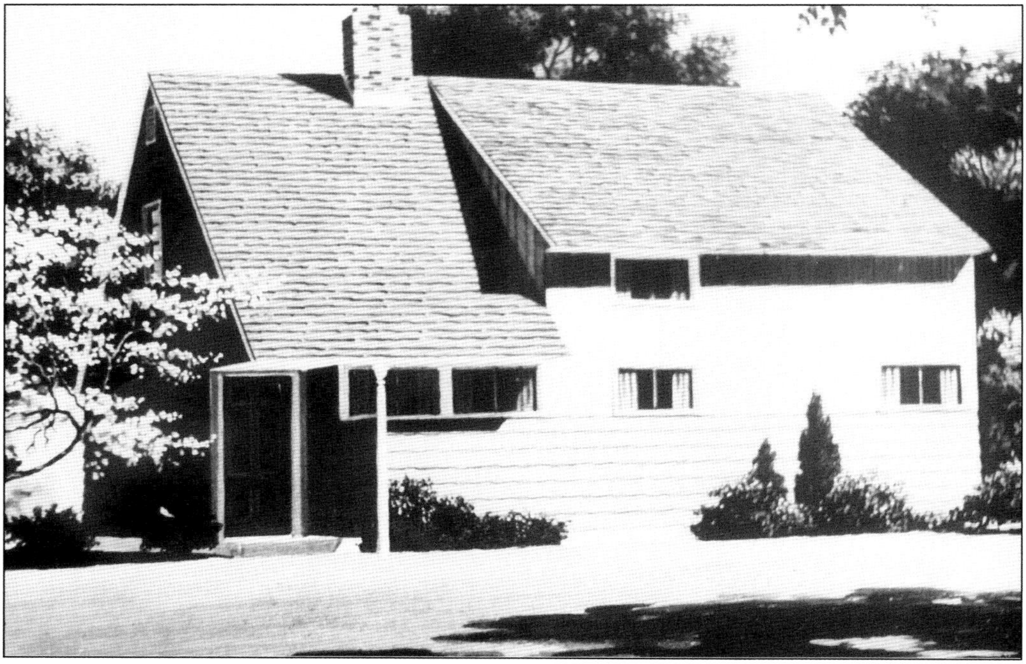

This drawing shows a 1951 Type 3 ranch. The 1951 ranch had a finished room in the attic. This model sold for $9,000. (Collection of the Levittown Library.)

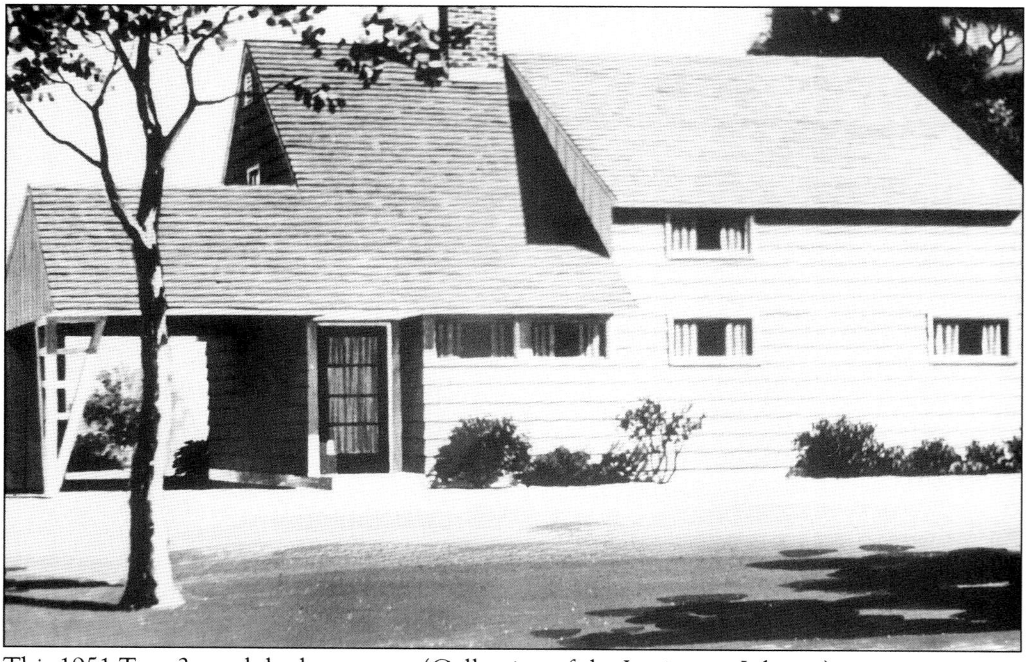

This 1951 Type 3 ranch had a carport. (Collection of the Levittown Library.)

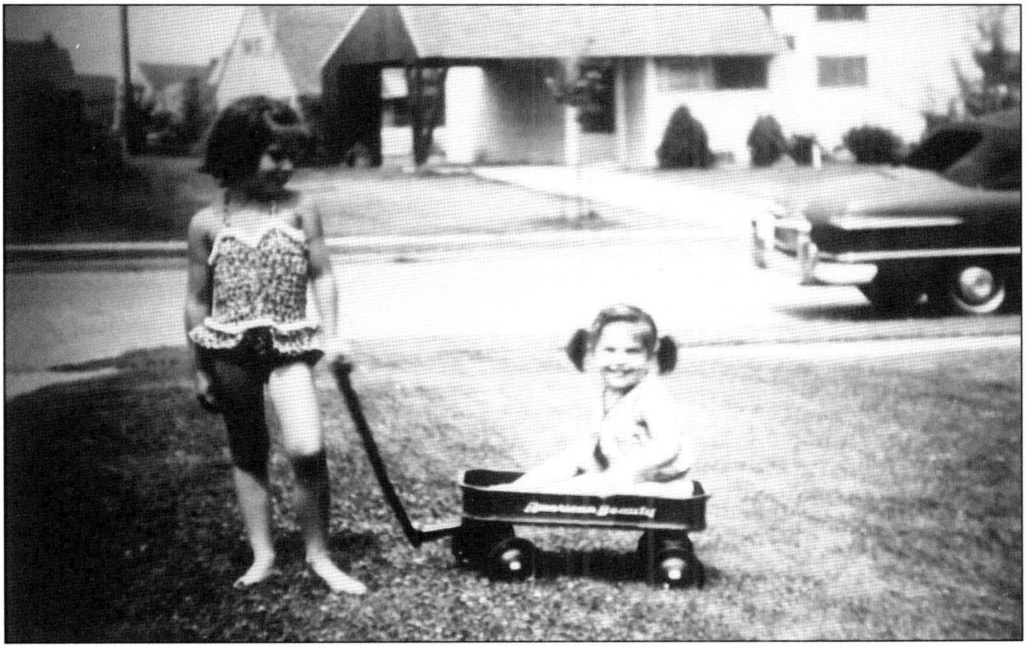

Four-year-old Joan Worthing pulls her sister Cathie, nearly two, in a wagon called an "American Beauty," which is a familiar piece of childhood nostalgia for many of the "baby boomer" generation. The sisters are wearing ruffled bathing suits, another piece of 1950s memorabilia. The Worthing family has been part of the Levittown development from the start. Parents Jerry and Clare Worthing rented a Cape, and soon purchased a ranch home. They went on to raise their daughters, and after a variety of extensions to their ranch, they still live in Levittown slightly more than 50 years later. (Collection of Clare and Jerry Worthing.)

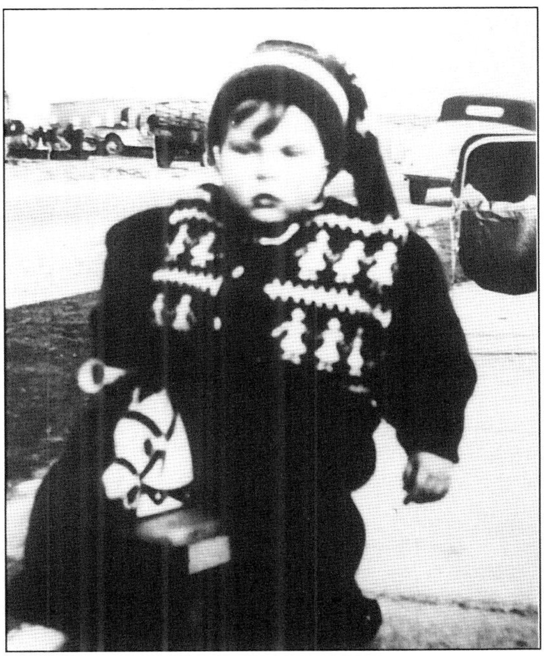

Carol Caveglia Price, a toddler in 1948, grew up in Levittown and went on to be head of reference at the Levittown Library. (Collection of Carol Price.)

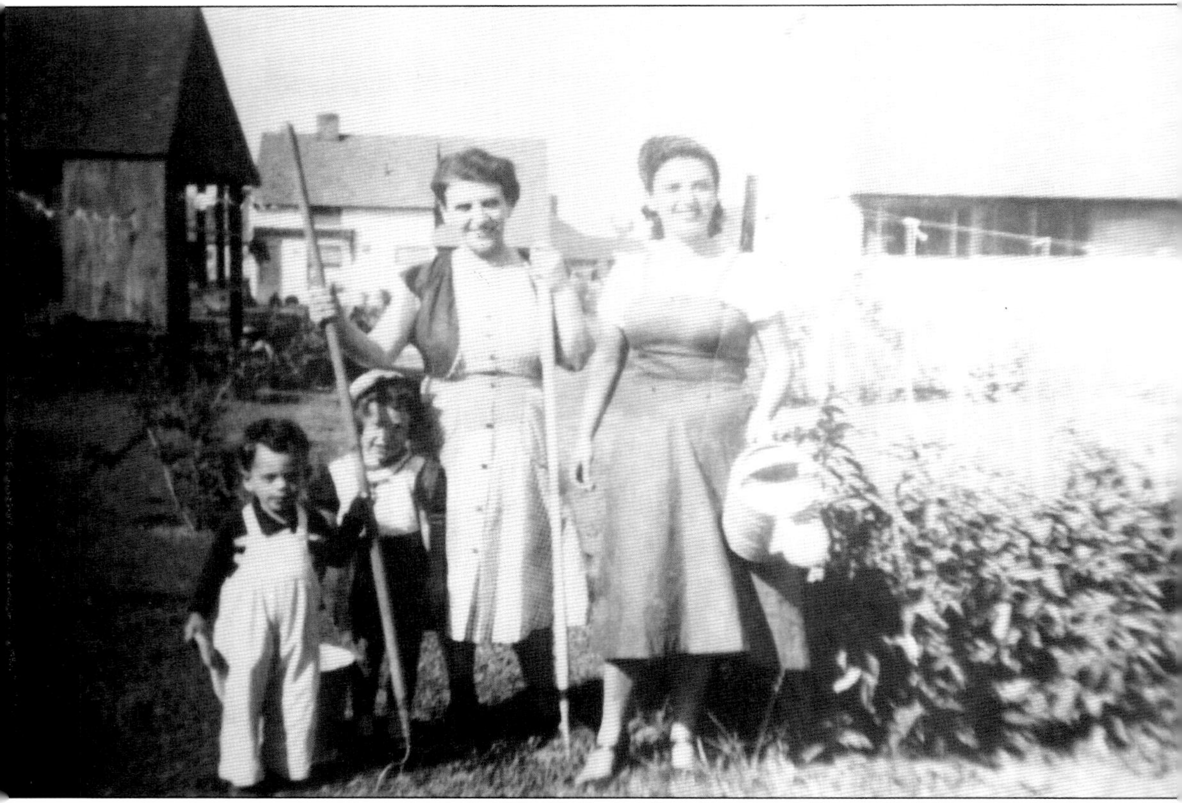

A pioneer who would go on to international fame was Billy Joel. He is shown here with Judy (his older sister), Rebecca Nyman (his maternal grandmother), and Rosalind Nyman Joel (his mother). In a 1993 interview at Hofstra University, Joel said he remembers his mother telling him they "were moving to the country." The Joels lived at 20 Meeting Lane in Hicksville, where he grew up. (Courtesy of Billy Joel.)

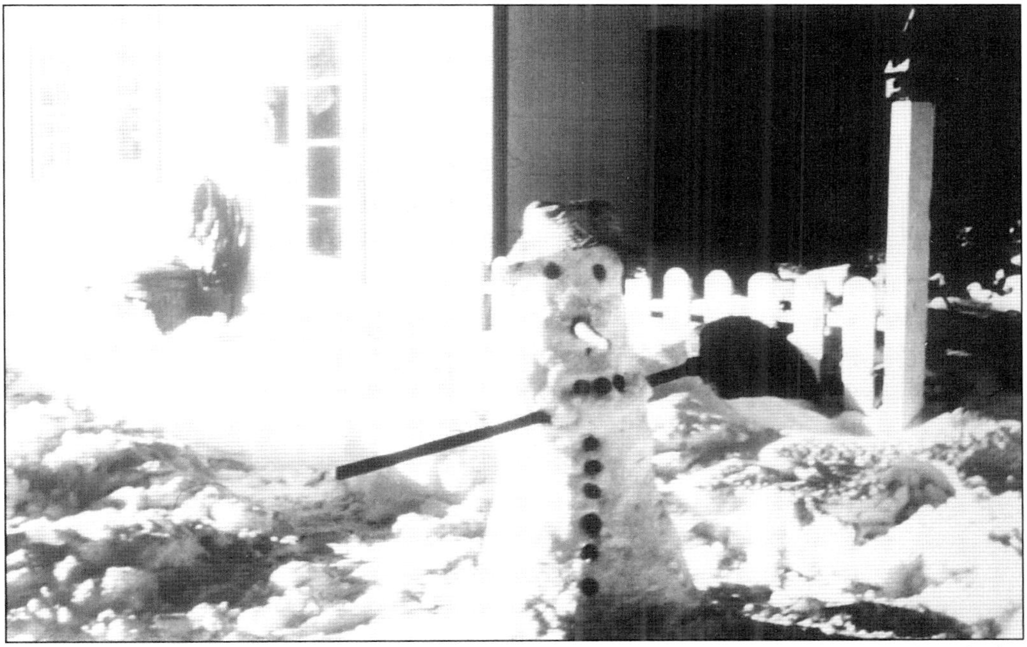

Snowmen are an eternal part of childhood, and this snowman, generously bedecked with the requisite coal, carrot, and a not-quite-stove-pipe hat, accompanies the birdhouse that came with the Type 4 Cape. In the background is the small section of rounded picket fence that also came with the Type 4 Cape. (Collection of the Levittown Library.)

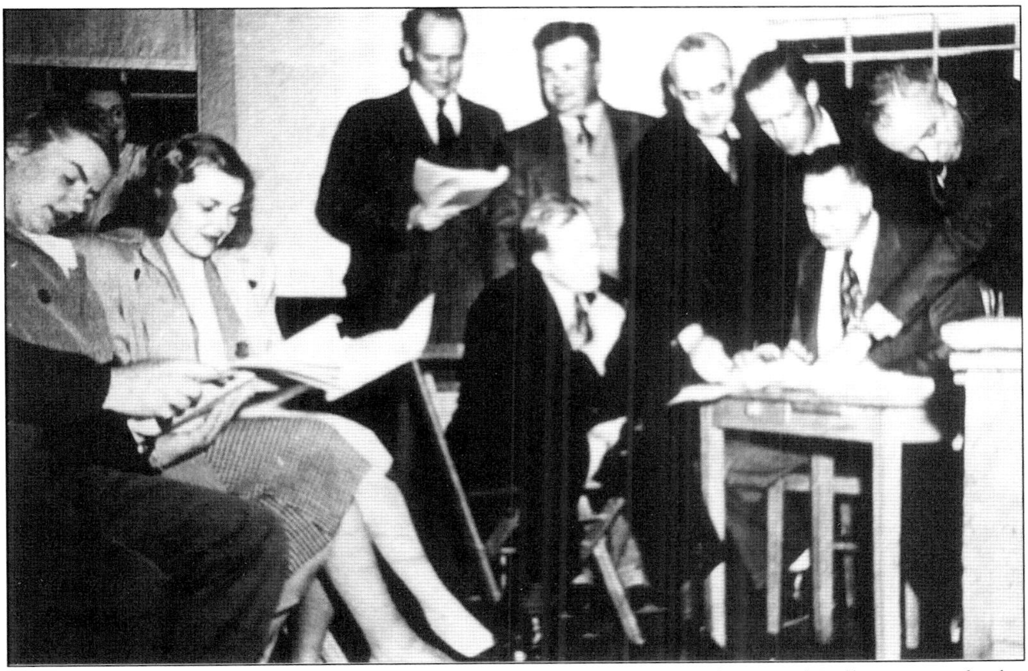

The school board votes in the days before voting machines. (Collection of the Levittown Library.)

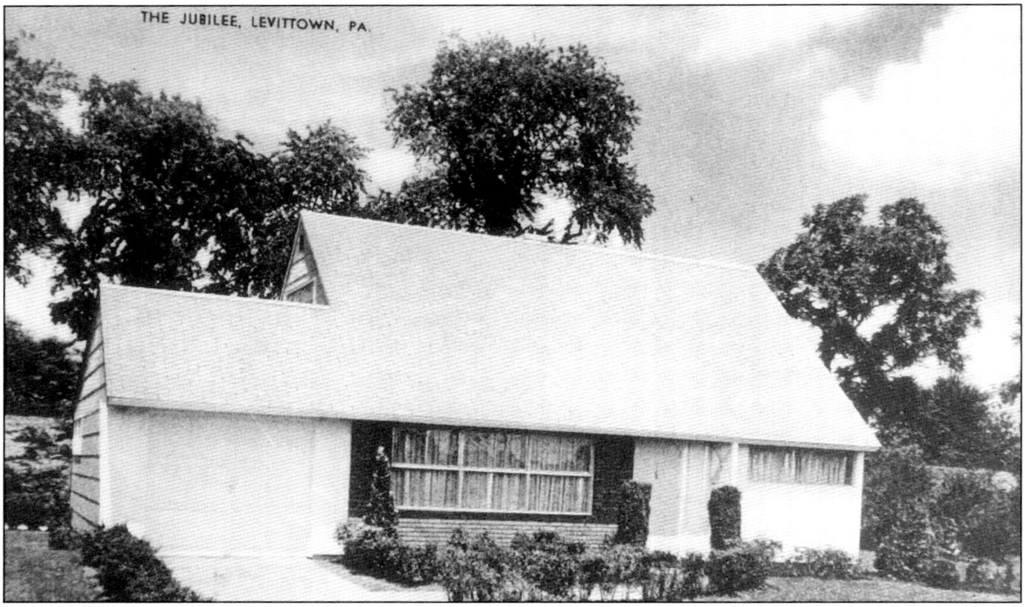

The success the Levitts experienced in Levittown led them to move on to other pastures. In 1952, the Levitts began construction in Levittown, Pennsylvania, where they duplicated their Long Island success. Levitt would build 17,311 homes in Bucks County, coming amazingly close to the 17,447 homes of the original Levittown. The postcard shows a "Jubilee" model, which bears a striking resemblance to the original Cape. This model sold for $10,990. In 1993, the Jubilee was selling in the mid-$90,000s. (Collection of Randall Gabrielan.)

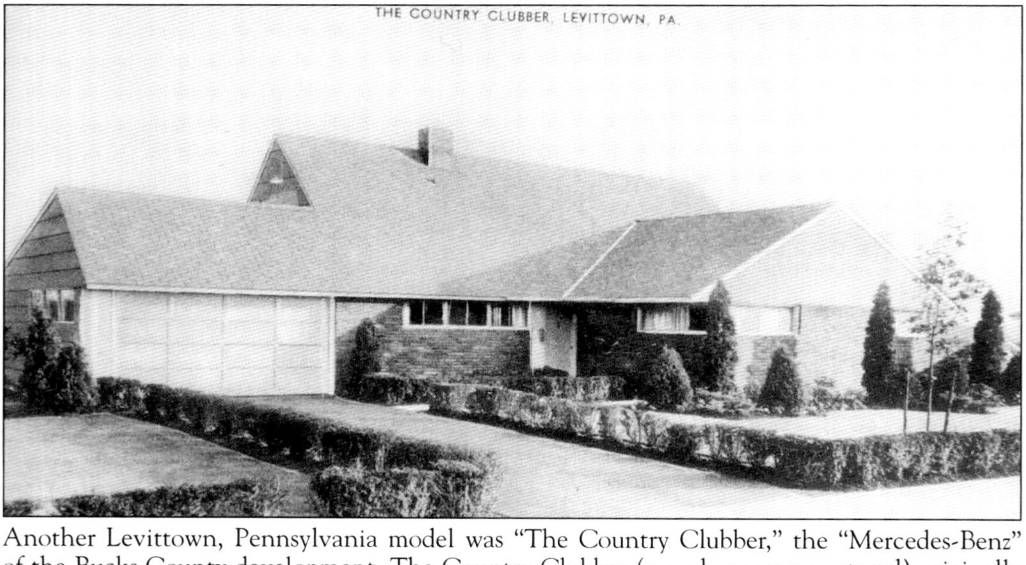

Another Levittown, Pennsylvania model was "The Country Clubber," the "Mercedes-Benz" of the Bucks County development. The Country Clubber (seen here on a postcard) originally sold for approximately $17,000. In 1993, Clubbers were selling for as much as $170,000. The windows were placed high "to discourage nosy neighbors." The development went into several municipalities including Falls, Tullytown, Bristol Township, and Middletown. Dealing with so many municipalities was said to have caused difficulties for Levitt. (Collection of Randall Gabrielan.)

Two

BUSINESS AS UNUSUAL

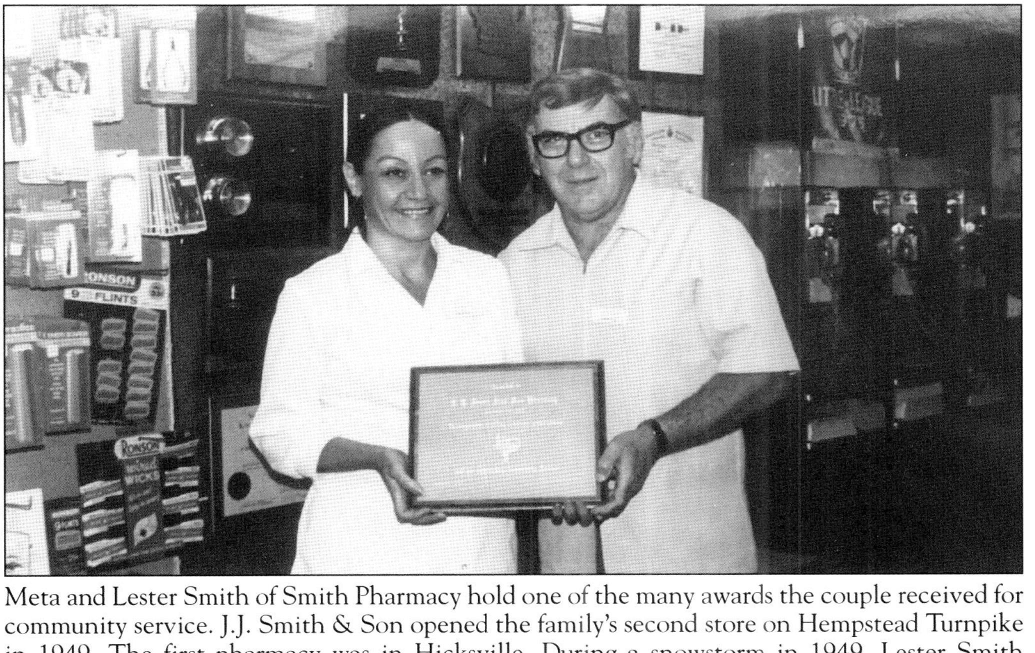

Meta and Lester Smith of Smith Pharmacy hold one of the many awards the couple received for community service. J.J. Smith & Son opened the family's second store on Hempstead Turnpike in 1949. The first pharmacy was in Hicksville. During a snowstorm in 1949, Lester Smith became a local hero when he got a snowplow and brought penicillin to a family in Hempstead. The trip back and forth from Levittown took seven hours. In an interview with Mark Sousa on Levittown's 40th anniversary, Smith said, "I remember staying open until midnight to accommodate the doctors who used to make housecalls." Lester Smith's death was mourned by many Levittowners. (Collection of Meta Smith.)

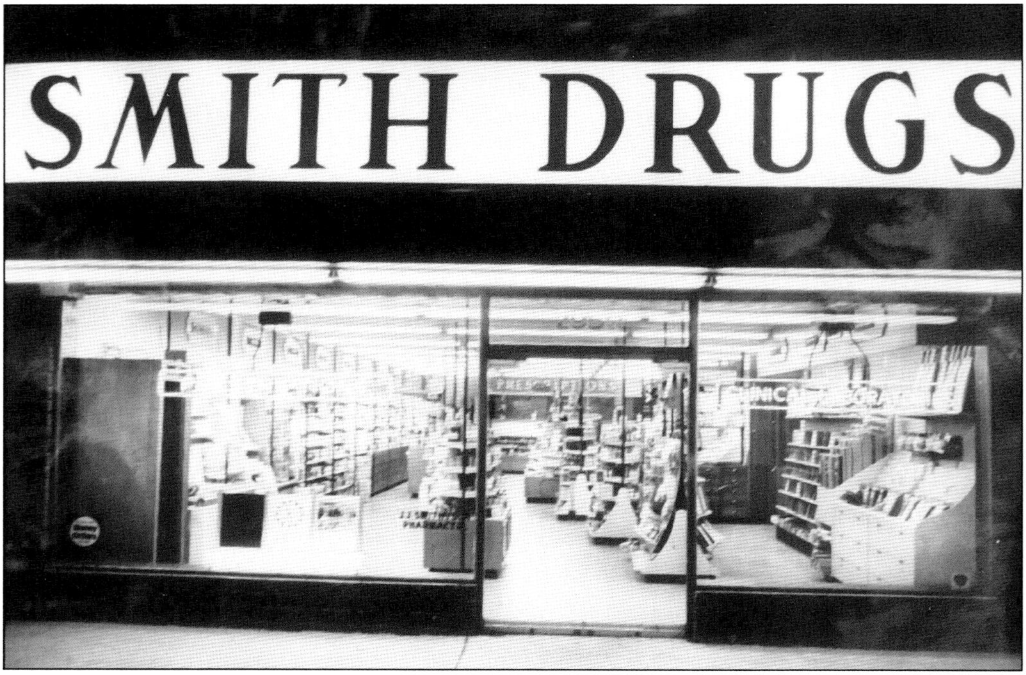

Here we see a dramatic nighttime shot of Smith Drugs. (Collection of Meta Smith.)

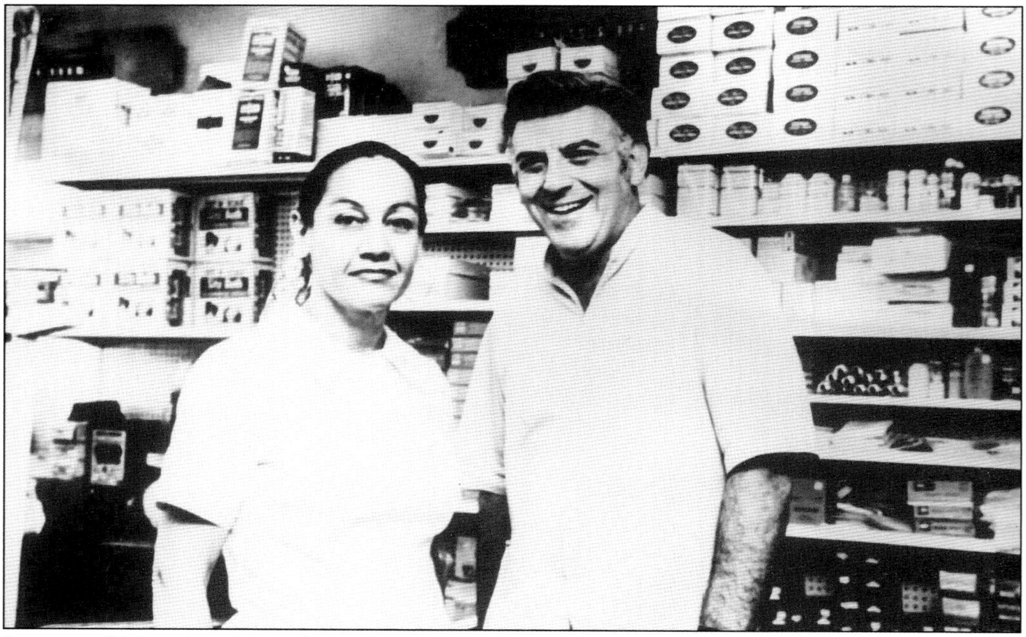
Lester and Meta Smith are shown here in a similar pose, a few years earlier than the photograph on the previous page. Both the Smiths were licensed pharmacists. Meta remembers working long hours, at times alternating shifts. The couple was involved in many Levittown activities such as the Exchange Club. Lester was one of the chairpersons for the town's 20th anniversary celebration. (Collection of Meta Smith.)

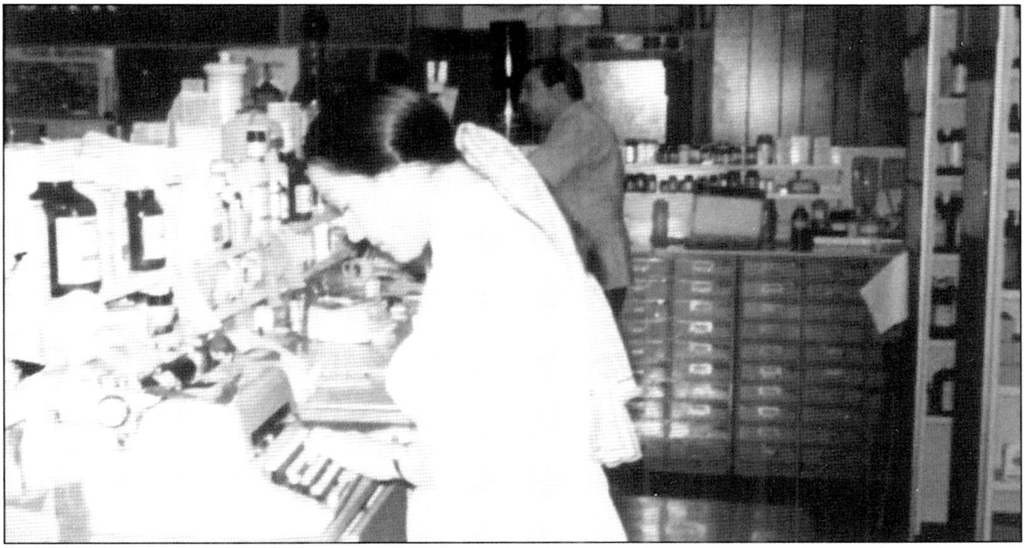

In the days before advanced computer technology, pharmacist Meta Smith typed prescription labels. Today, this kind of labor-intensive activity is no longer necessary. It is possible to look up a person's pharmaceutical record and possible drug interactions with a quick entry. Thirty or 40 years ago, drugstores relied upon record keeping and a great deal of work to accomplish the same result. (Collection of Meta Smith.)

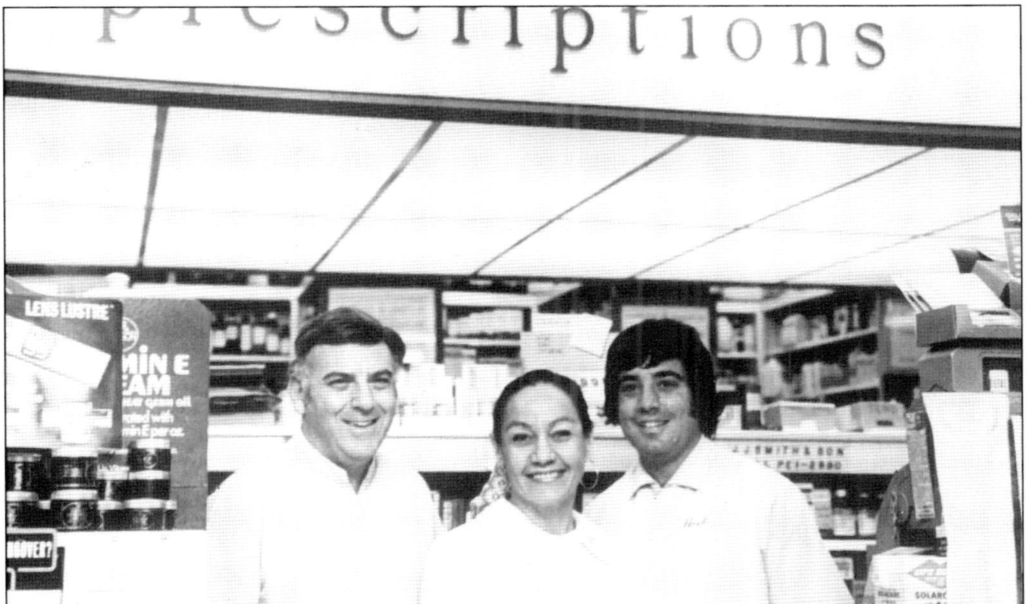

In this 1980s photograph we see Meta, Lester, and their son Neil in the family pharmacy. By this time, Smith Pharmacy had become a fixture in Levittown. The three were now licensed pharmacists. Meta describes the early days in which she and Lester would often work separate shifts. She also describes an atmosphere not unlike the old general store during flu season, when area doctors would gather at the pharmacy as they took a break between calls. Despite their busy life at the pharmacy, the Smiths raised six children. (Collection of Meta Smith.)

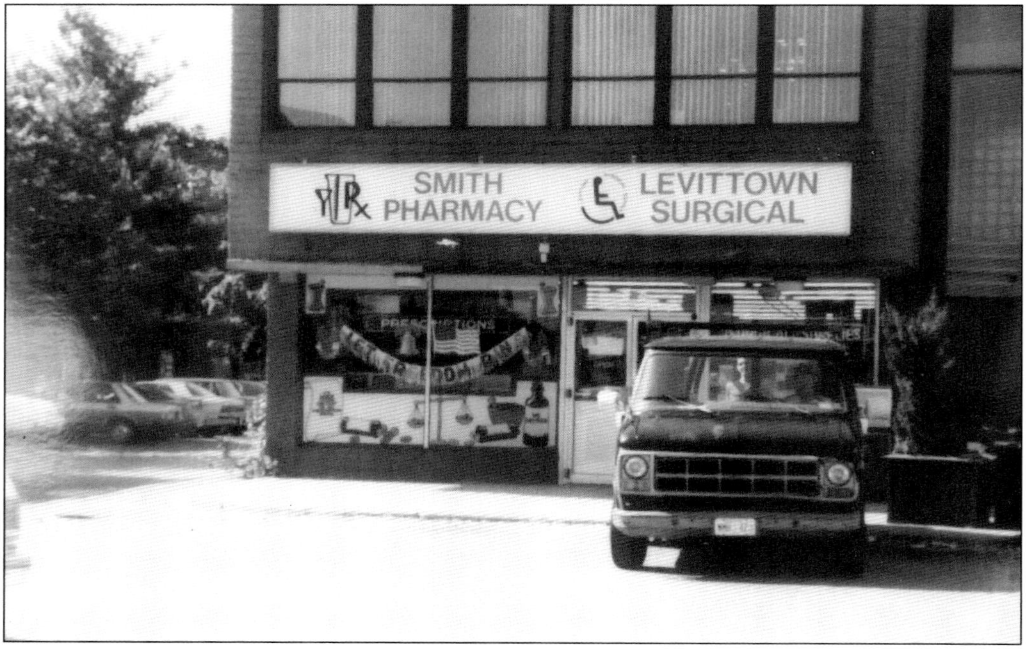

Pictured here is the Smith Pharmacy and Levittown Surgical Supply. (Collection of Meta Smith.)

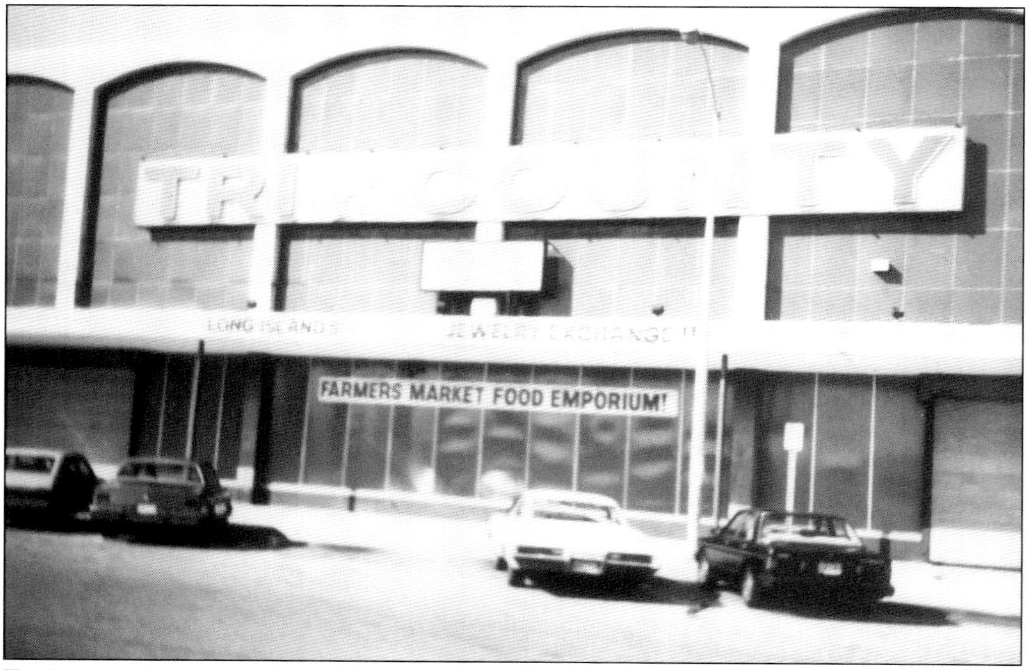

Tri-County Auction occupies the former Mays Department Store. Mays, a welcome addition for many former city-dwellers, was a well-known retail chain and nearly the equivalent of today's malls. For city folk used to walking to the corner for their needs, suburban life was a bit of a culture shock. (Collection of the Levittown Library.)

A favorite occupation of Levittowners was home improvement. In this advertisement, Herbert Richheimer, a building contractor, exhibits his craftsmanship. In the upper left is a photograph of an attic room completed by Richheimer for Mr. and Mrs. Donald Schaur of Rose Lane. The garage and breezeway pictured in the upper right were added to the Sapede home on Old Farm Drive. The room in the lower right corner is a dining room extension added to the home of the Sandler family on Harbor Lane. All of these additions were popular renovation projects. (Collection of the Levittown Library.)

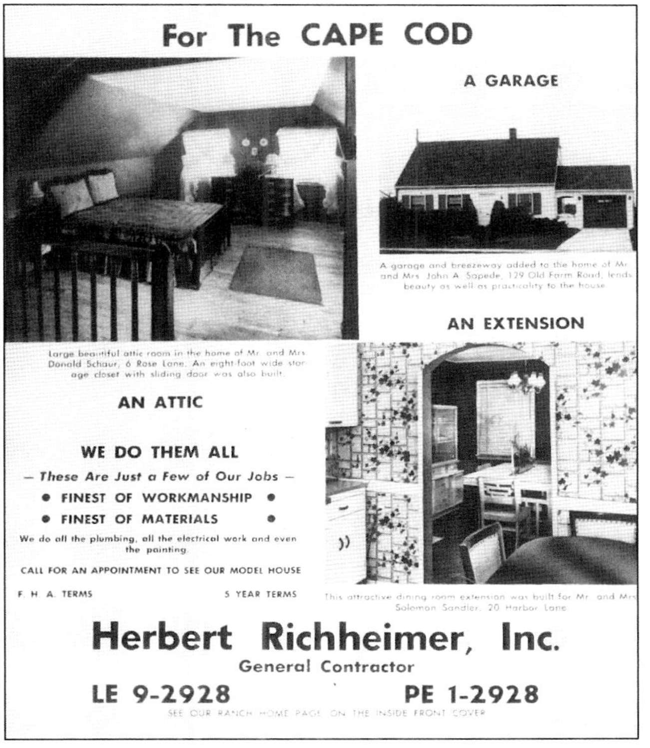

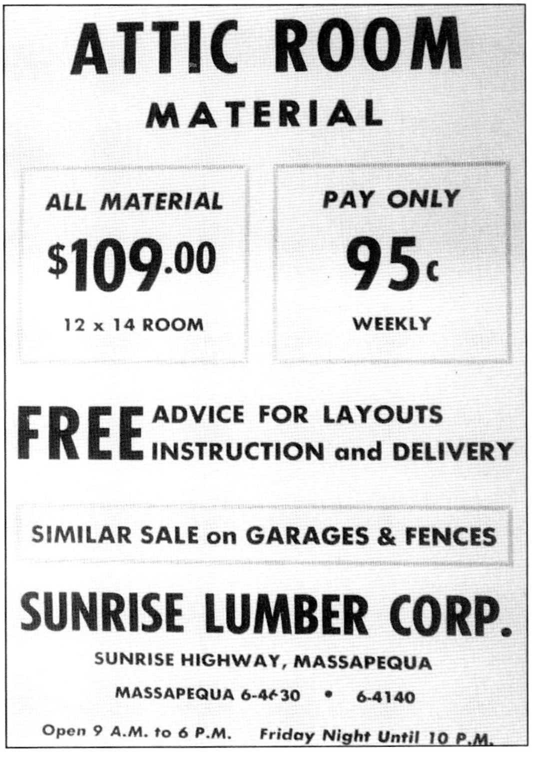

The Sunrise Lumber Corp. on Sunrise Highway in Massapequa advertised material needed to finish a 12-by-14-foot attic room for $109. Many businesses boomed as a result of the need Levittown created for services and building materials of all kinds. While many Levittowners became do-it-yourselfers, others turned to professionals for help. Alfred H. Parsons became known as the premier designer of Levittown home improvements. Trained in architecture at Pratt Institute, Parsons founded Parsons Plan Service. By 1957, Parsons had designed nearly 4,000 home improvements in Levittown. (Collection of the Levittown Library.)

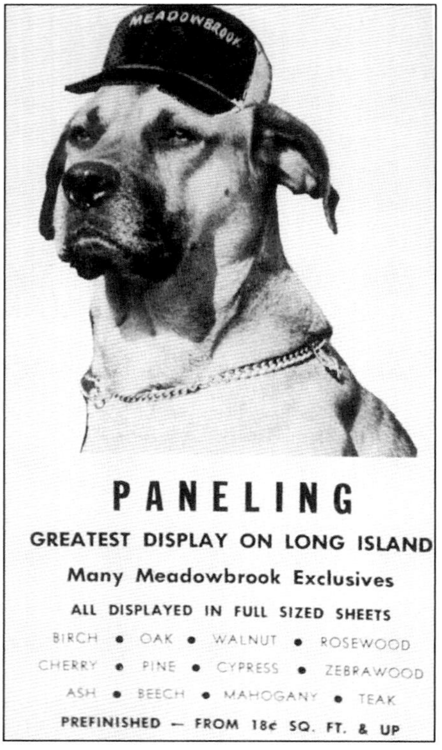

Meadowbrook Building Supply used creative advertising featuring a homeowner's best friend wearing a Meadowbrook cap. The ad for paneling, including birch rosewood, cherry, mahogany, and zebrawood, demonstrates the enormous popularity wood paneling enjoyed from the 1950s through the 1960s and 1970s. Alfred Parsons noted the most popular improvements were the squared kitchen, playrooms, and enlarged living rooms. He would tell prospective homeowners what he thought their options were, draw up plans, and get the necessary building permits. (Collection of the Levittown Library.)

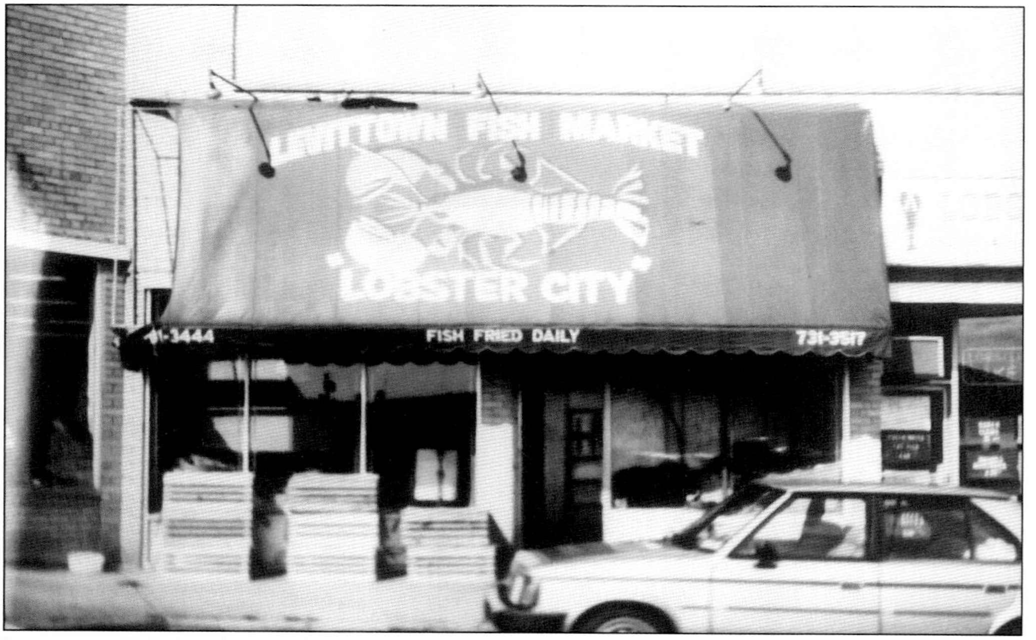

Levittown Fish Market "Lobster City" has been a longtime fixture in Levittown. Open seven days a week, the store is located on Gardiners Avenue. The store's specialties are prepared dishes and fried seafood. (Collection of the Levittown Library.)

Franklin National Bank of Long Island advertised low-cost, home-improvement loans. The thorn in the rose of home improvement was the need for cash to finance the projects. Home-improvement loans, which were the financial precursors of home equity loans, provided the means for valued additions and alterations. (Collection of the Levittown Library.)

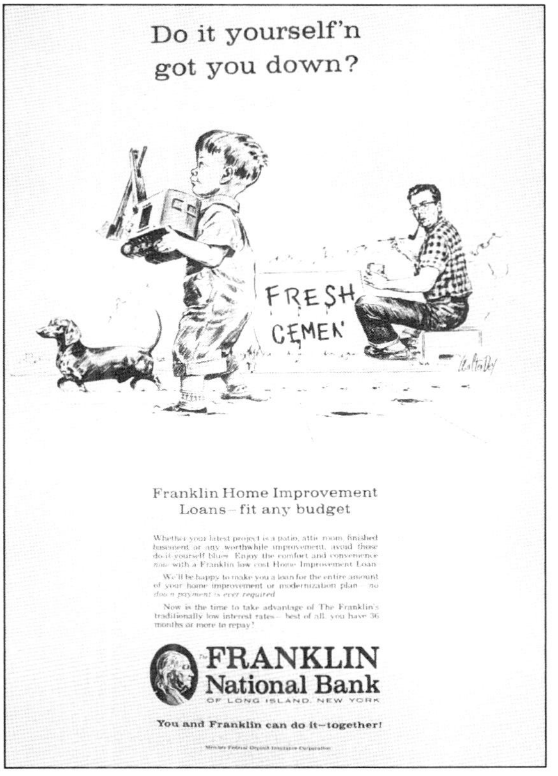

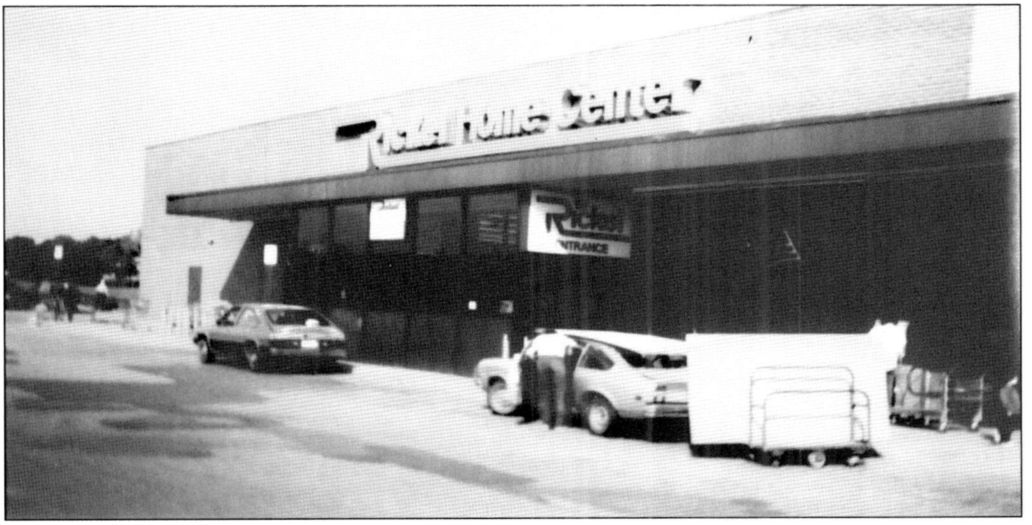

The entrance of Rickels Home Center, another bastion for the do-it-yourselfer, was one of many "welcome mats" in stores such as Rickels and Channel, which especially in suburban communities took the place of the small hardware store. Here we see a brave homeowner loading Sheetrock onto the roof of a small hatchback car. The extent of homeowner mania could possibly be measured by the need to purchase a station wagon, but only if it could safely accommodate a sheet of plywood with the back seats turned down. (Collection of the Levittown Library.)

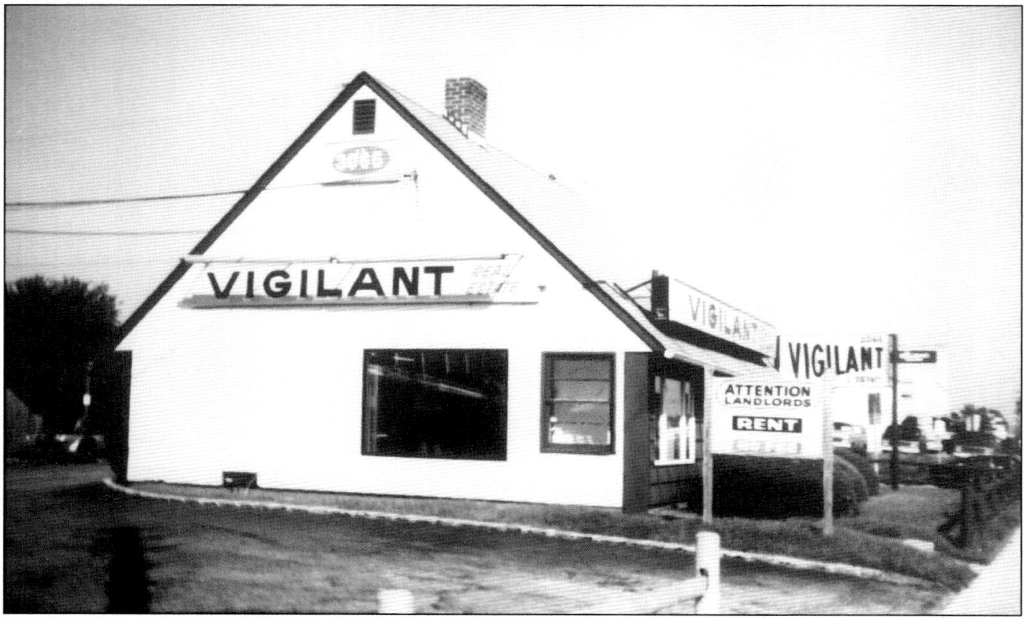

Vigilant Real Estate on Hempstead Turnpike was one of the many real estate offices founded to handle the burgeoning sale and resale of homes in Levittown. (Collection of the Levittown Library.)

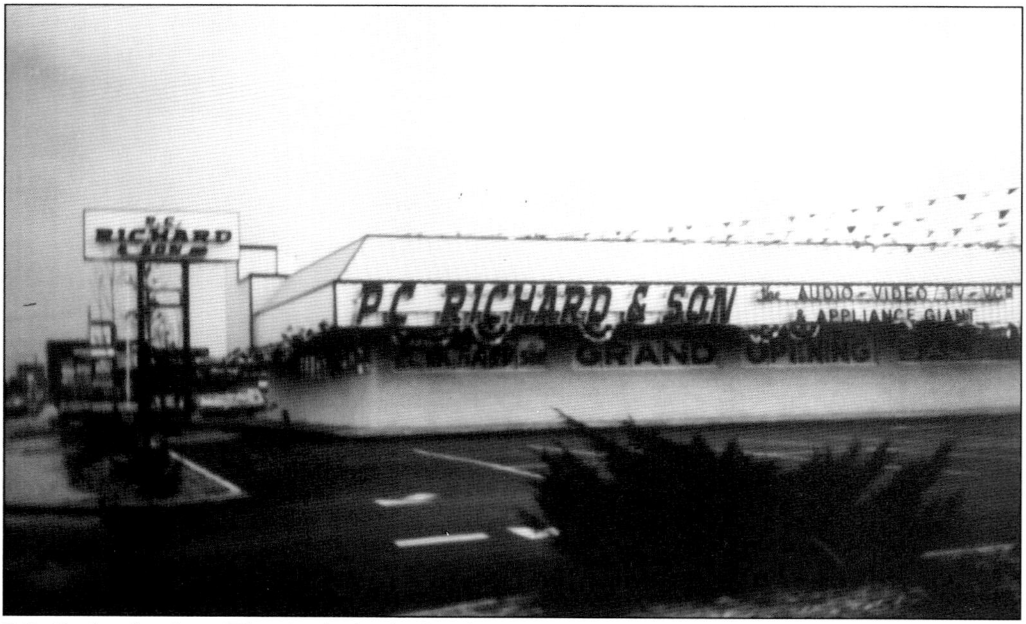

P.C. Richard, a.k.a. "The Audio/Video/TV/VCR/and Appliance Giant," is shown in this early 1988 photograph on Hempstead Turnpike, just east of Shelter Lane. In a few short decades, since the 12-inch Admiral television was a selling point of the Levitt ranch, the world of audio-visual equipment exploded. Unlike the young vets and their families, who felt fortunate to own a small television, today's average family owns several televisions, sophisticated stereo equipment, a camcorder, and VCRs. (Collection of the Levittown Library.)

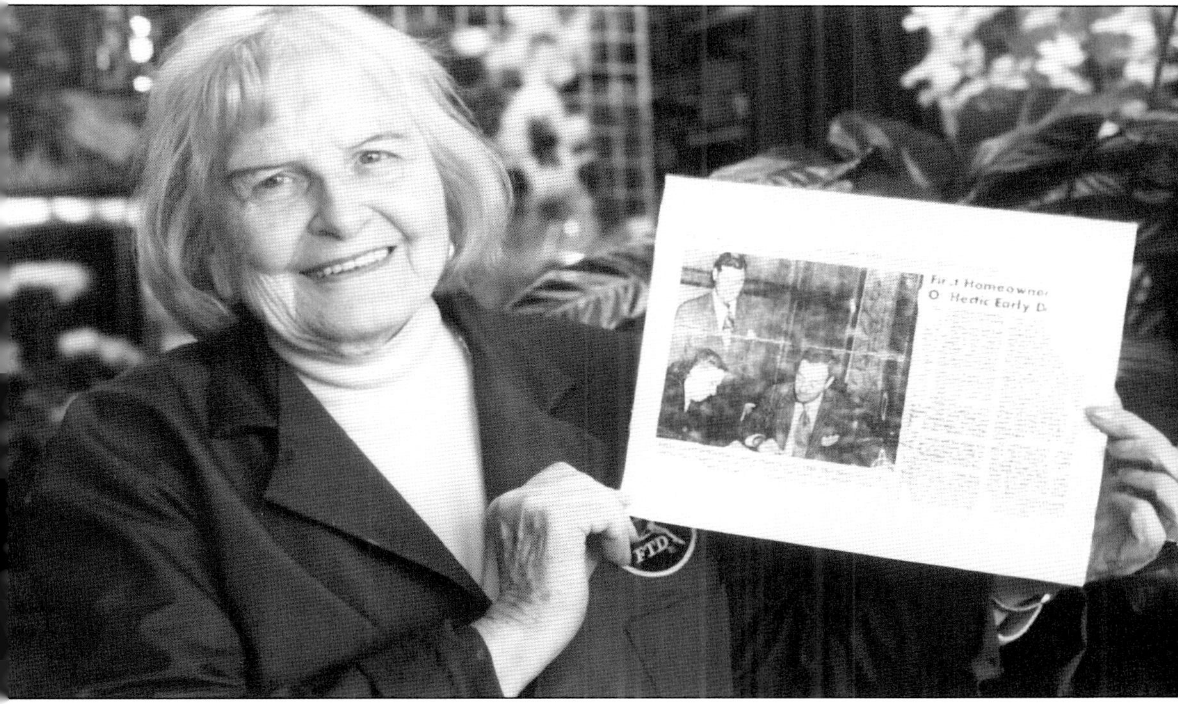

Original Levittowner Mary Heron Quinn holds a newspaper clipping of her brother Phil Heron and sister Adele with William Levitt signing a deed to their new Cape Cod. Mary, who purchased the home with her brother and sister, was working at the time and unable to attend the closing. To the authors' great delight, Mrs. Quinn made it into her own photograph 50 years later. She still works at the store founded by her brother, a much-loved Levittown pioneer. Today, Flowers by Phil is owned by Mary's son Robert Quinn. (Photograph by Tova Navarra.)

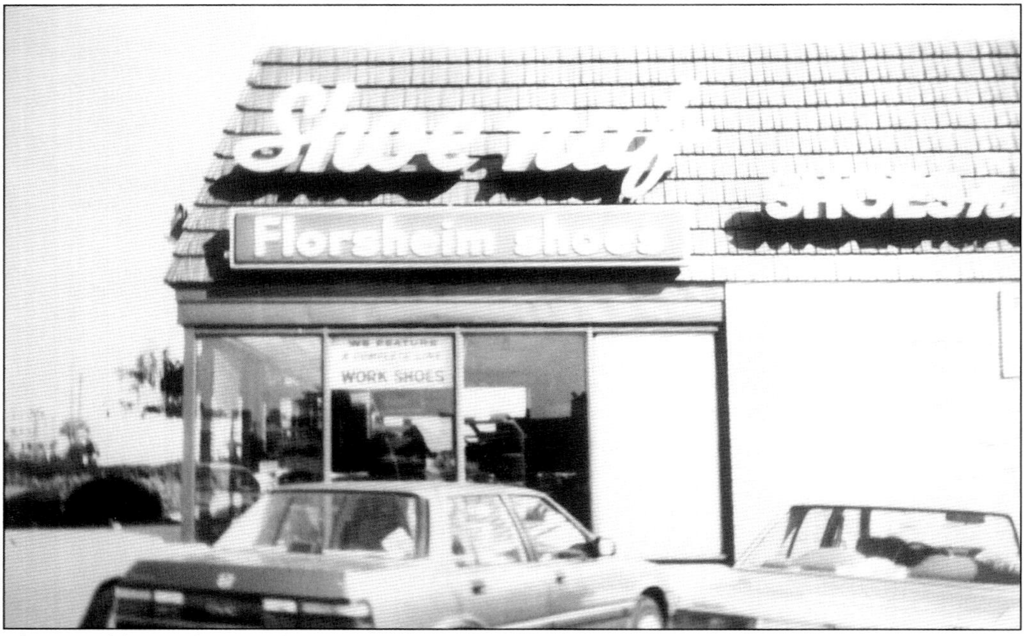

Shoe-Nuf, located west of Center Lane and Hempstead Turnpike, featured Florsheim shoes, a well-known brand. (Collection of the Levittown Library.)

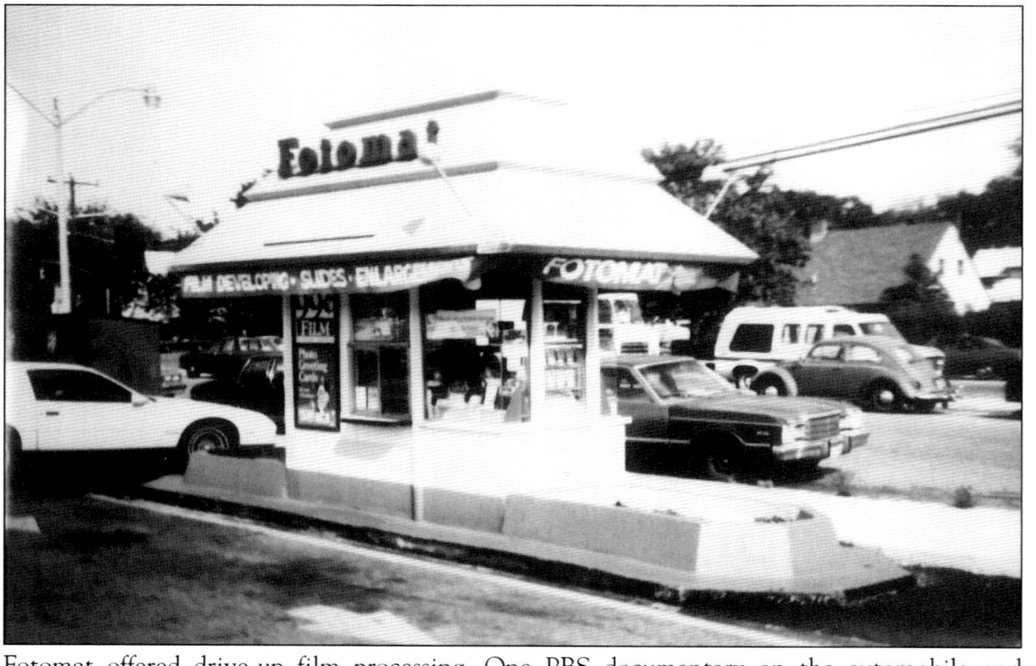

Fotomat offered drive-up film processing. One PBS documentary on the automobile and the changes it brought in the 20th century made specific mention of Levittown and the transportation ease that the automobile provided people. Many businesses really blossomed with the use of drive-up services, such as fast-food franchises and banks. (Collection of the Levittown Library.)

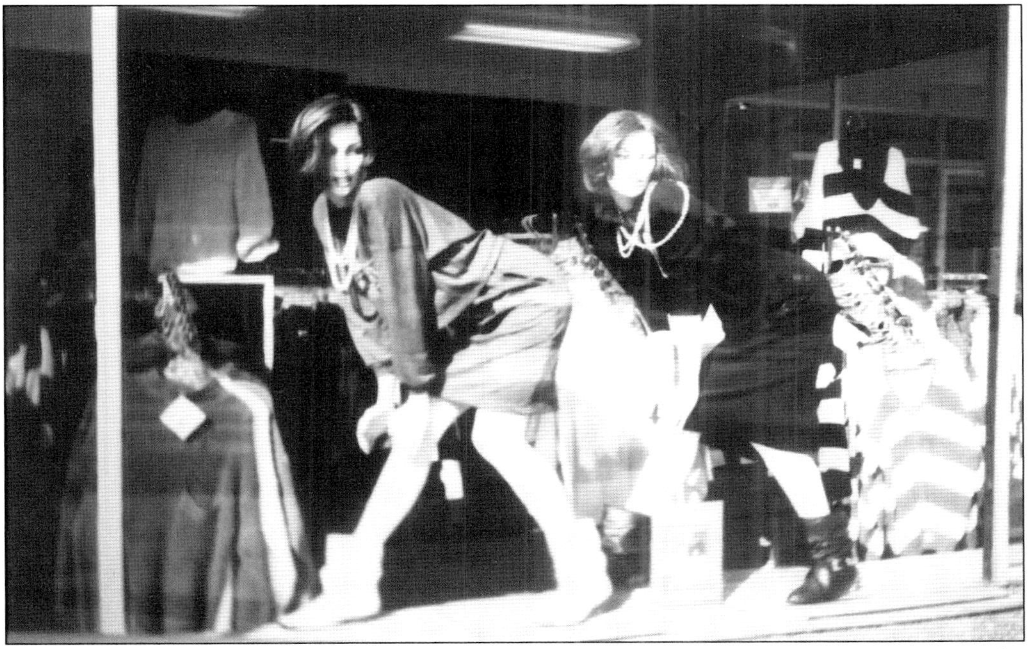

Mannequins pose seductively in this J.C. Penney windowfront. (Collection of the Levittown Library.)

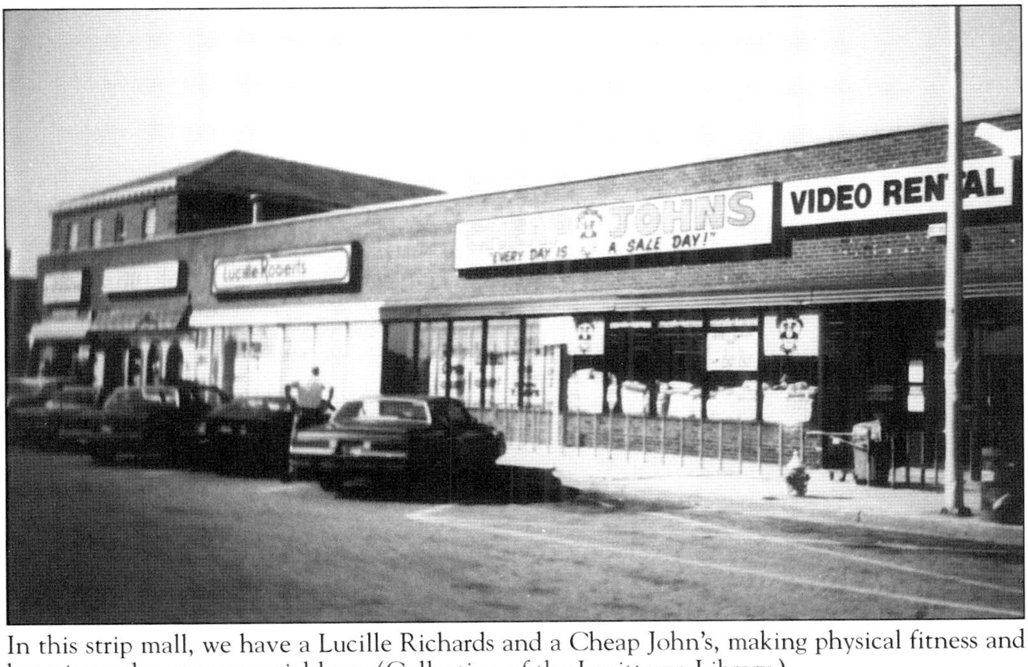

In this strip mall, we have a Lucille Richards and a Cheap John's, making physical fitness and bargains rather strange neighbors. (Collection of the Levittown Library.)

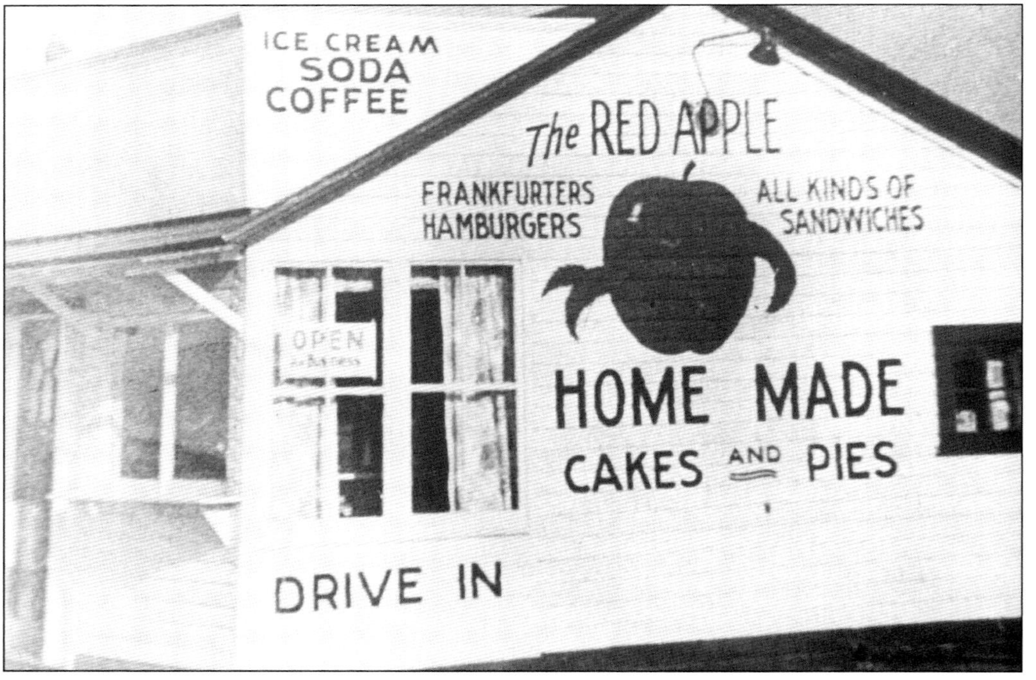

The Red Apple Restaurant was one of the few businesses in the early days of Levittown. It went on to become Caruso's and later Steve's Steak House. The original Red Apple featured frankfurters, hamburgers, homemade pies, all kinds of sandwiches, ice cream, coffee, and soda. (Collection of the Levittown Library.)

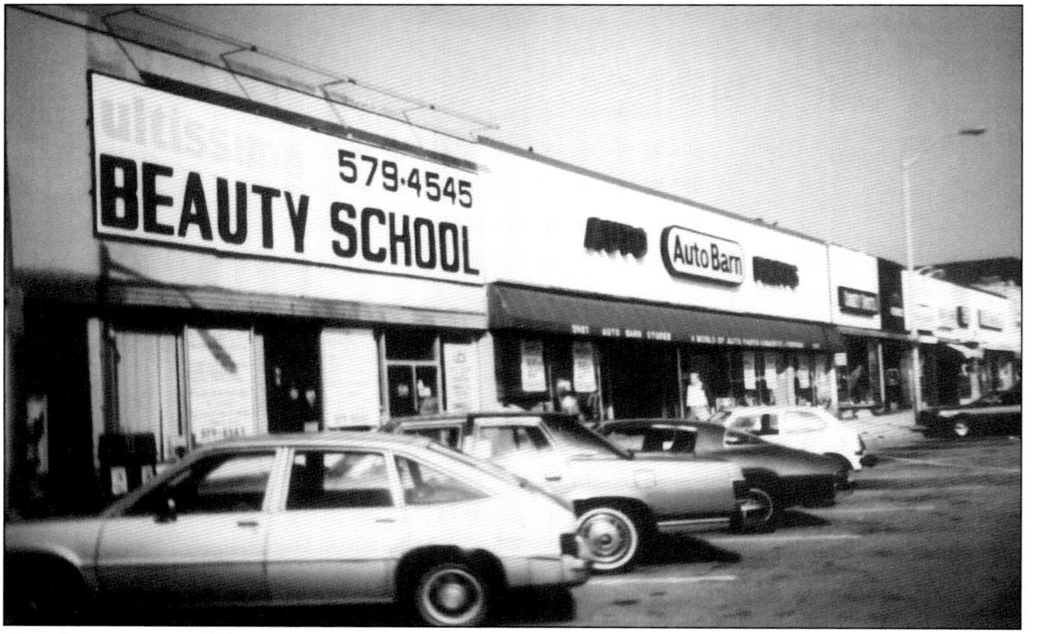

Another strip mall boasts the Ultissima Beauty School, next to Auto Barn Auto Supply. (Collection of the Levittown Library.)

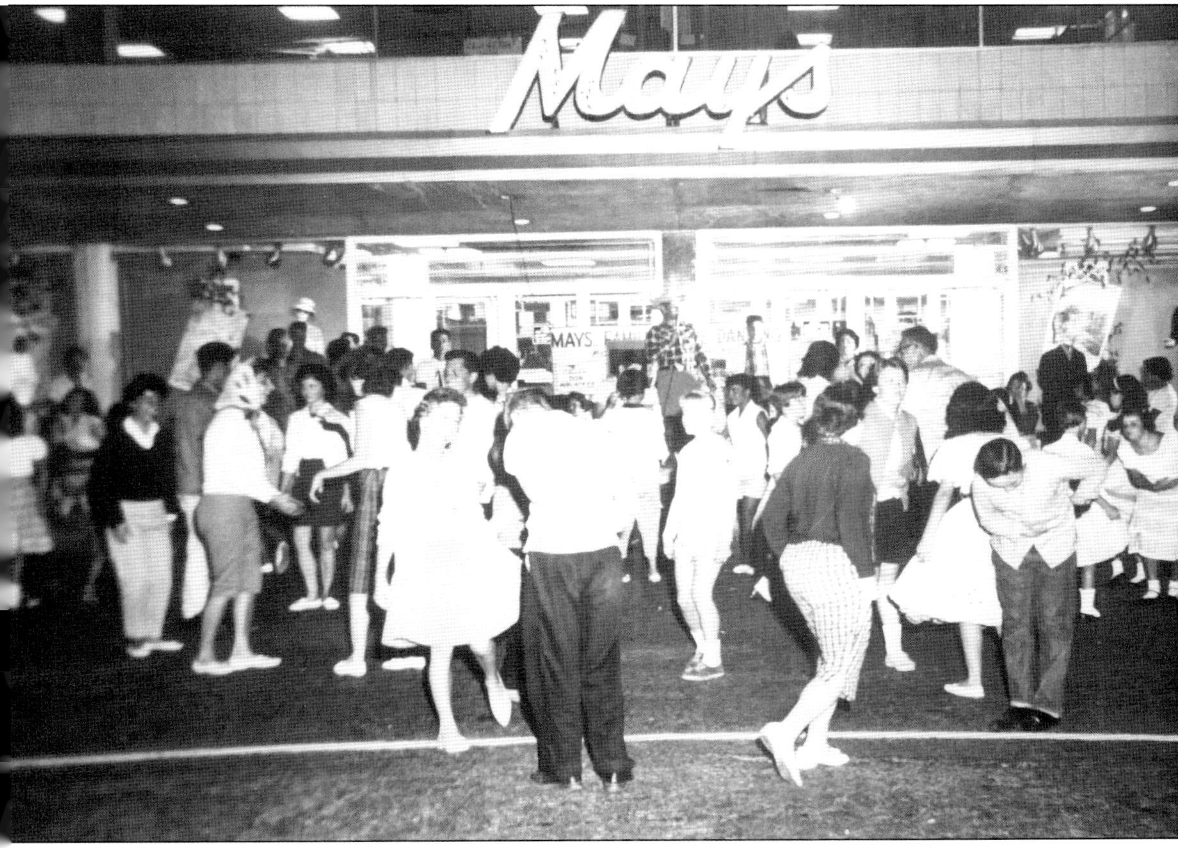

Square dancers do-si-do their talents in front of Mays on Hempstead Turnpike. The event was part of the activities to celebrate the 20th anniversary of Levittown. (Collection of the Levittown Library.)

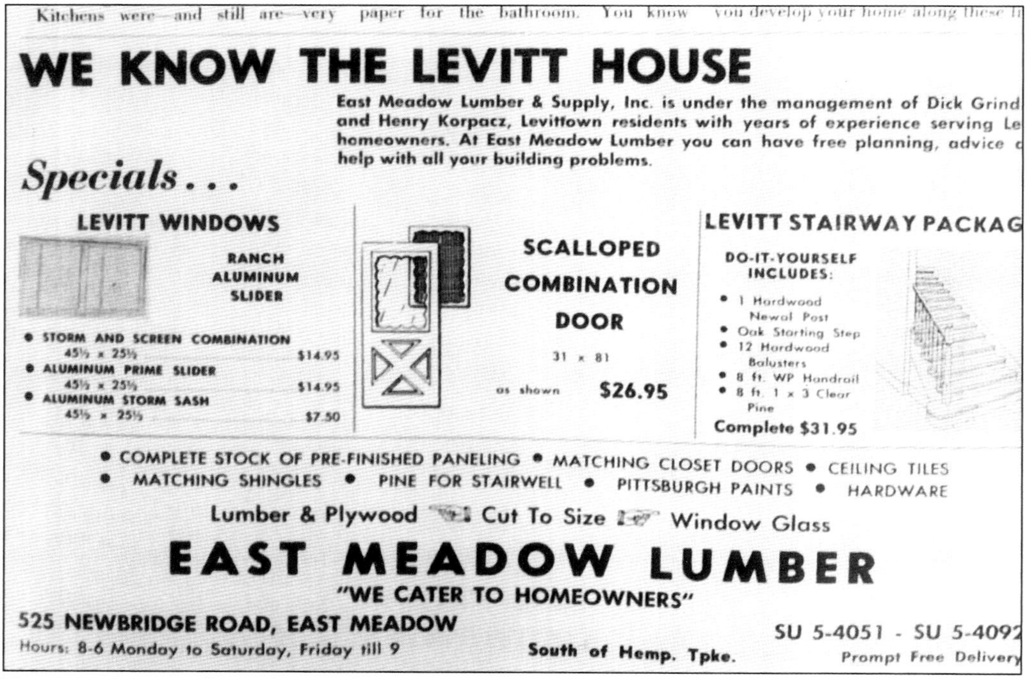

East Meadow Lumber advertised a line of products geared to the Levitt homeowner. The ad features a stairway package for the do-it-yourselfer for $31.95 and slider windows for $14.95. (Collection of the Levittown Library.)

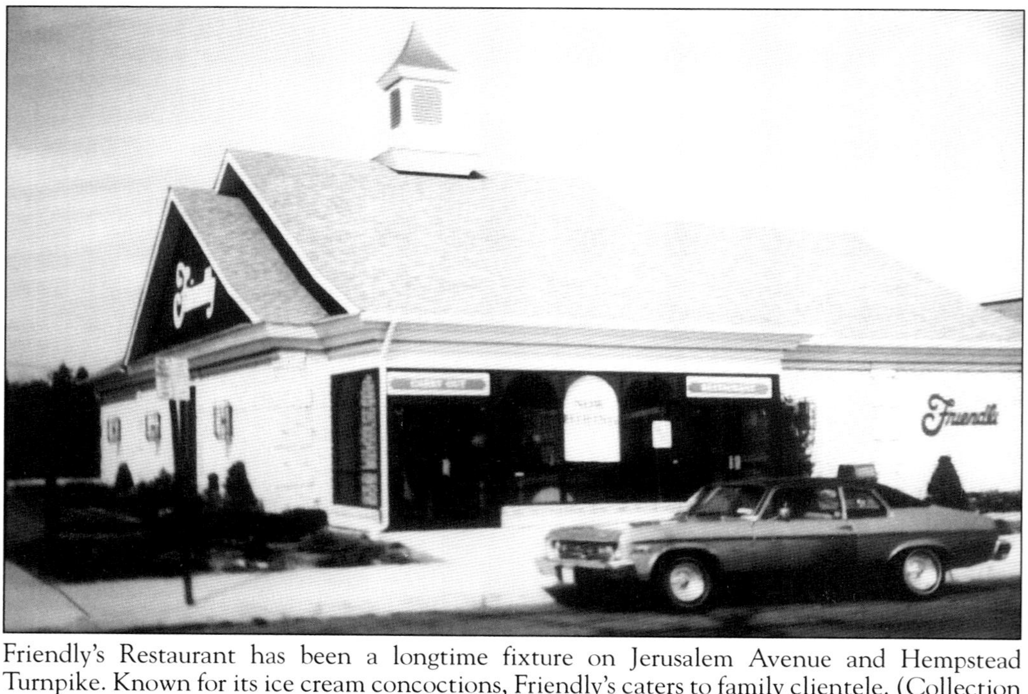

Friendly's Restaurant has been a longtime fixture on Jerusalem Avenue and Hempstead Turnpike. Known for its ice cream concoctions, Friendly's caters to family clientele. (Collection of the Levittown Library.)

Three

The Nuzzi Perspective

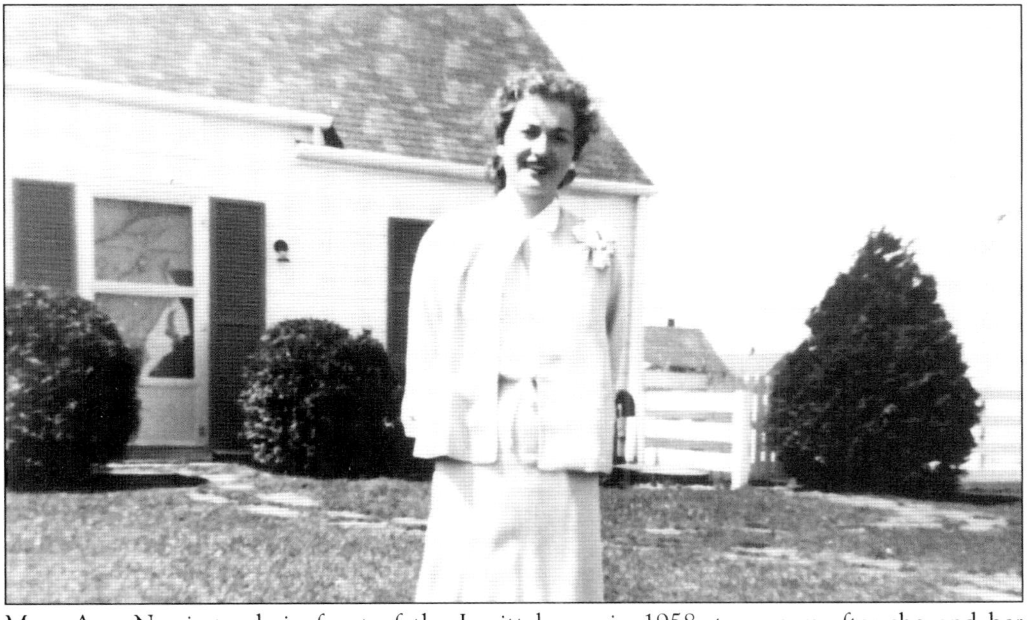

Mary Ann Nuzzi stands in front of the Levitt house in 1958, two years after she and her husband, Tony, bought it. They had a four-month-old son, Anthony. The house was originally rented until 1954, then purchased by the previous owners. The Nuzzis owned one car that Tony used to drive to his workplace. Mary Ann walked to the South Village Green with the baby carriage to shop for their needs at the Sunrise Supermarket, barbershop, stationary store, dry cleaners, hardware store, and the Levittown Public Library. (Collection of Mary Ann and Tony Nuzzi.)

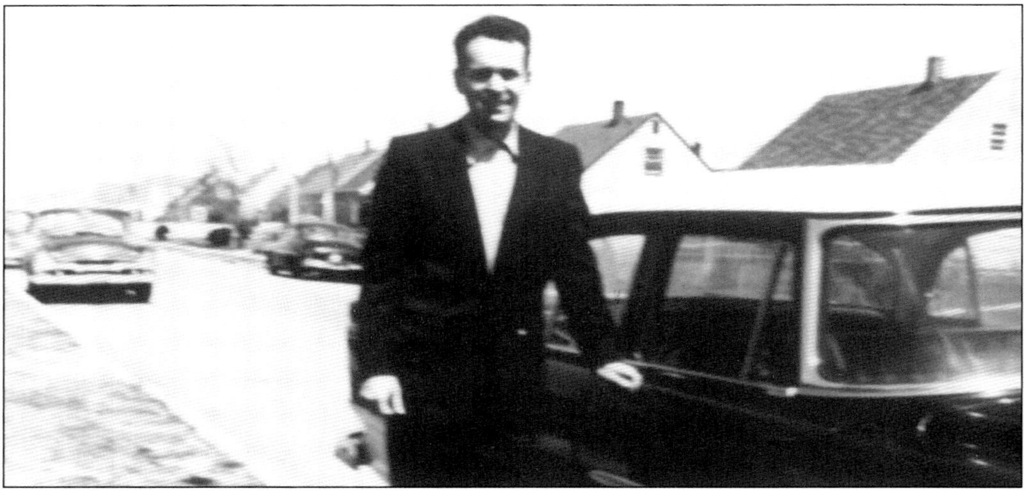

Tony Nuzzi is pictured next to the family car in 1958. Mary Ann recalls that initially Tony commuted to Queens by car. She said, "Tony joined the Nassau County Police Department in 1960 and retired in 1987. He worked rotating shifts for 27 years. Like many Levittowners, he pursued higher education and in 1974, he received an A.S. in criminal justice from Nassau Community College, and in 1978, a B.S. in behavioral science from the New York Institute of Technology." (Collection of Mary Ann and Tony Nuzzi.)

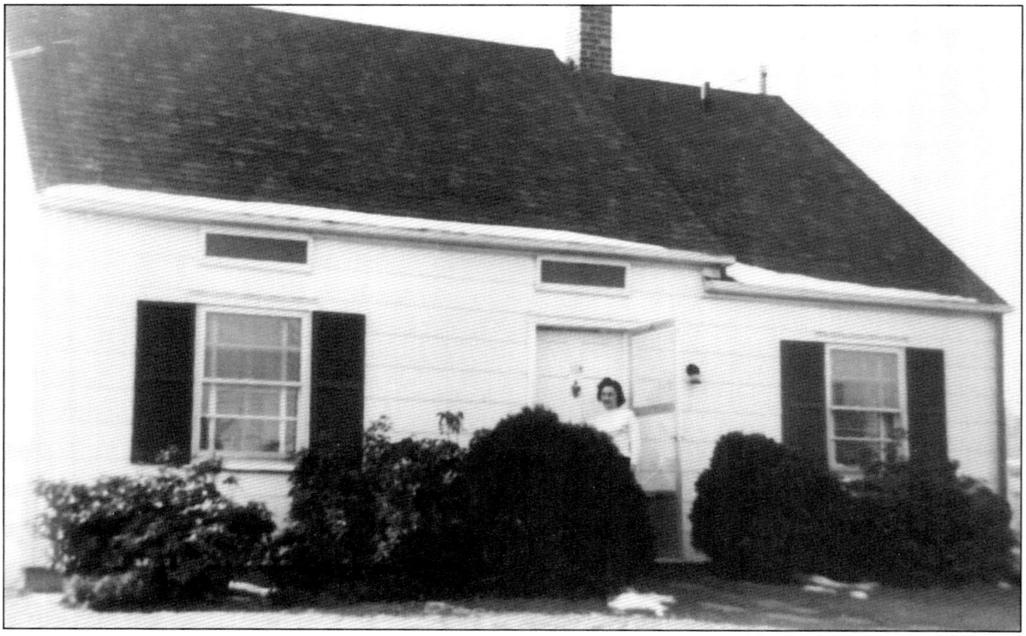

A young Mary Ann Nuzzi is shown in front of the family's newly purchased Levitt Cape Cod at 118 Ranch Lane. "I was a stay-at-home mother involved in school, community, gardening, sewing—a typical '50s mom," she said. "Hempstead Turnpike was originally two lanes in each direction. It was later widened and property was taken from the backyards of some homes. There was still some farming on Hempstead Turnpike then. We all dried clothes outdoors on backyard dryers or clotheslines." Fifty years later, the Nuzzis still own the same home with many additions and alterations. (Collection of Mary Ann and Tony Nuzzi.)

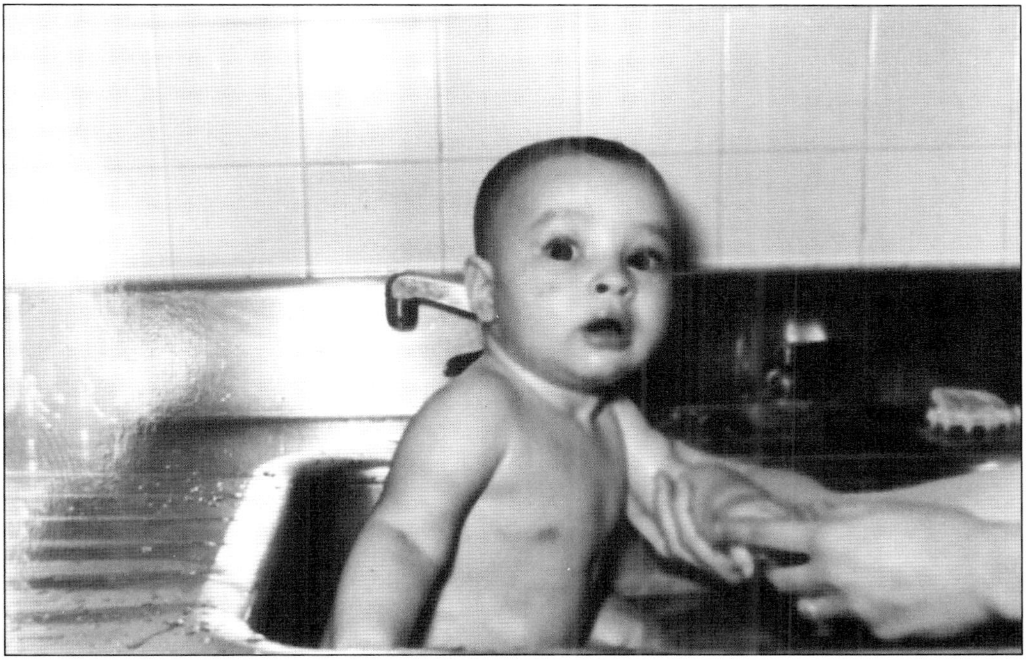

The baby in the bath is Anthony, the first of the Nuzzi children, in the trademark Tracey stainless-steel sink. The photograph was taken in 1957. (Collection of Mary Ann and Tony Nuzzi.)

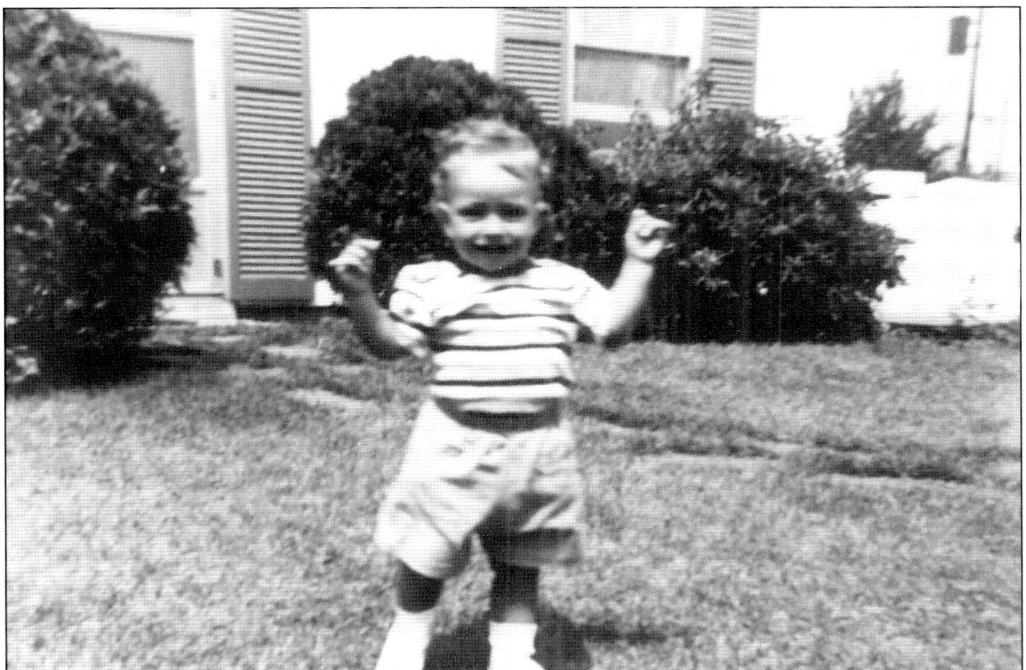

This photograph taken in July 1957 captures Anthony toddling about on the lawn. (Collection of Mary Ann and Tony Nuzzi.)

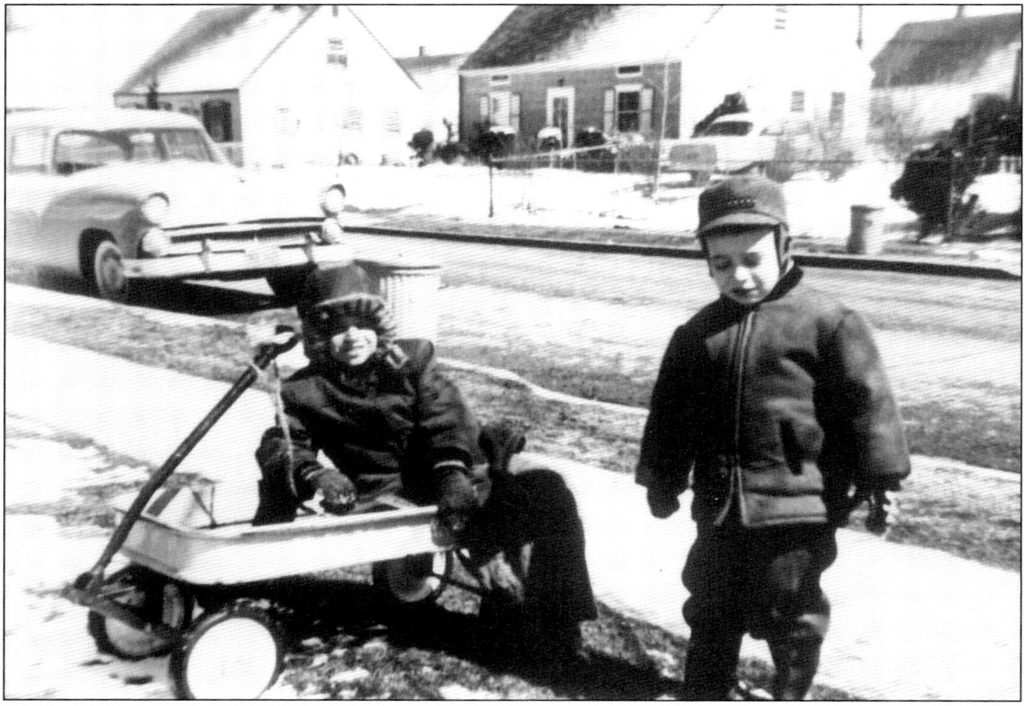

Shown here in this April 1959 photograph are Anthony and his friend Arthur Yankis in a wagon. "Many, many playmates for children lived on each block," said Mary Ann Nuzzi, ". . . mostly young families. Neighbors were friendly and helpful." (Collection of Mary Ann and Tony Nuzzi.)

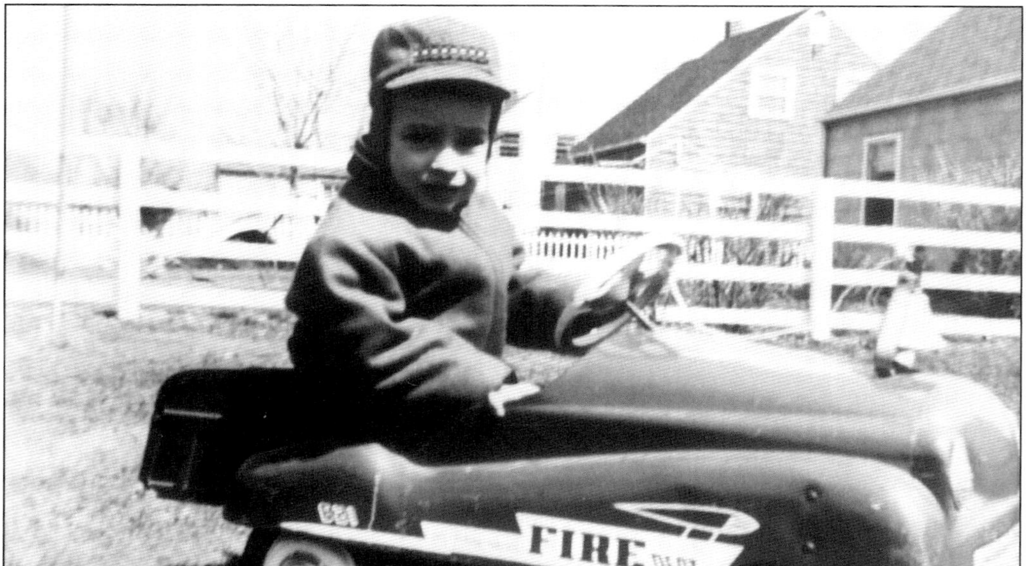

Anthony Nuzzi is captain of his own firetruck in this photograph taken in 1959 in the backyard of the Nuzzi home. A clothes dryer is visible on the left. (Collection of Mary Ann and Tony Nuzzi.)

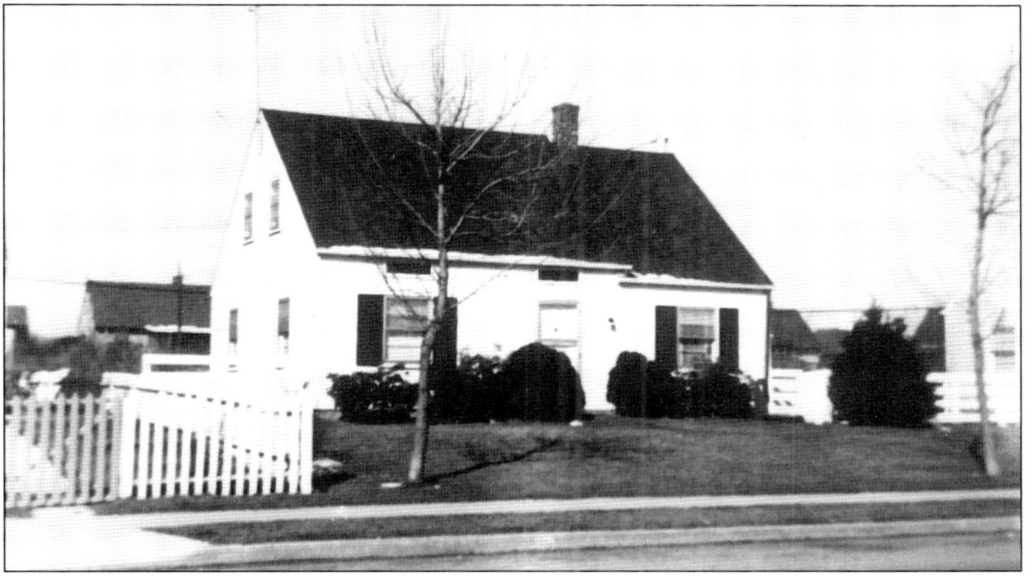

Another photograph documents the Nuzzi home soon after it was purchased. (Collection of Mary Ann and Tony Nuzzi.)

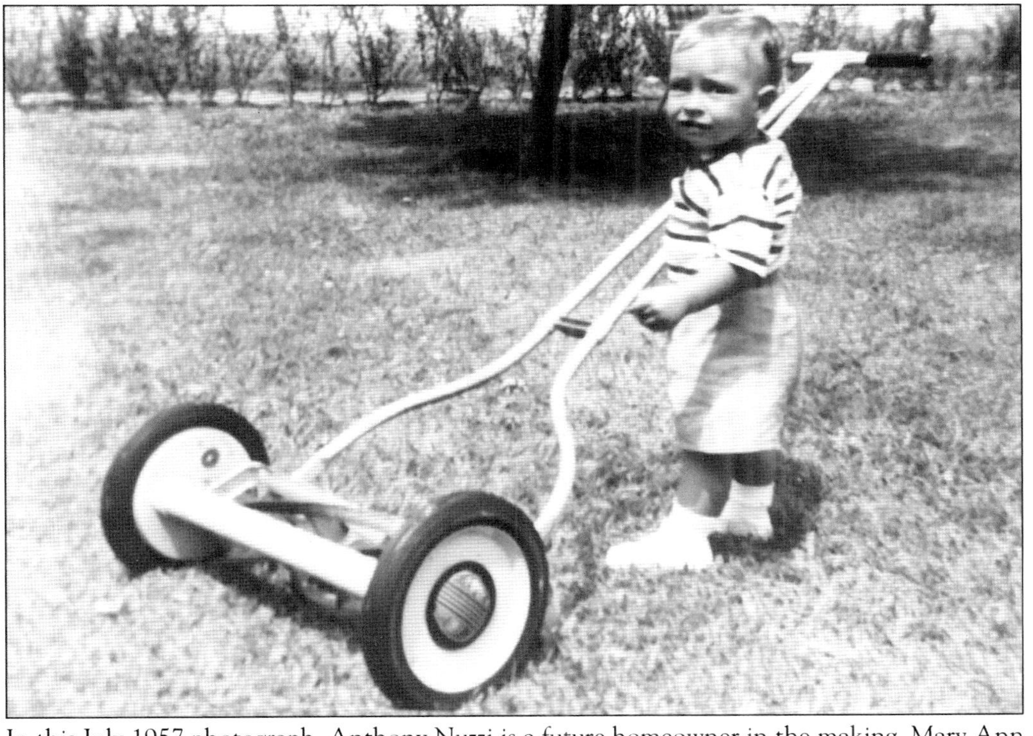

In this July 1957 photograph, Anthony Nuzzi is a future homeowner in the making. Mary Ann noted, "We used this lawnmower for at least 20 years." One of the early Levitt "laws" was that lawns had to be kept well. When a homeowner did not comply, the Levitts would have the grass cut and send a bill to the owner. Gradually, such regulations spelled out in the covenant that homeowners signed were not enforced. (Collection of Mary Ann and Tony Nuzzi.)

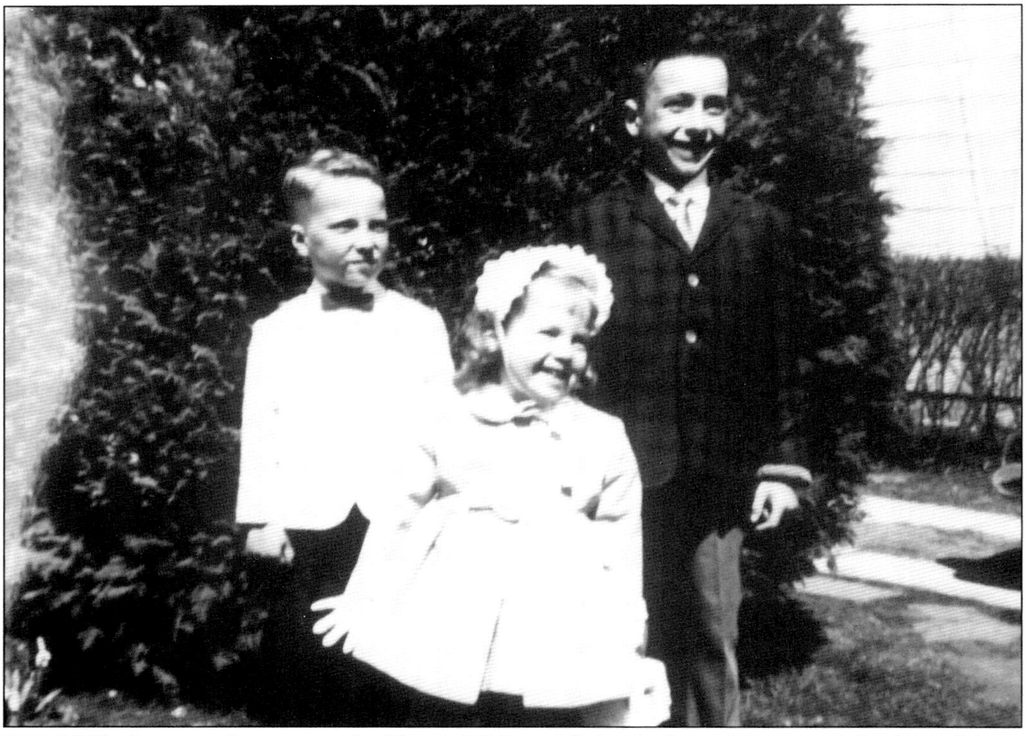

This 1963 photograph captures the Nuzzi children, Michael, Anne-Marie, and Anthony Nuzzi, on Easter Sunday. (Collection of Mary Ann and Tony Nuzzi.)

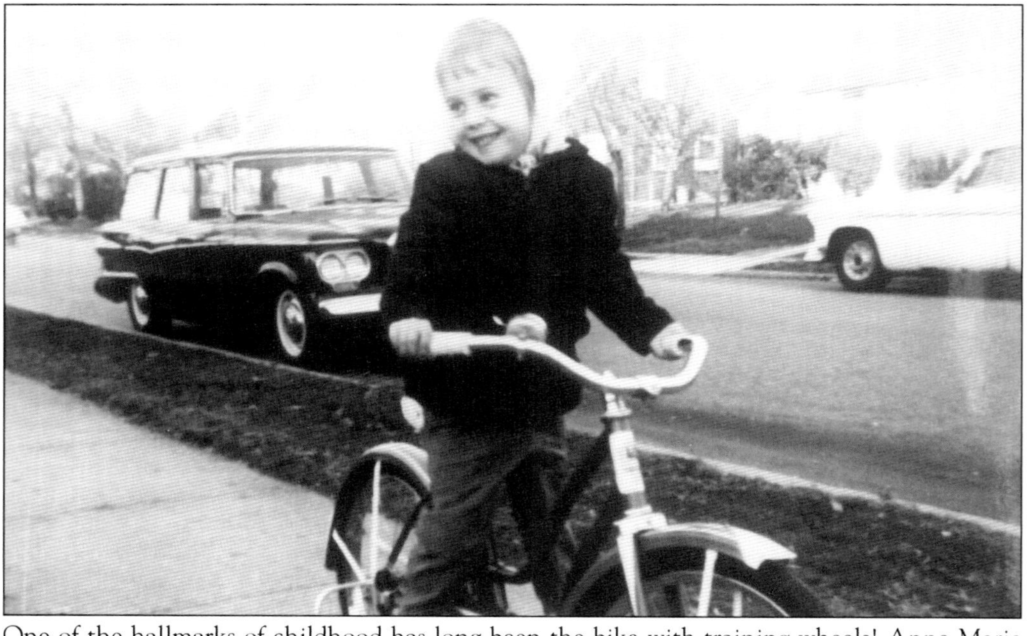

One of the hallmarks of childhood has long been the bike with training wheels! Anne-Marie Nuzzi is moving at her own speed in this November 1964 photograph. (Collection of Mary Ann and Tony Nuzzi.)

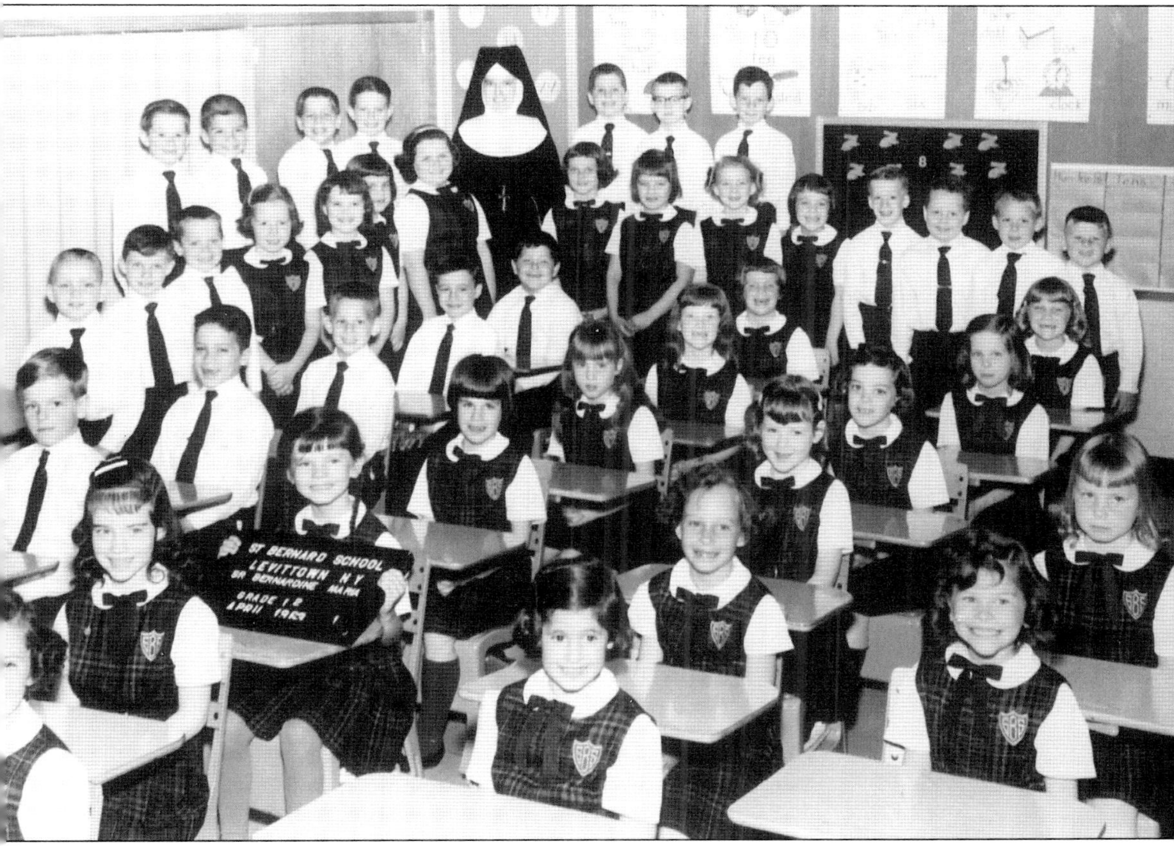

There were 42 students in the 1963 first-grade class at the new St. Bernard School. This photograph, taken in April 1963, shows this class with their teacher, Sister Bernardine Maria. Anthony Nuzzi is in the first row in the fourth seat from the left. (Collection of Mary Ann and Tony Nuzzi.)

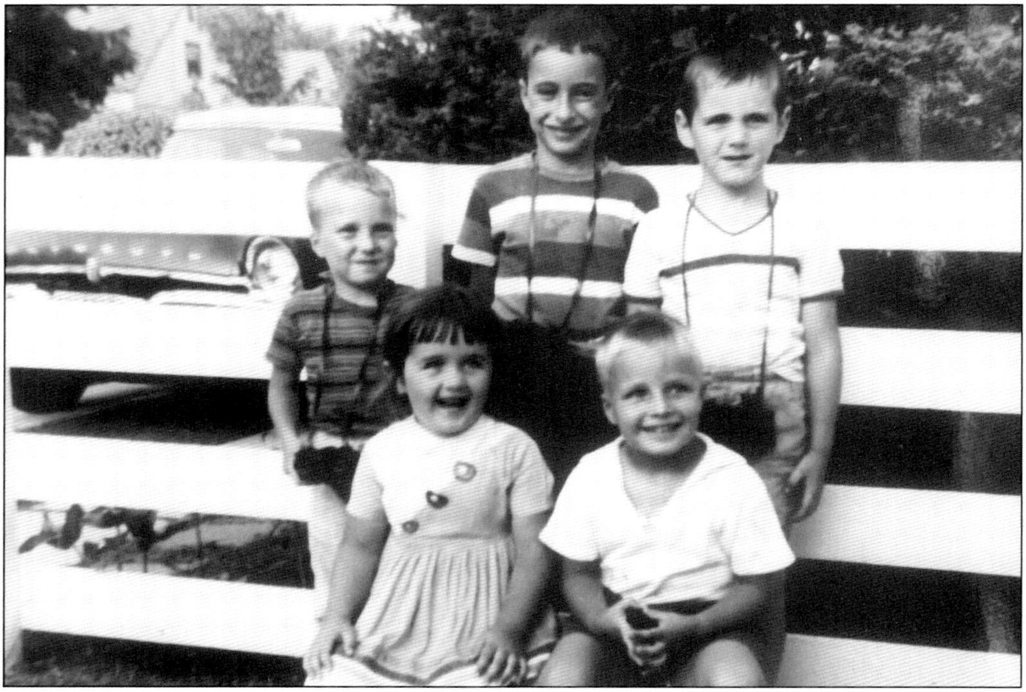

Pictured in this July 1963 photograph are playmates Pamela Naughton, Eric Krall, Michael Nuzzi, Anthony Nuzzi, and Richard Naughton. Mary Ann recalls one of the benefits of growing up in Levittown: "Children took Red Cross swimming lessons free at South Village Green pool." (Collection of Mary Ann and Tony Nuzzi.)

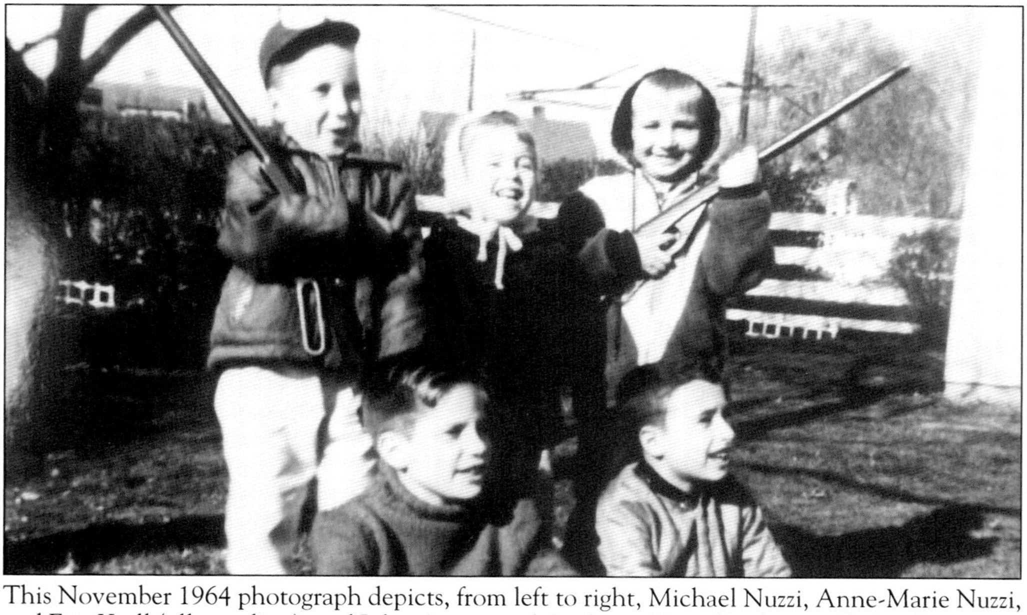

This November 1964 photograph depicts, from left to right, Michael Nuzzi, Anne-Marie Nuzzi, and Eric Krall (all standing), and John Aresca and Anthony Nuzzi (both seated). (Collection of Mary Ann and Tony Nuzzi.)

Anne-Marie Nuzzi received her First Communion in May 1968, at the original St. Bernard Church (a side view). (Collection of Mary Ann and Tony Nuzzi.)

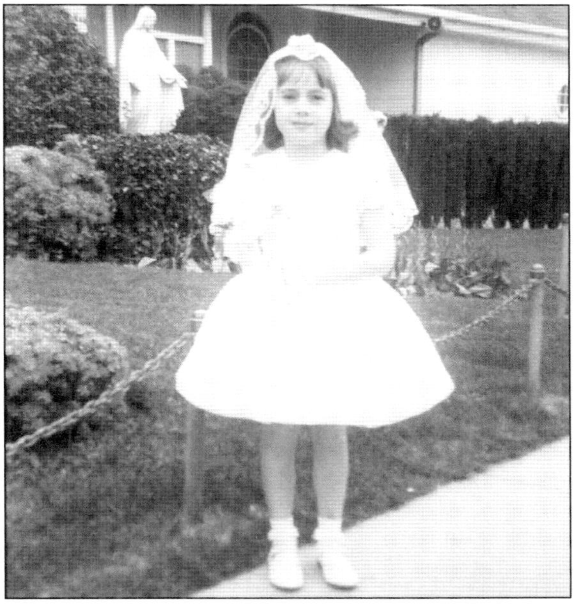

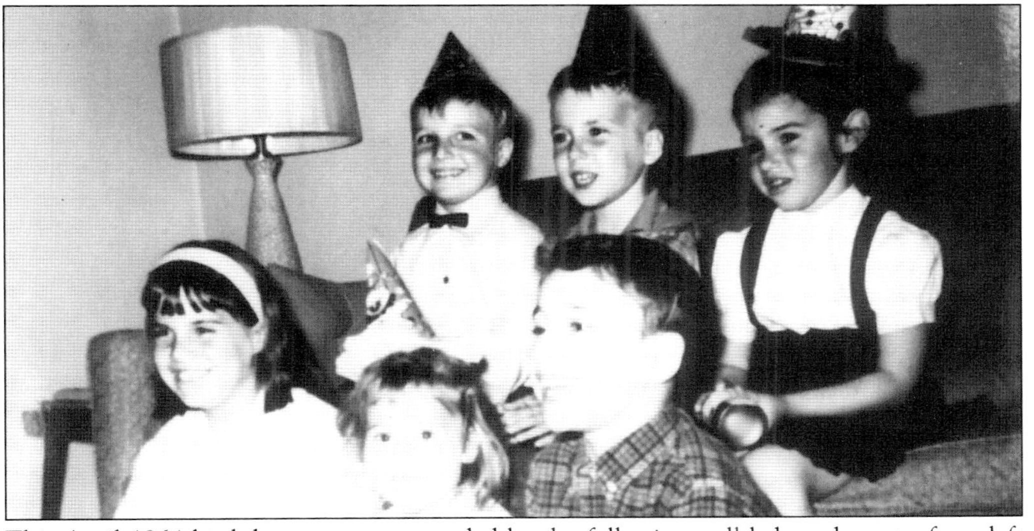

This April 1964 birthday party was attended by the following well-behaved guests, from left to right: (bottom row) Joyce Gerardi, Anne-Marie Nuzzi, and Anthony Nuzzi; (top row) Eric Krall, Michael Nuzzi, and Marie-Elena Gerardi. An important part of any parent's life is finding a pediatrician. Mary Ann said, "Our family doctor was Robert V. DiPasca, M.D. He began his practice when he came out of the service. His office was (and still is) in an original Levittown Cape Cod, at 84 Tanners Lane, near the South Village. He's been in Levittown since it was built. He delivered my three youngest children and saw us though illnesses, ailments, pneumonia, etc. He made house calls with his nurse, Kathy Dormer. His office was always crowded, especially in August when children went for their school check-ups. Going to the doctor was more like a visit to a friend's house. You always met others you knew there. Doctor usually had Jerry Vale songs playing, and a huge tropical fish tank in one of the examination rooms fascinated the kids. He is a part of Levittown history, a special, caring person who loves what he does."

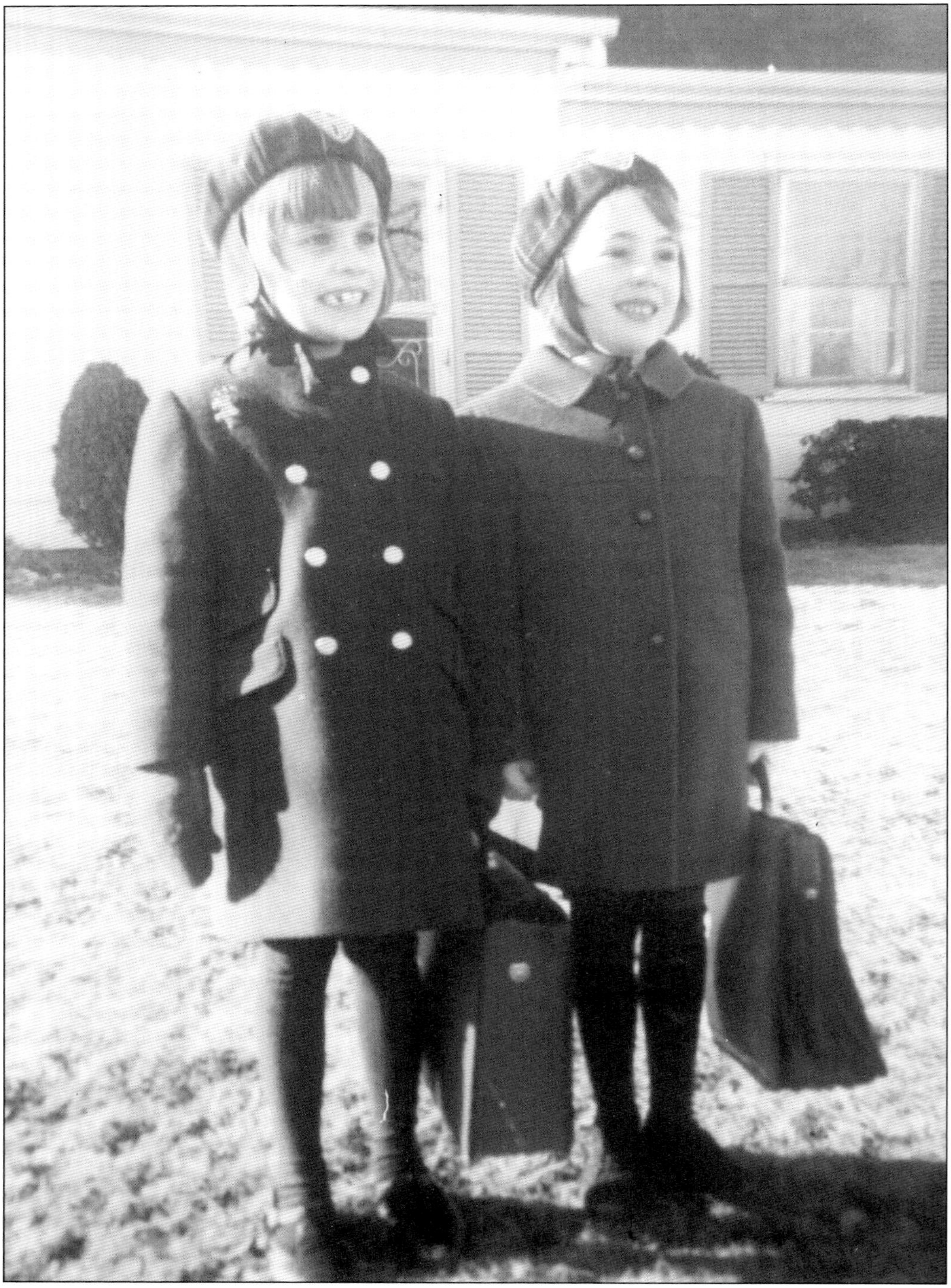

This January 1968 photograph shows St. Bernard students Lisa Aresca and Anne-Marie Nuzzi. "There were seven little girls almost the same age on the block," said Mary Ann. "Four of those families still live in the same houses. We are now all grandparents. The 20th high school reunion for the girls will be held November 1998." (Collection of Mary Ann and Tony Nuzzi.)

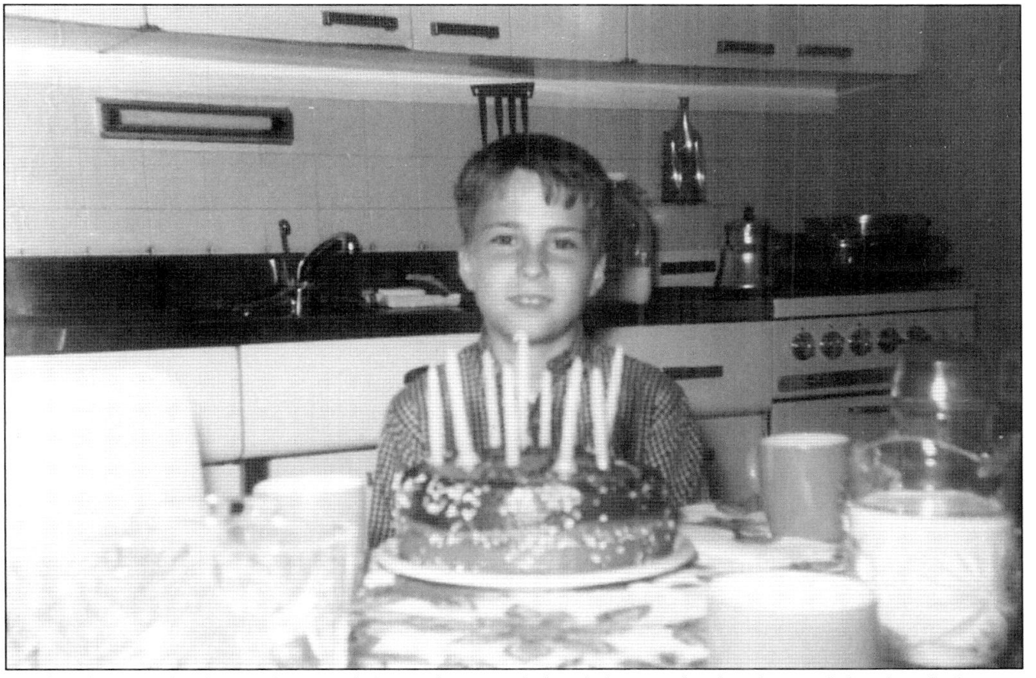

Michael Nuzzi looks ready to celebrate his ninth birthday in the kitchen of the family home. In the background are the famous Tracey steel cabinets the Levitts installed in their homes. (Collection of Mary Ann and Tony Nuzzi.)

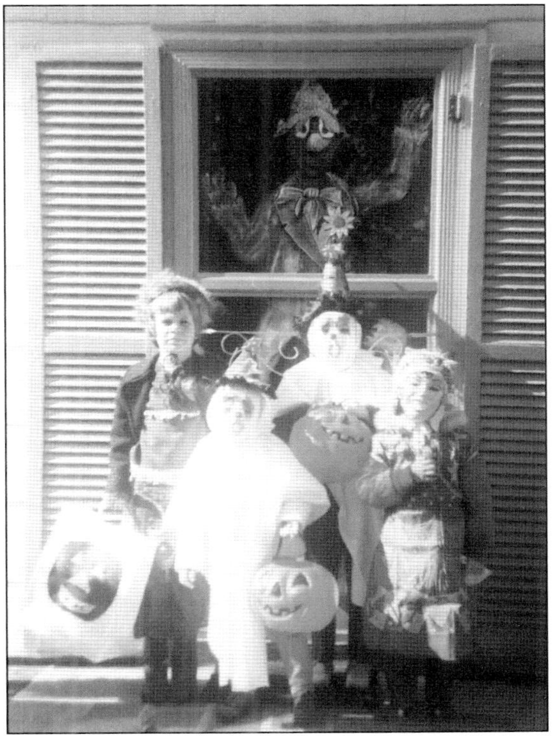

This Halloween 1968 photograph shows, from left to right, Lisa Aresca as a cowgirl, Susan Nuzzi and Anne-Marie Nuzzi as goblins, and Debbie Grier as a Mandarin. Debbie's brother Michael lives in the house today. (Collection of Mary Ann and Tony Nuzzi.)

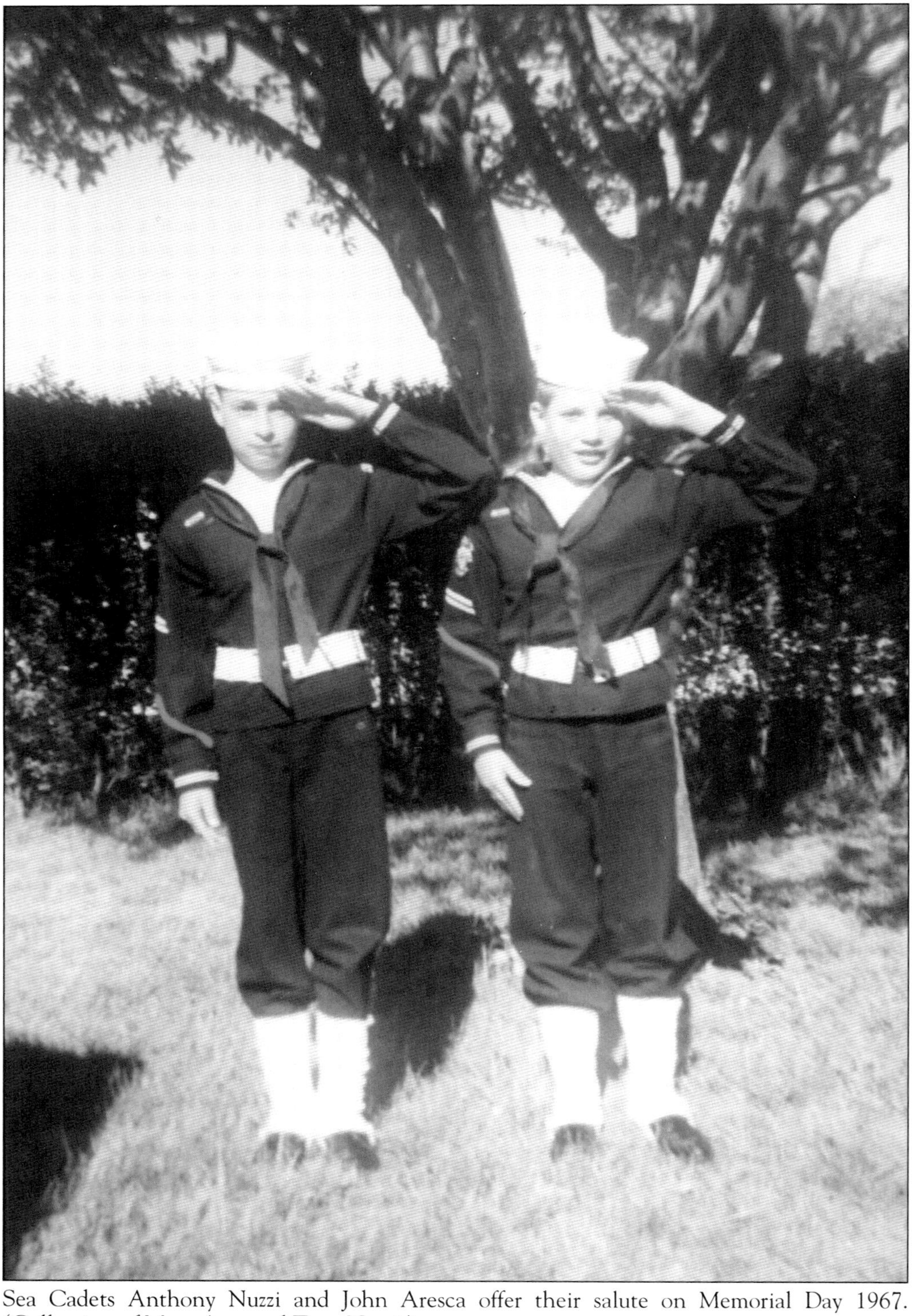

Sea Cadets Anthony Nuzzi and John Aresca offer their salute on Memorial Day 1967. (Collection of Mary Ann and Tony Nuzzi.)

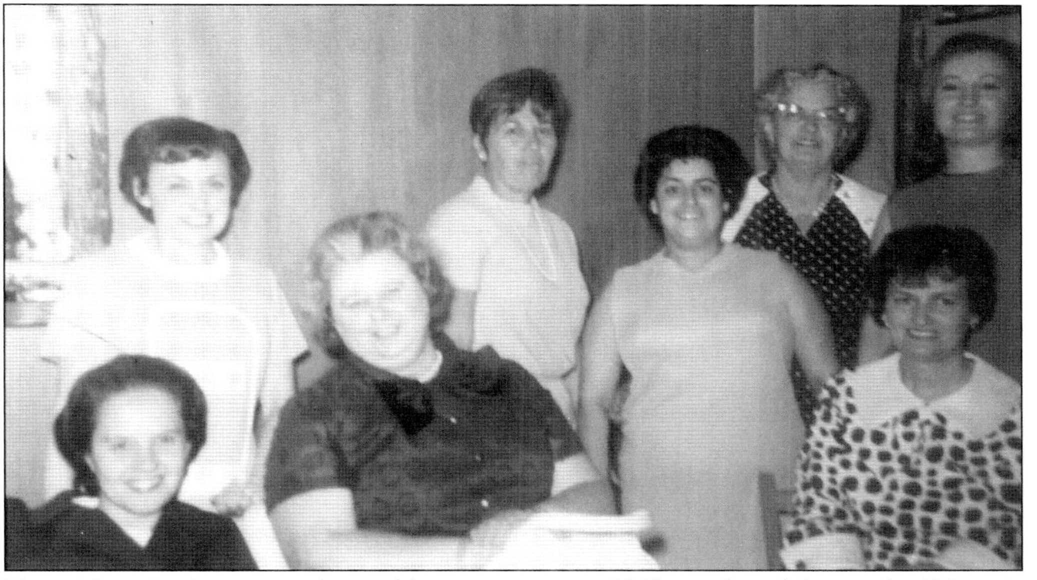

Using Mary Ann's own words, neighbors at a party in 1969 are, from left to right, "Virginia Gerardi, still residing in the same Levitt House, Luise Krall (deceased), Mickey Nichols, now residing in Florida (all seated); Elayne Singer, who lives in senior housing and whose married daughter Cindy lives in Levittown, Alba Aresca, still living in same house, Ruth Herscovit (deceased) whose married daughter Clare now lives in the family home, Marge Manley (deceased), and Mary Ann Nuzzi, still living in the same Levitt home (all standing)." (Collection of Mary Ann and Tony Nuzzi.)

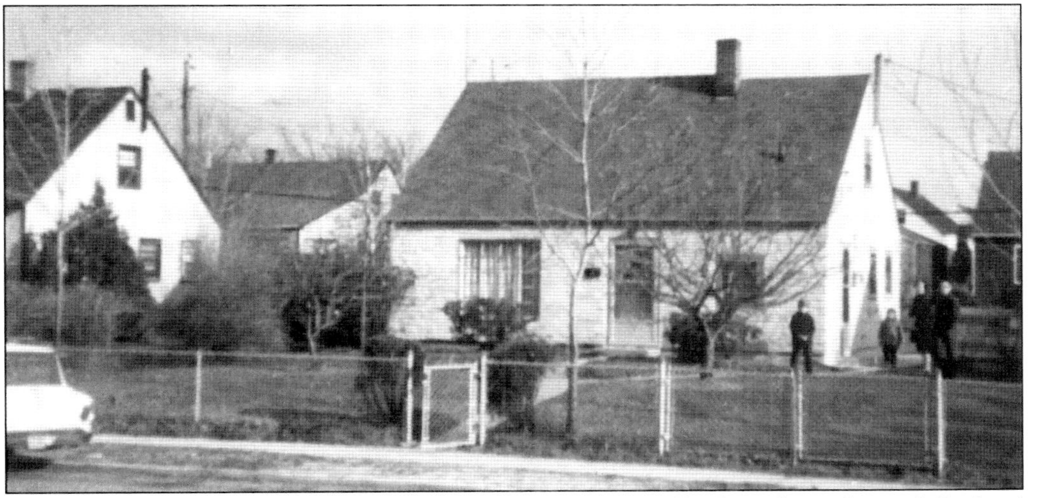

The Naughton Cape Cod in 1966 at 115 Ranch Lane was still relatively unchanged. Richard and Elizabeth Naughton describe how they became interested in Levittown: "In May 1946, my cousin Harold began working on the Levitt housing development. He performed general construction such as nailing Sheetrock, putting on roofs, etc., as required by the foreman. Harold was so impressed by the construction that he eventually bought a home on Old Oak Lane. After Harold, my brother Bill moved to Tailor Lane in 1956. In December 1961, we purchased our home for $13,900. Our monthly payment was $97, including taxes." (Collection of Mary Ann Nuzzi.)

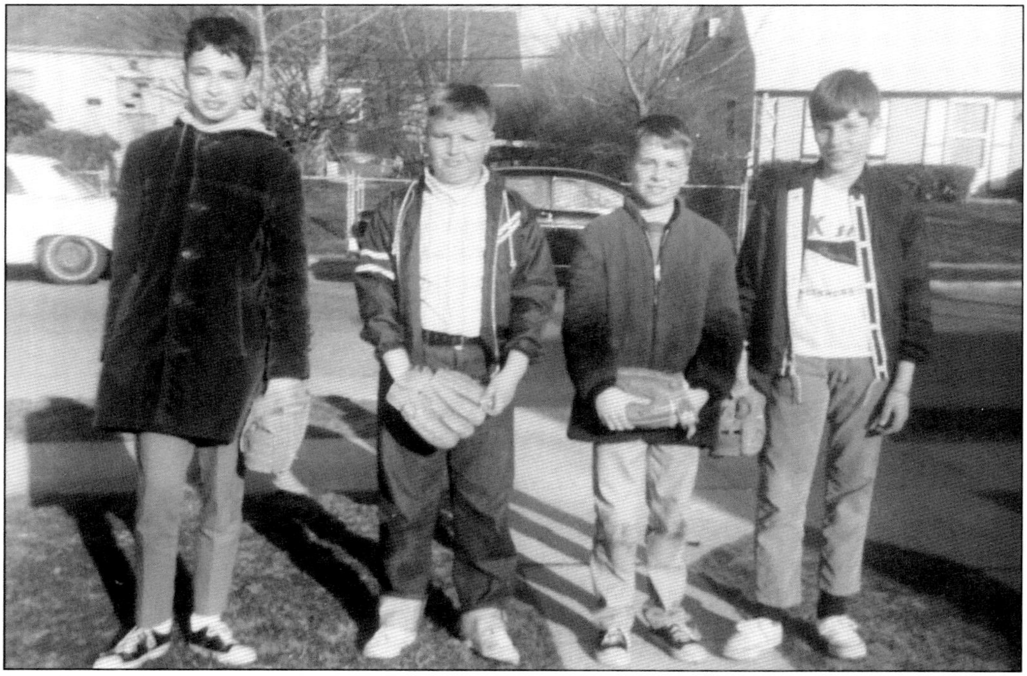

The "Boys of Summer" are seen in this 1969 photograph. From left to right are Anthony Nuzzi, Eric Krall, Michael Nuzzi, and John Aresca. (Collection of Mary Ann and Tony Nuzzi.)

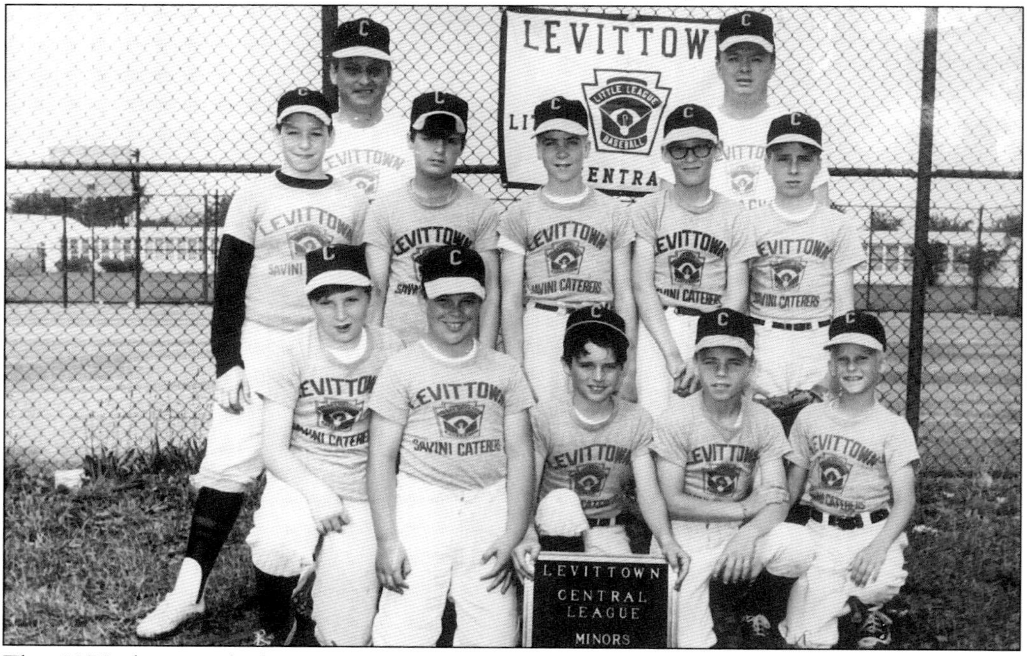

This 1970 photograph shows one Levittown Little League team from the Central League. The team was sponsored by Savini Caterers. Michael Nuzzi is in the top row at the extreme right. Top row center is John Dillon, now Father John Dillon, a priest in the Rockville Centre diocese. (Collection of Mary Ann and Tony Nuzzi.)

Michael Nuzzi is a convincing hobo for Halloween 1968. Said his mom: "My son Michael married a Levittown girl, Eileen Grogan. Her family still lives in Levittown. Michael graduated from Polytechnic Institute of New York with both a B.S. and a M.S. in civil engineering. Today, he is a professional engineer, married and has two daughters." (Collection of Mary Ann and Tony Nuzzi.)

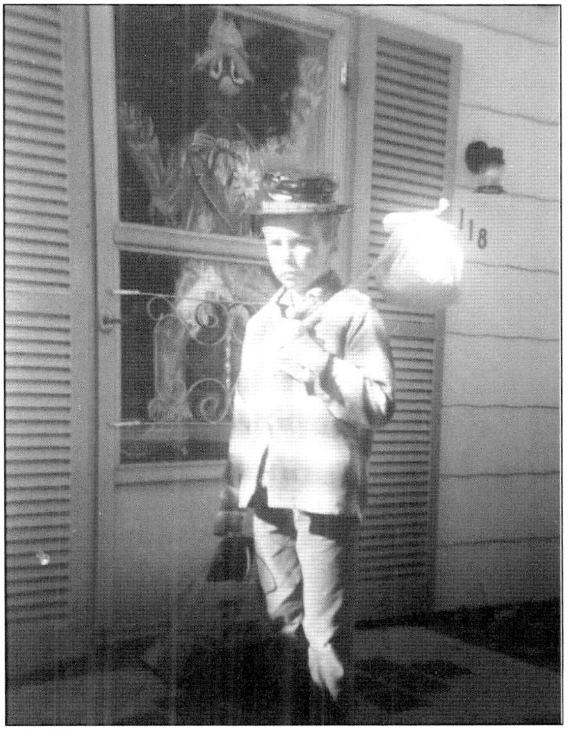

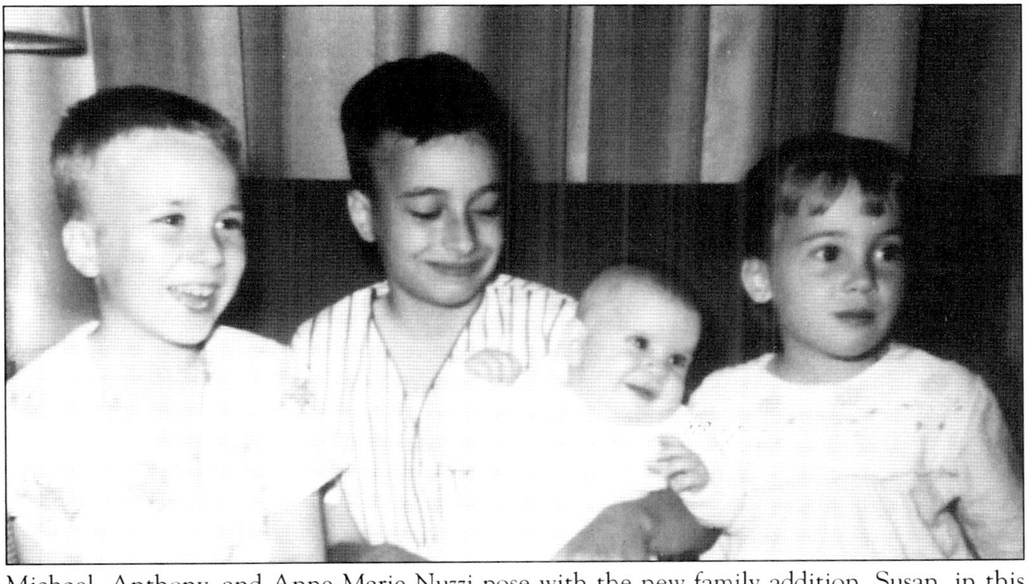

Michael, Anthony, and Anne-Marie Nuzzi pose with the new family addition, Susan, in this 1965 photograph. Mary Ann notes: "We raised four children in Levittown—Anthony, born July 1956, Michael, born April 1959, Anne-Marie, born in November 1960, and Susan, born in January 1960. The children all attended Abbey Lane School for kindergarten, St. Bernard School from first to eighth grade, and graduated from Levittown Memorial High School. They all excelled in school and had full or partial scholarships for college. Thanks to St. Bernard School and Levittown Memorial High School!" (Collection of Mary Ann and Tony Nuzzi.)

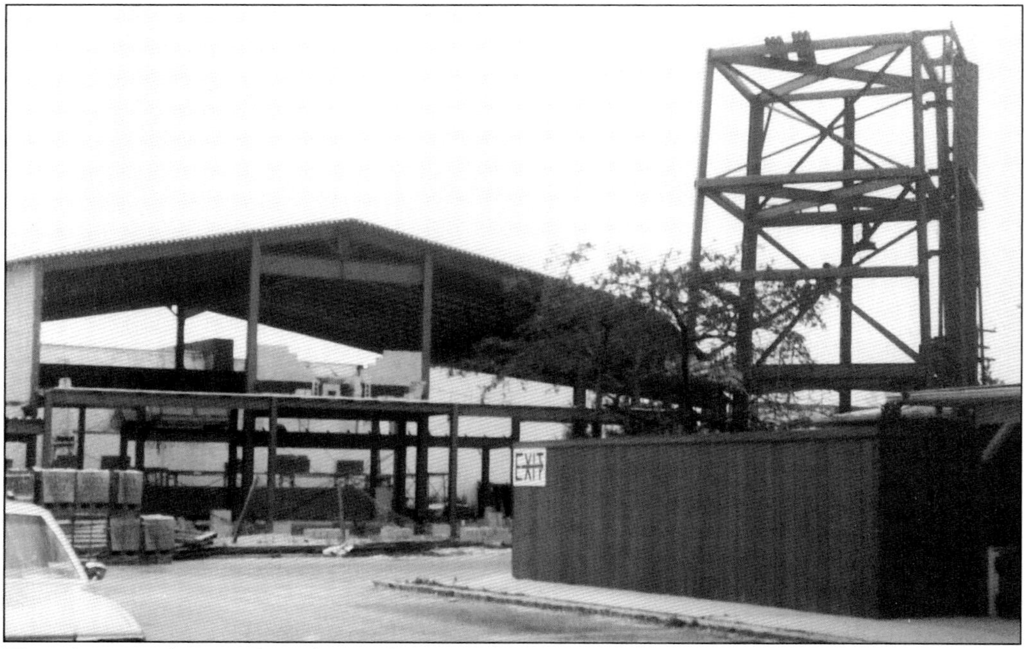

This photograph was taken during the construction of the new church of St. Bernard in 1984. (Collection of Mary Ann and Tony Nuzzi.)

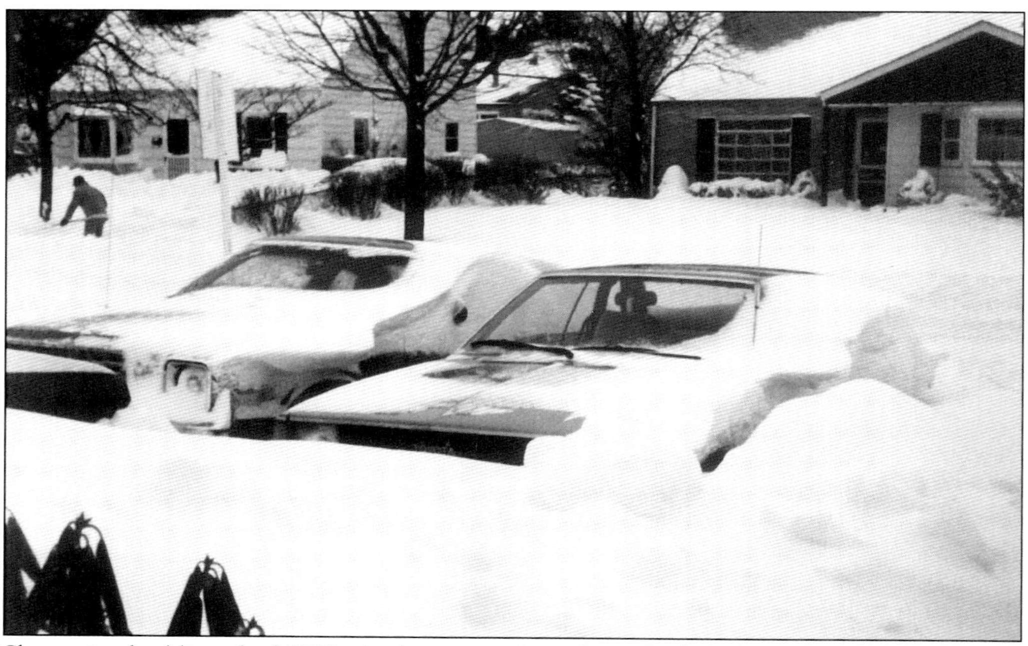

Shown in the blizzard of 1983, the house on the right is Dick and Betty Naughton's at 115 Ranch Lane before its latest renovation. (Collection of Mary Ann and Tony Nuzzi.)

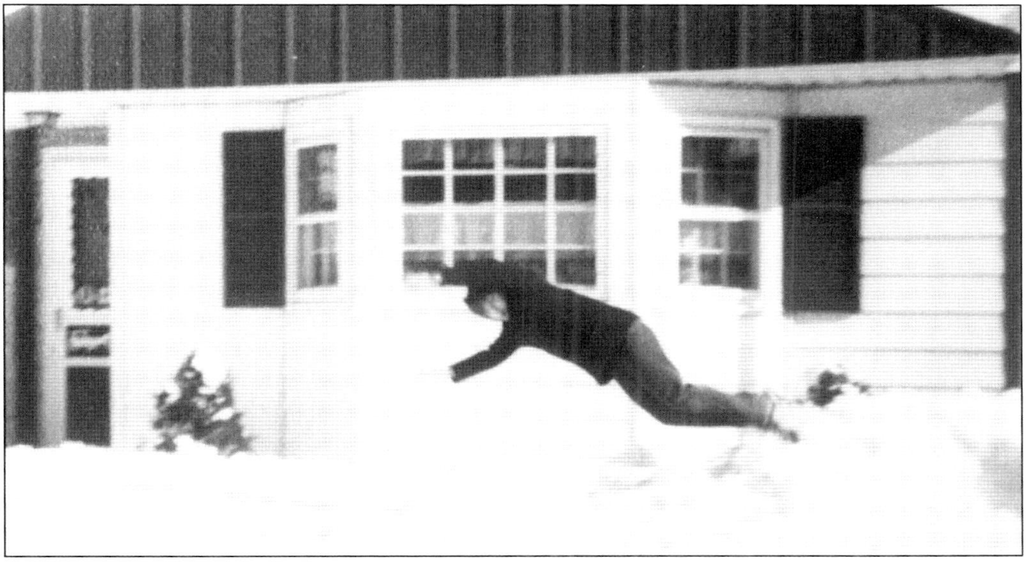

By 1974, the Naughton home had a significant addition to the side and front. Note the child flying through the air. Dick Naughton said, "In the beginning of 1963, since I was in the Air Force, I was shipped out to Turkey. We decided to keep the house and rent it out. We rented it through John Pergola, Real Estate. We moved back in September 1973 when I returned from the Air Force. At that time, we made our first expansion, including extending the kitchen to the side and front. We also had a garage built and put up aluminum siding. During the period we were away from Levittown, my mother, my sister and two of my cousins bought homes in Levittown. Needless to say, when our children attended the local schools, our names were well known." (Collection of Mary Ann and Tony Nuzzi.)

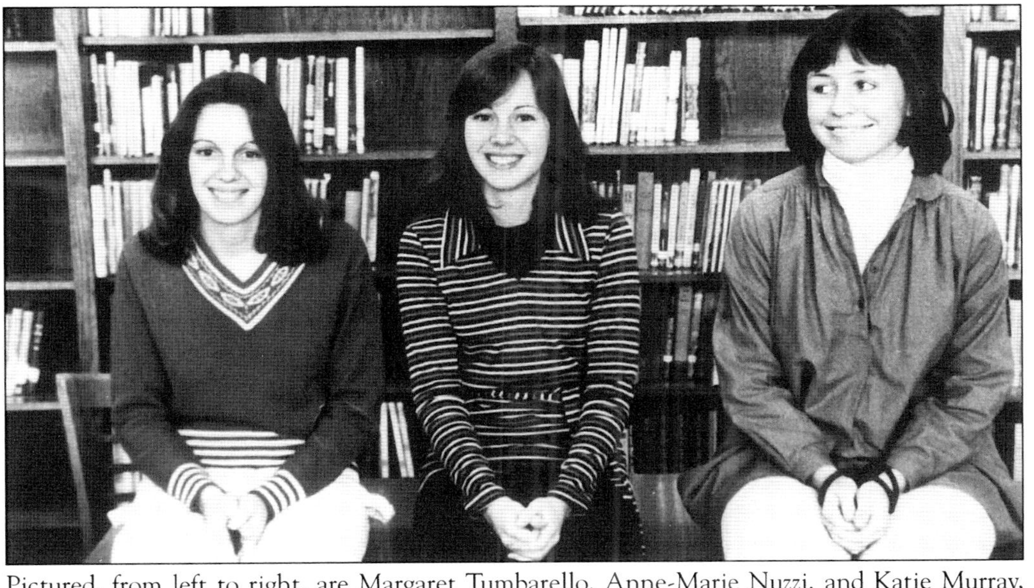

Pictured, from left to right, are Margaret Tumbarello, Anne-Marie Nuzzi, and Katie Murray, today the New York State assemblywoman Kathleen Murray. The students were members of the *Spotlight*, the school newspaper committee of Levittown Memorial High School in 1978. (Collection of Mary Ann and Tony Nuzzi.)

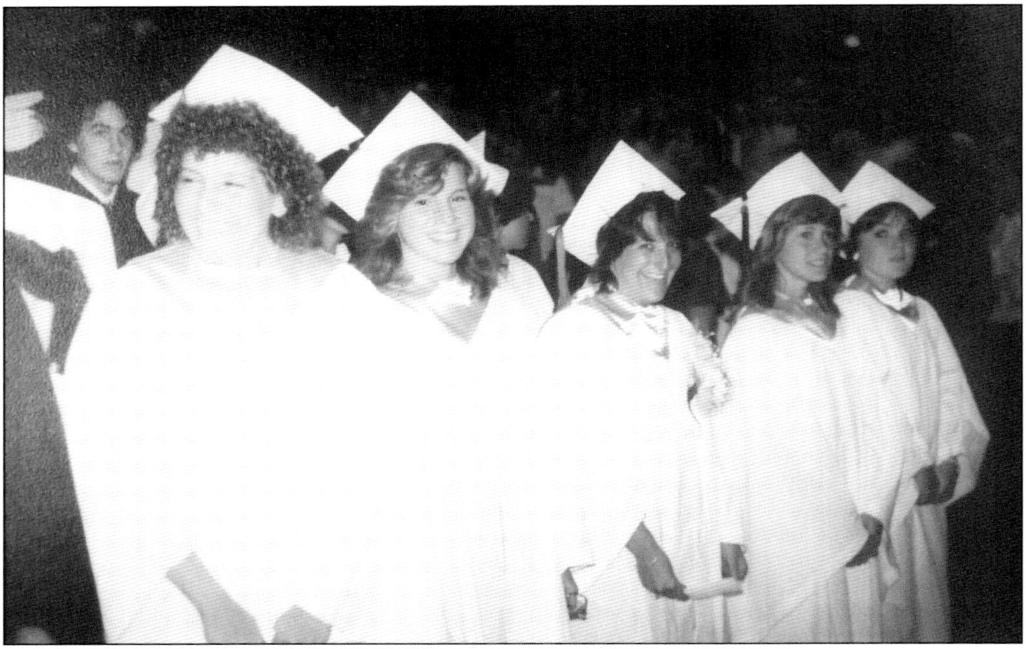

This June 1983 photograph shows students from the last graduating class of Levittown Memorial High School. The school building is now used for administration offices, BOCES classes, a senior center, and adult education classes. Pictured from left to right are Robin Forster, Susan Nuzzi, Lori Shapiro, Loraine Vestutti, and Sharon O'Gallagher. (Collection of Mary Ann and Tony Nuzzi.)

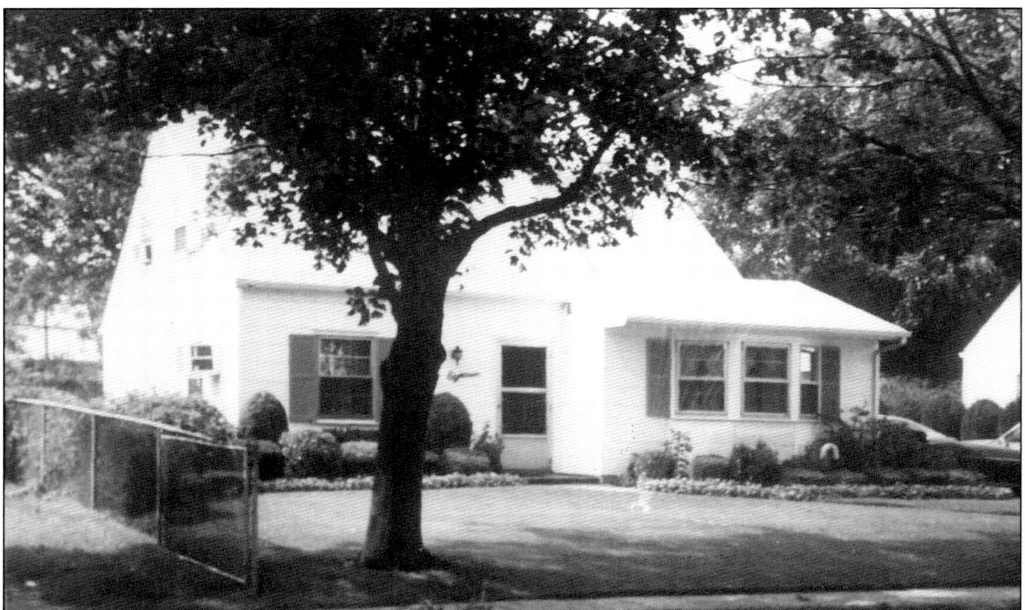

This photograph, taken in September 1981, is of the Nuzzi house with it first extension, a kitchen that was added on the right side of the house in 1971. A garage was added in 1962. (Collection of Mary Ann and Tony Nuzzi.)

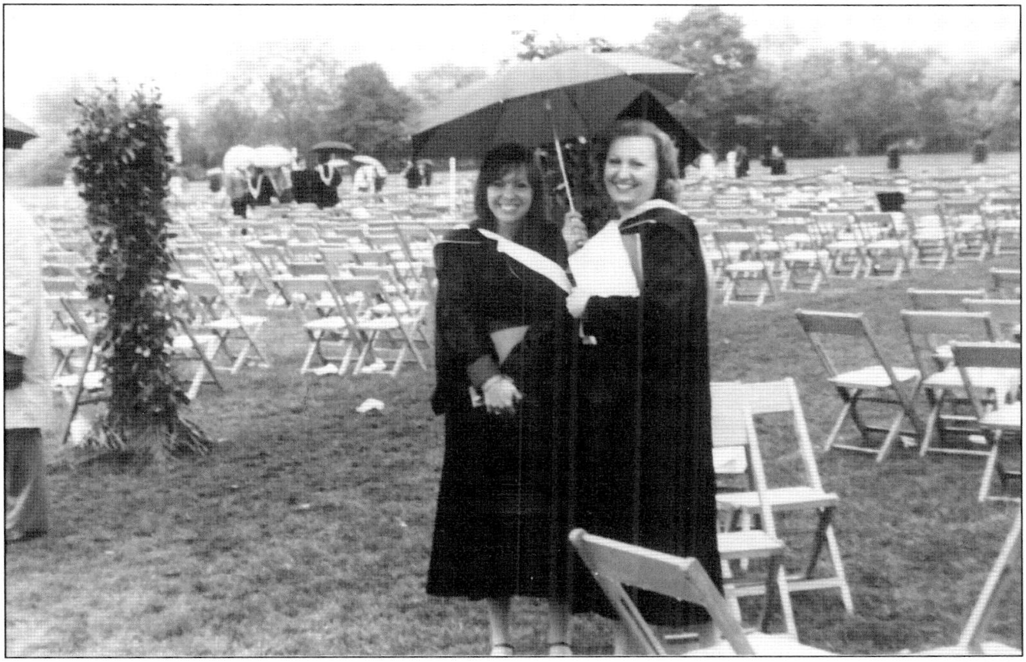

Proud mom Mary Ann Nuzzi and her daughter Anne-Marie both graduated from Adelphi University in May 1982. Mary Ann earned a degree in accounting, and Anne-Marie a degree in art. They attended the outdoor ceremony on a rainy May day. (Collection of Mary Ann and Tony Nuzzi.)

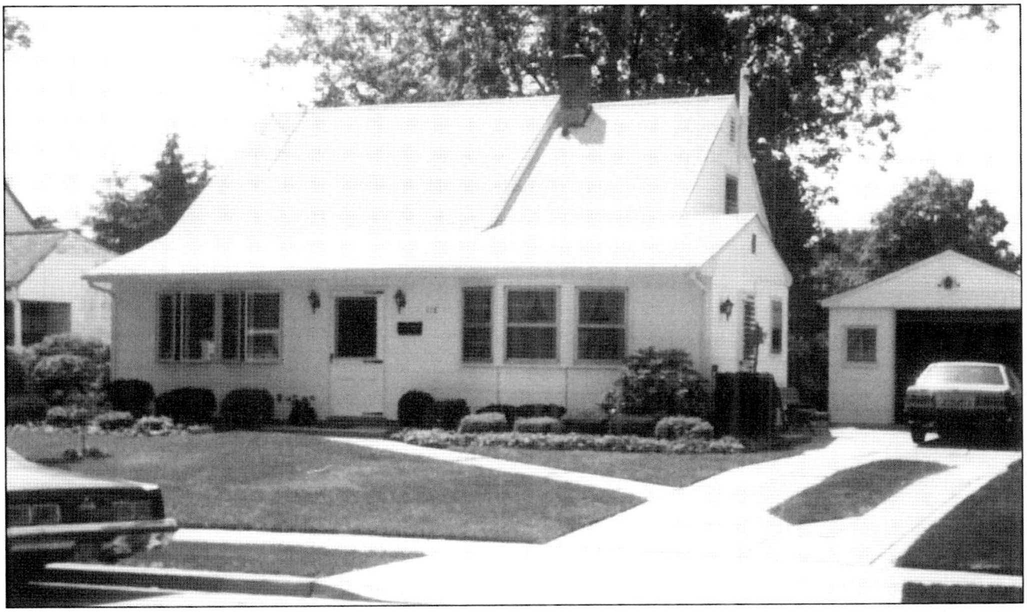

Pictured here is the Nuzzis' Levittown Cape with garage. In Joseph D'Agnese's article "The Great Cape" (This Old House, January/February 1999) he says: "In our mind's eye, we all know what a house looks like. When someone says 'home,' Americans picture a Cape Cod." (Collection of Mary Ann and Tony Nuzzi.)

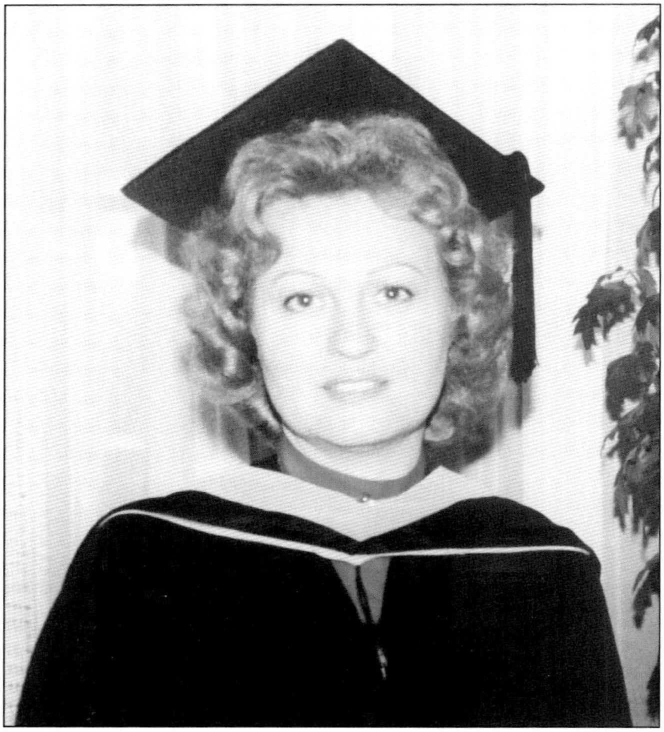

Mary Ann Nuzzi, in cap and gown, graduated summa cum laude. She said, "Tony and I both attended college while the children were also in college. It was a busy time. We bought a second car when the children were ready for college. That car went to all the colleges they attended. It was passed down from one to another as they graduated. Later on, we ended up with five cars in the driveway, garage, and on the street." (Collection of Mary Ann and Tony Nuzzi.)

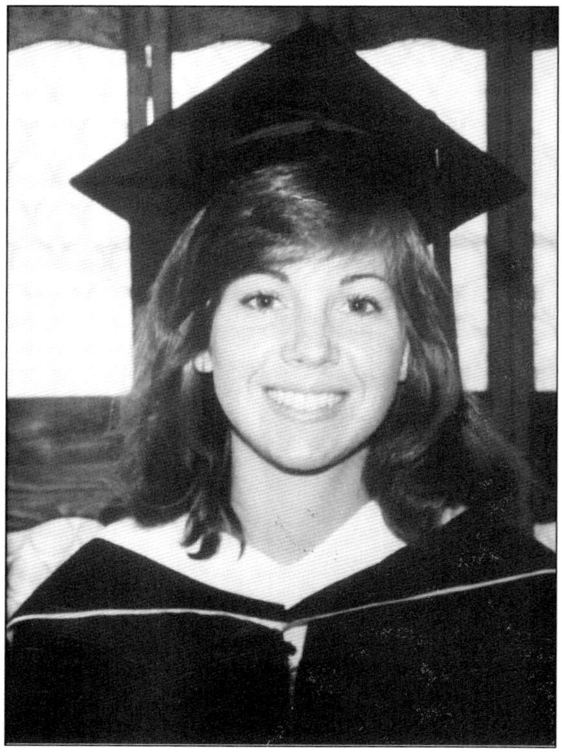

Anne-Marie in her cap and gown graduated magna cum laude. (Collection of Mary Ann and Tony Nuzzi.)

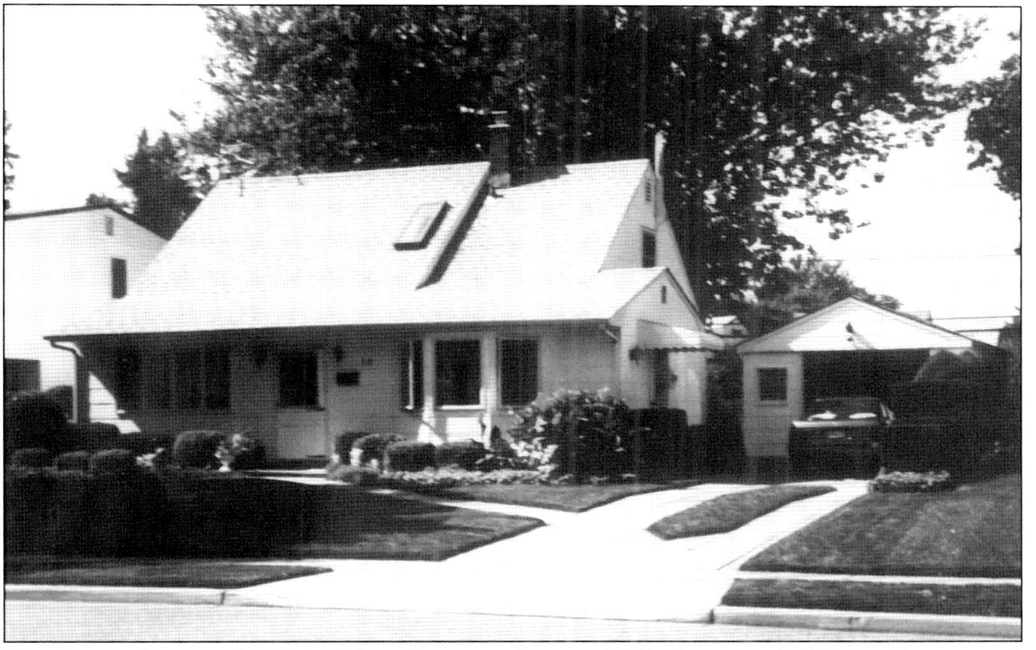

The latest photograph of the Nuzzi home, taken in 1995, shows a skylight and new roof. (Collection of Mary Ann and Tony Nuzzi.)

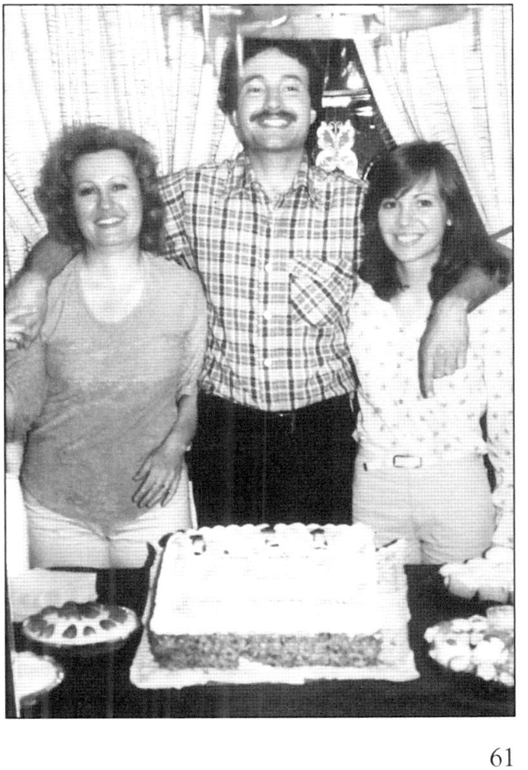

In 1982, the Nuzzi family celebrated three college graduations. Mother and daughter Mary Ann and Anne-Marie graduated with bachelor's degrees from Adelphi, and son Anthony graduated with a Master's of Business Administration from the University of Maryland. (Collection of Mary Ann and Tony Nuzzi.)

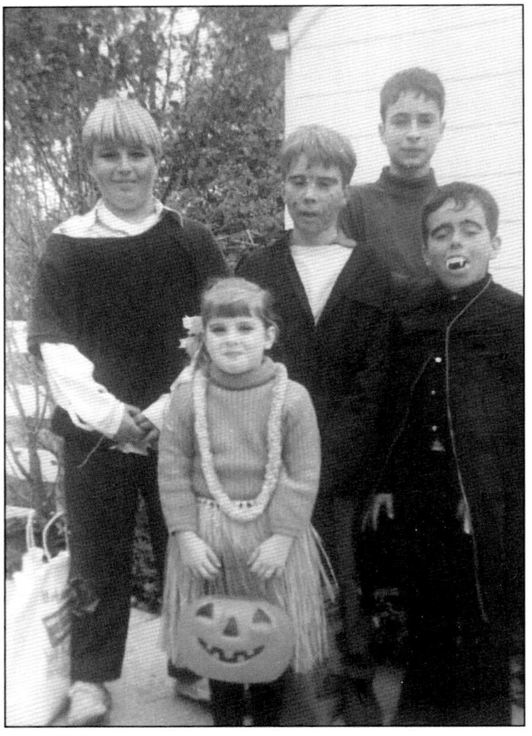

This 1970 Halloween shot shows the following trick-or-treaters from left to right, Eric Krall, Susan, Michael, and Anthony Nuzzi, and Scott Elsner. Scott is Count Dracula and has the fangs to prove it, while Susan wears a hula skirt. (Collection of Mary Ann and Tony Nuzzi.)

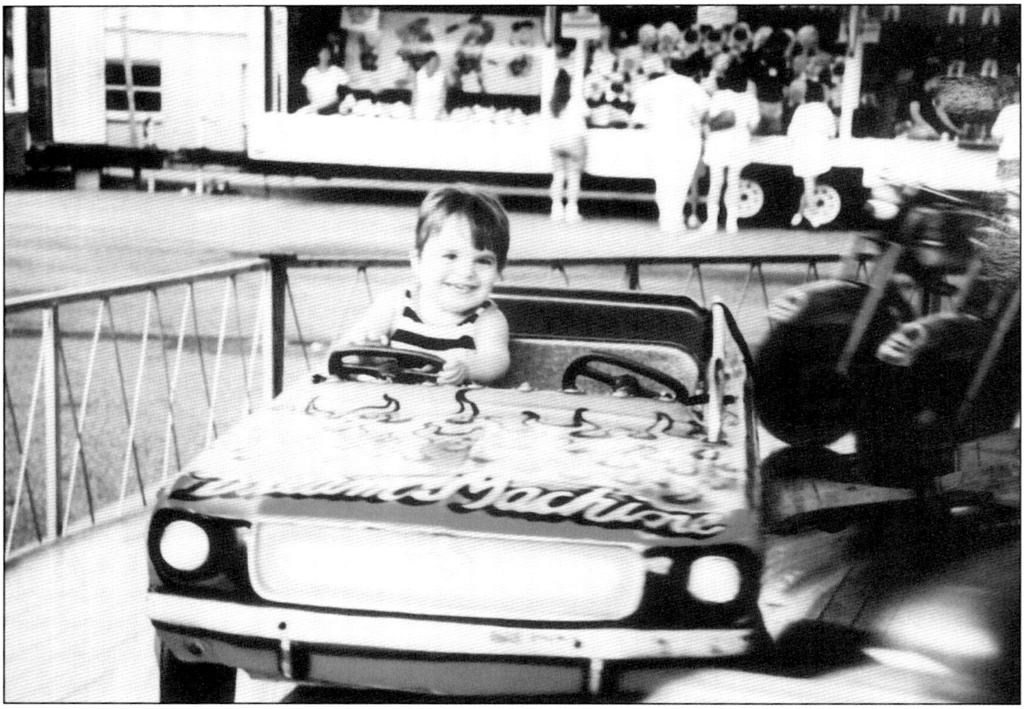

Michael Brzezinski, grandson of the Nuzzis, is riding high at the 1993 St. Bernard Bazaar. Michael is the son of Anne-Marie and Jim. (Collection of Mary Ann and Tony Nuzzi.)

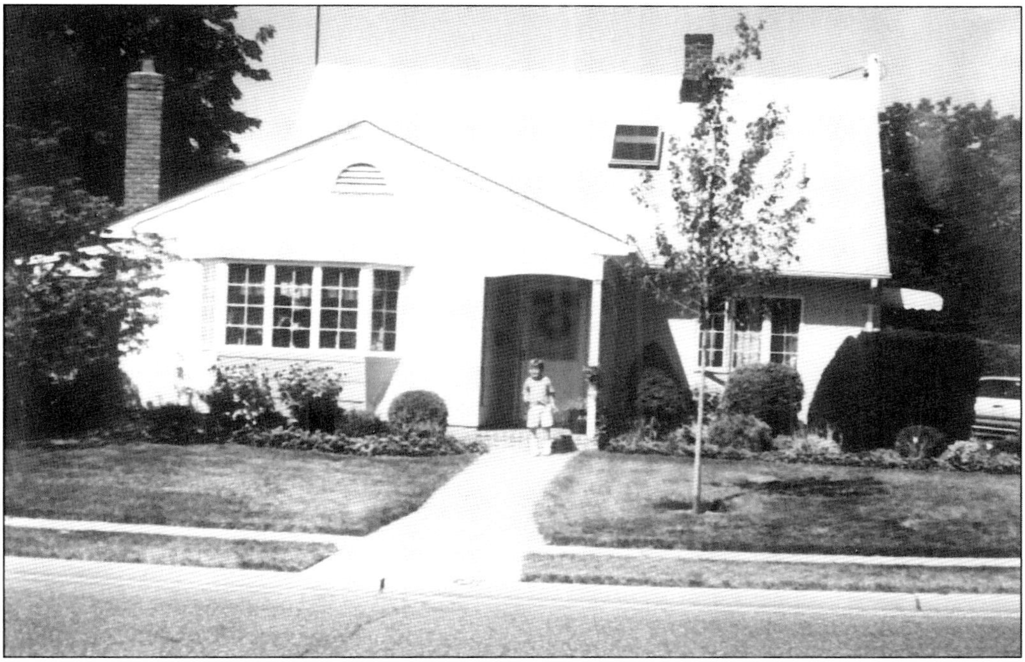

The Nuzzi legacy in Levittown continues as their daughter Anne-Marie lives at 130 Hickory Lane. Grandson Michael is pictured in the doorway of this home. (Collection of Mary Ann and Tony Nuzzi.)

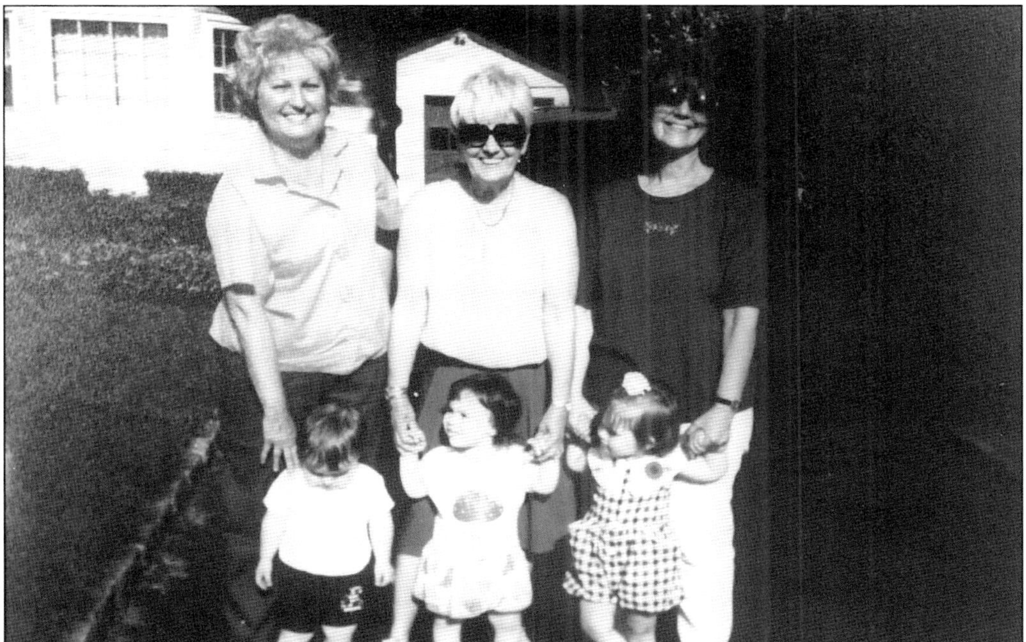

Longtime neighbors Mary Ann Nuzzi (in Levittown since 1956), Alba Aresca (since 1951), and Betty Naughton (since 1961) posed in the summer of 1992 with their grandchildren, all their daughters' babies. (Collection of Mary Ann and Tony Nuzzi.)

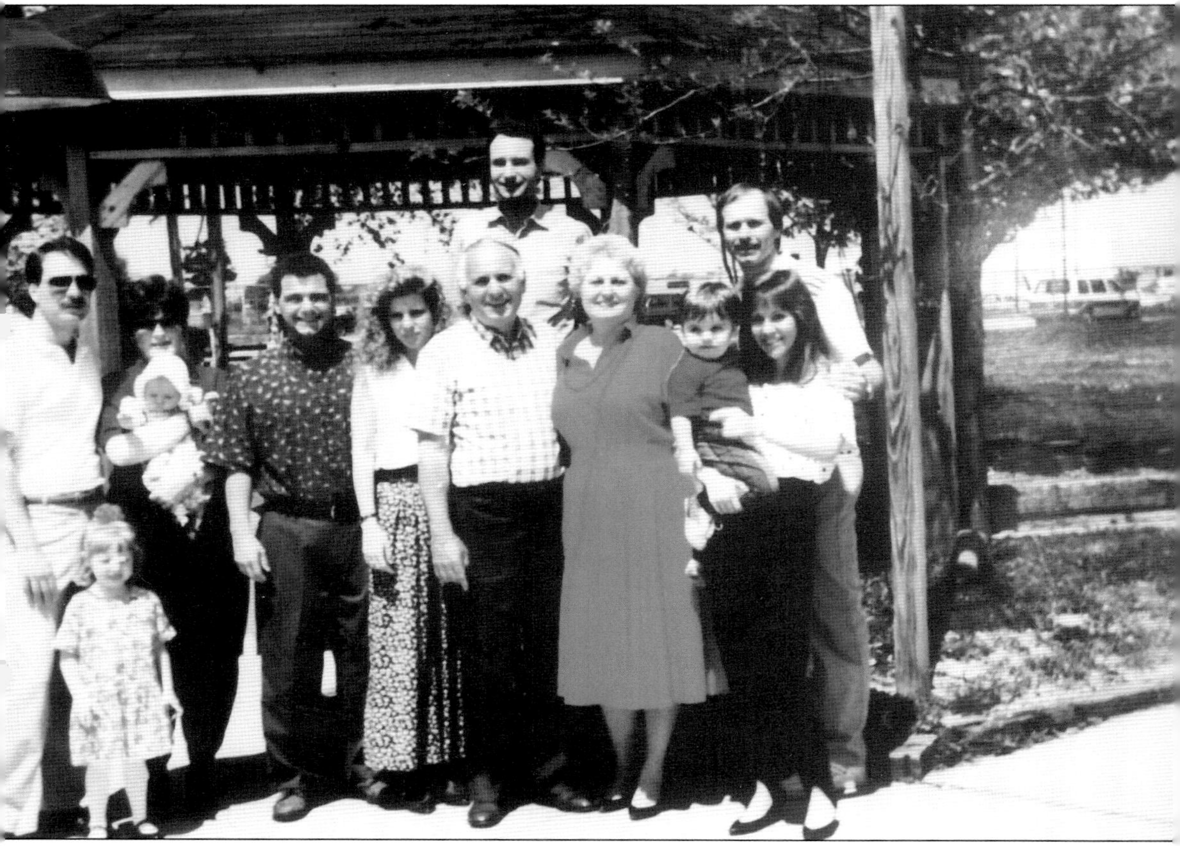

Here's to the Nuzzi family! "Our family has four generations living in Levittown," said Mary Ann. "My mother, Ann Cancelliere, lives in a garden apartment in Levittown. Daughter Anne-Marie lives in Levittown with husband Jim Brzezinski and two sons, Michael and Matthew, on Hickory Lane." The Brzezinskis bought their house in 1987. And last, but certainly, not least, Mary Ann and Tony still live in their much-improved Cape that was purchased in 1956. (Collection of Mary Ann and Tony Nuzzi.)

Four

AS THE COMMUNITY TURNS

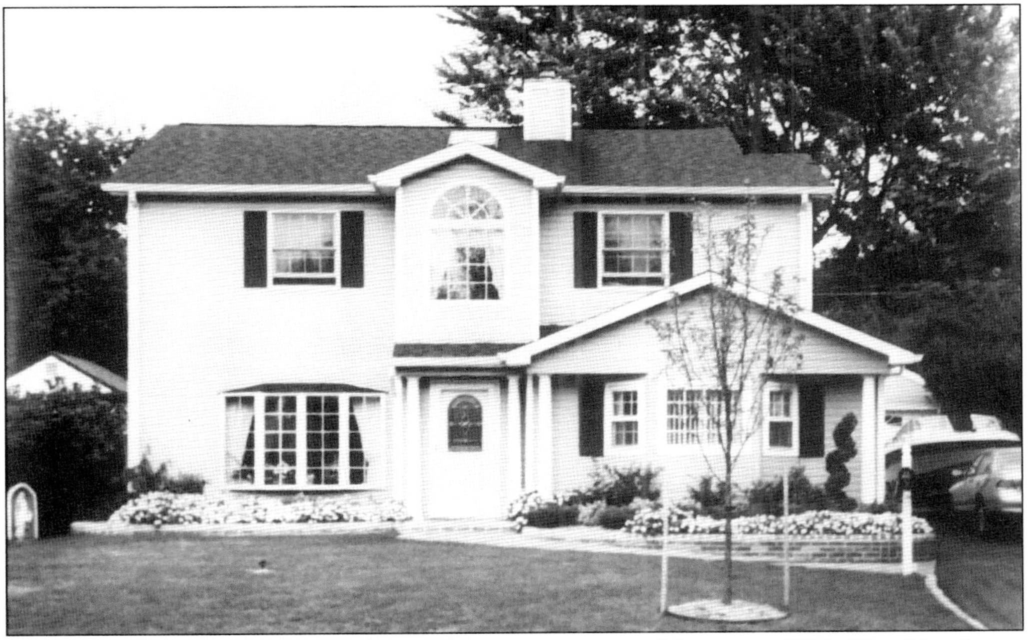

The Naughton home sports its last and very impressive addition in 1998. The Naughtons said, "In October 1996, we again had construction on our house which put it into its present condition. It should be noted that many of our neighbors from 1961 are still our neighbors today. Our children who played and grew up together are scattered all over the United States, but we parents are still neighbors together." Dick has worked at the Levittown Post Office since 1973, when he retired from the Air Force. (Collection of Mary Ann and Tony Nuzzi.)

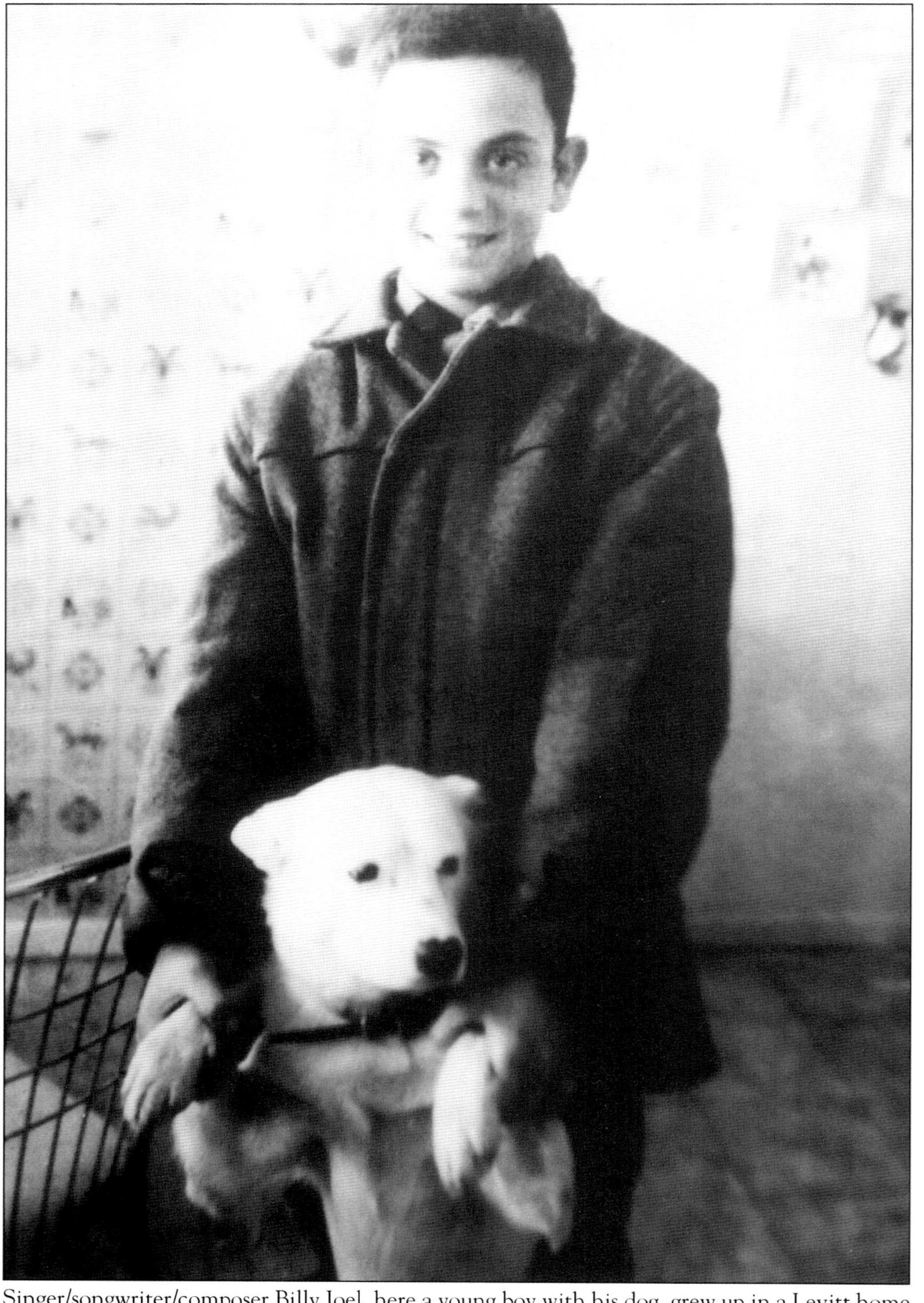

Singer/songwriter/composer Billy Joel, here a young boy with his dog, grew up in a Levitt home in Hicksville, Long Island. (Courtesy of Billy Joel.)

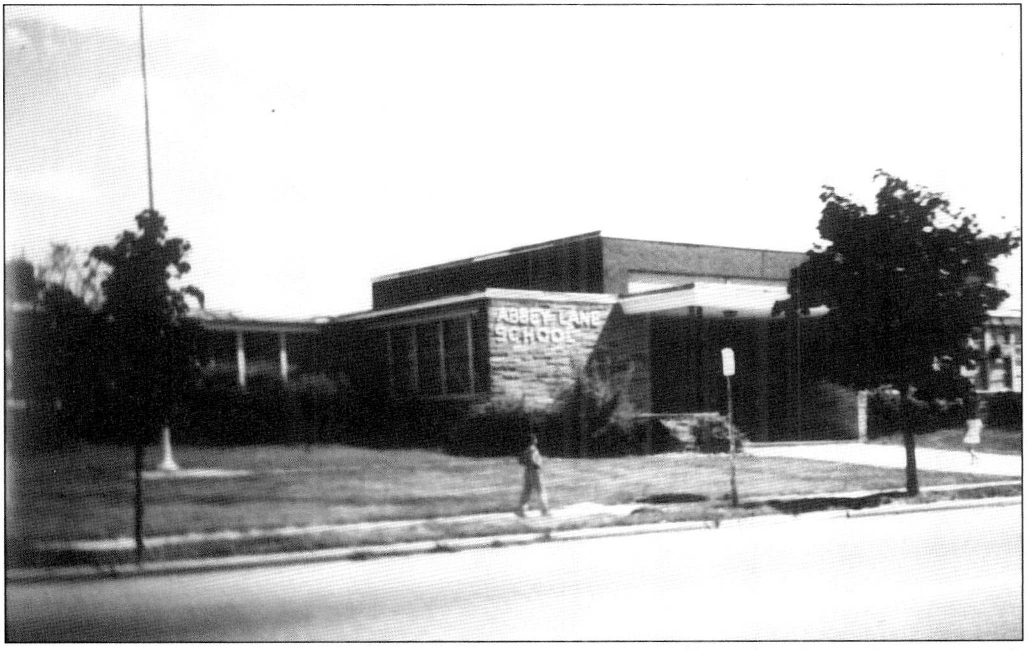

The Abbey Lane School opened in November 1949. It was followed in December 1949 with the Gardiners Avenue School. (Collection of the Levittown Library.)

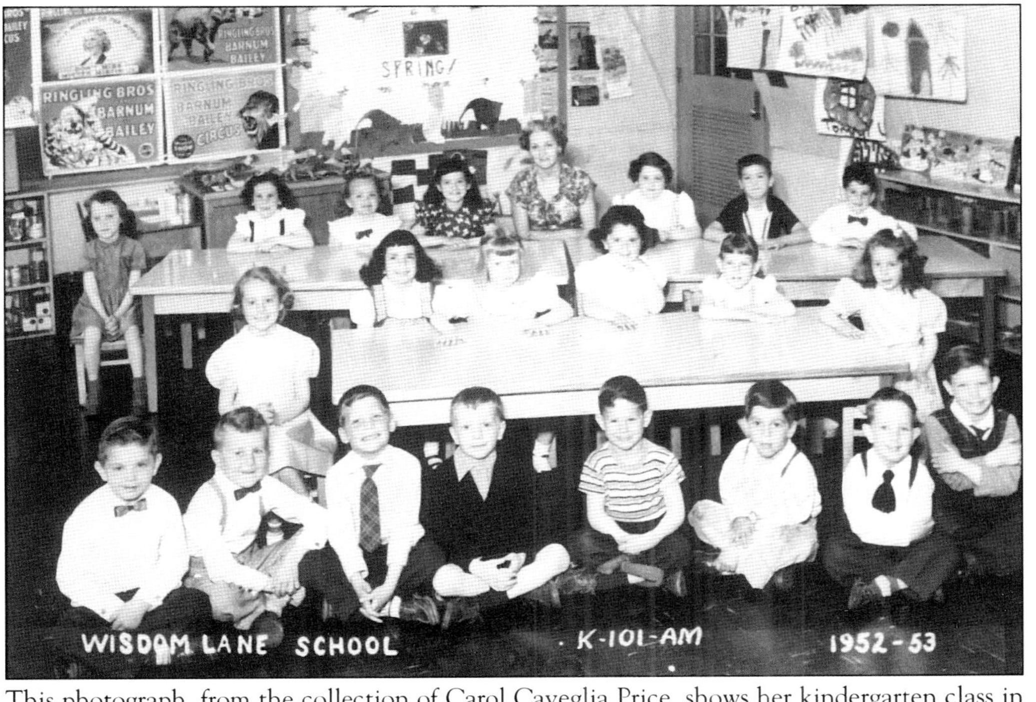

This photograph, from the collection of Carol Caveglia Price, shows her kindergarten class in the spring of 1953 in the Wisdom Lane School, when the school was still in the Quonset hut. Carol is in the second row, second from the right, with bangs and braids. (Collection of Carol Caveglia Price.)

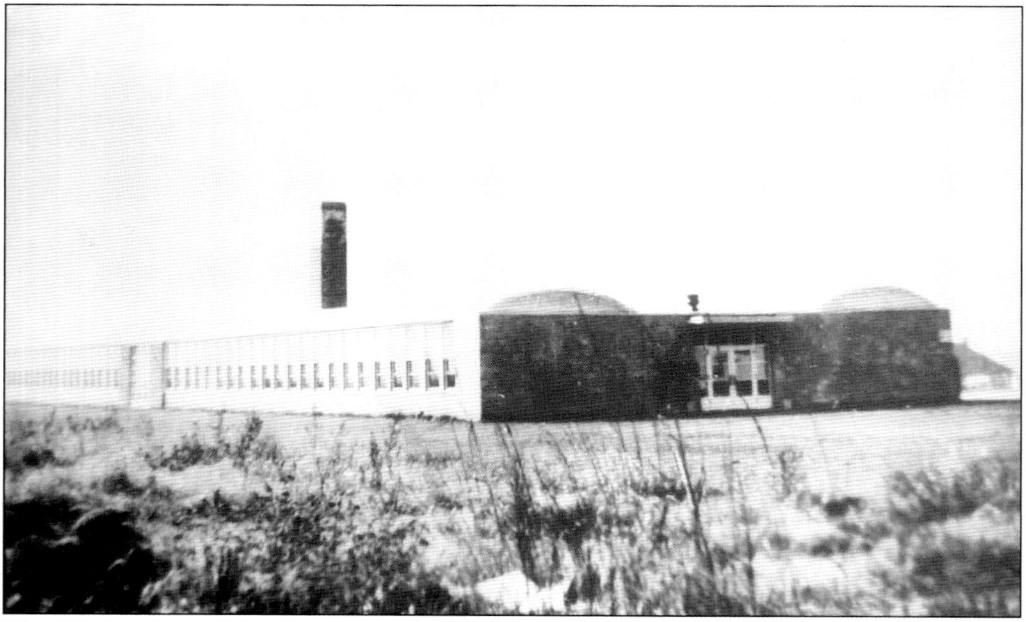

The Wisdom Lane School opened in eight Quonset huts on November 3, 1948. The school offered grades kindergarten through third, with two classrooms in each of the huts to make up a total of 16 classes. There were double sessions to accommodate the 600 students. Sybil Rosenblum, who taught kindergarten at the school, had her daughter with her and kept her for the second session. (Collection of Carol Caveglia Price.)

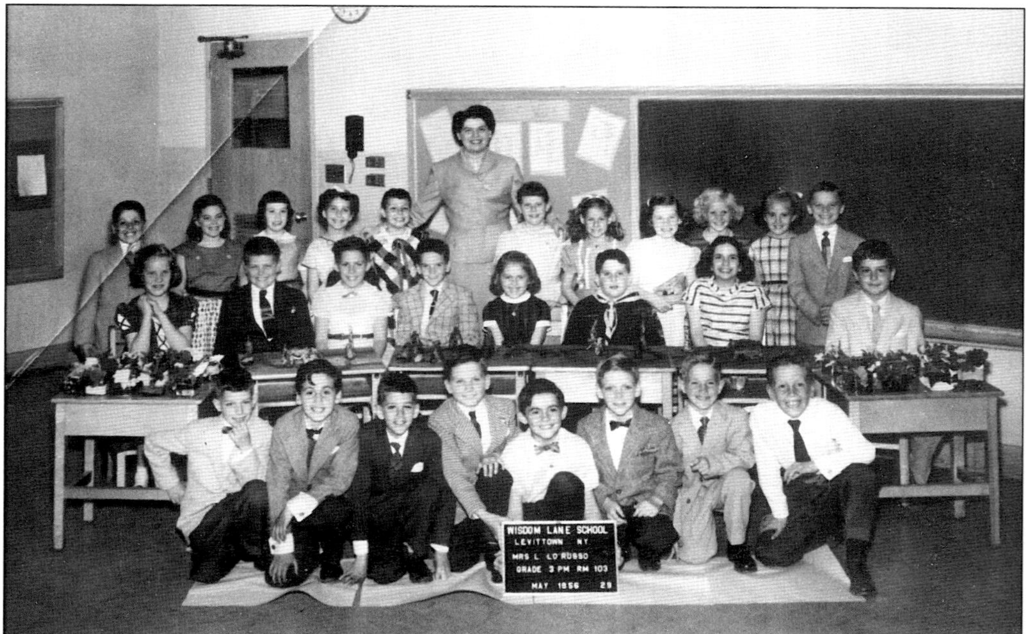

This May 1956 photograph shows the third grade of Wisdom Lane School in its new building on Center Lane. In this snapshot, Carol is in the second row, second from the right, with bangs and braids. (Collection of Carol Caveglia Price.)

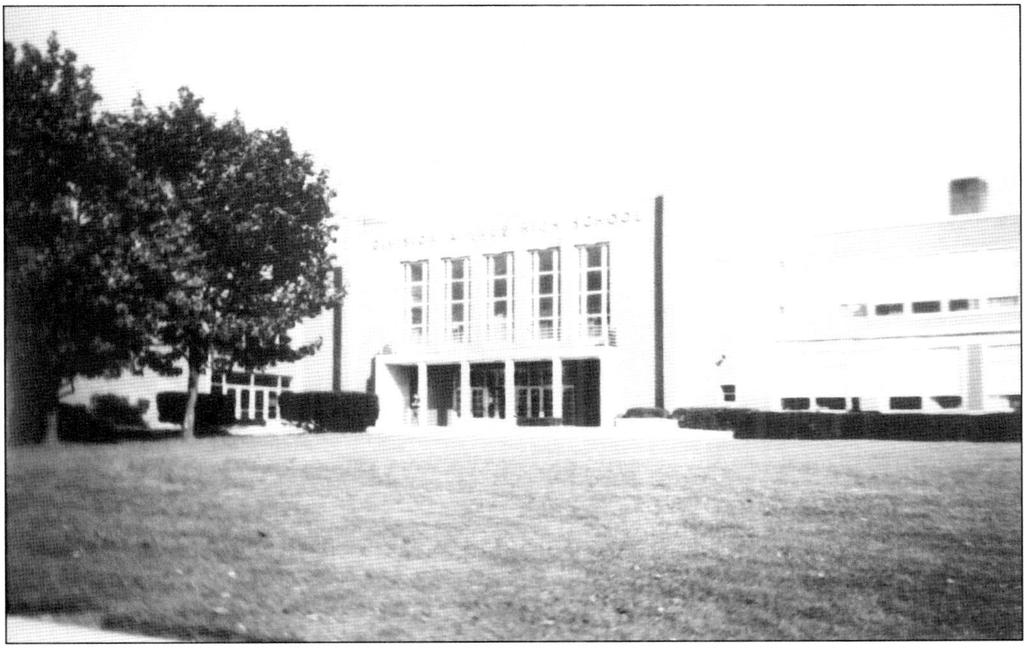

Pictured here is the Division Avenue High School. (Collection of the Levittown Library.)

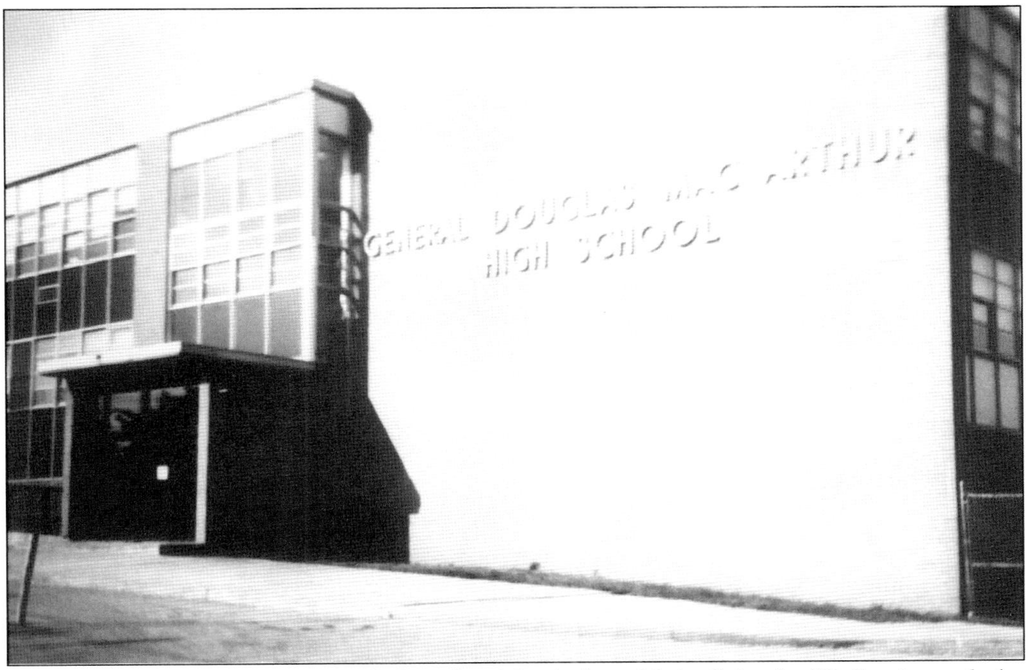

This is a view of the General Douglas MacArthur High School. (Collection of the Levittown Library.)

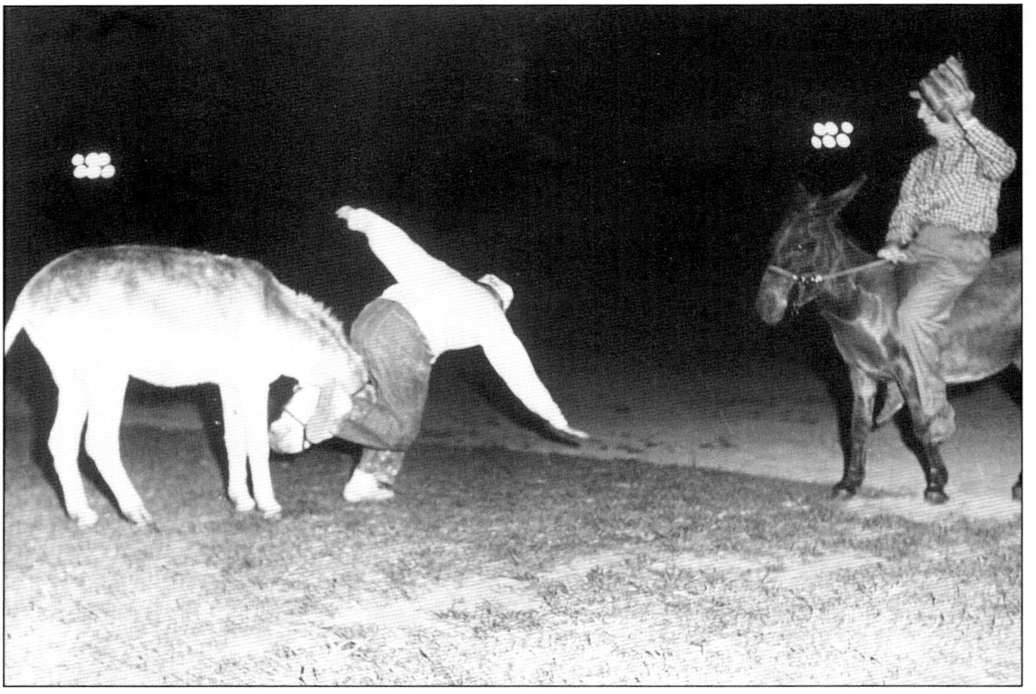

A scene of "playing ball on donkey" is captured in this photograph. (Collection of the Levittown Library.)

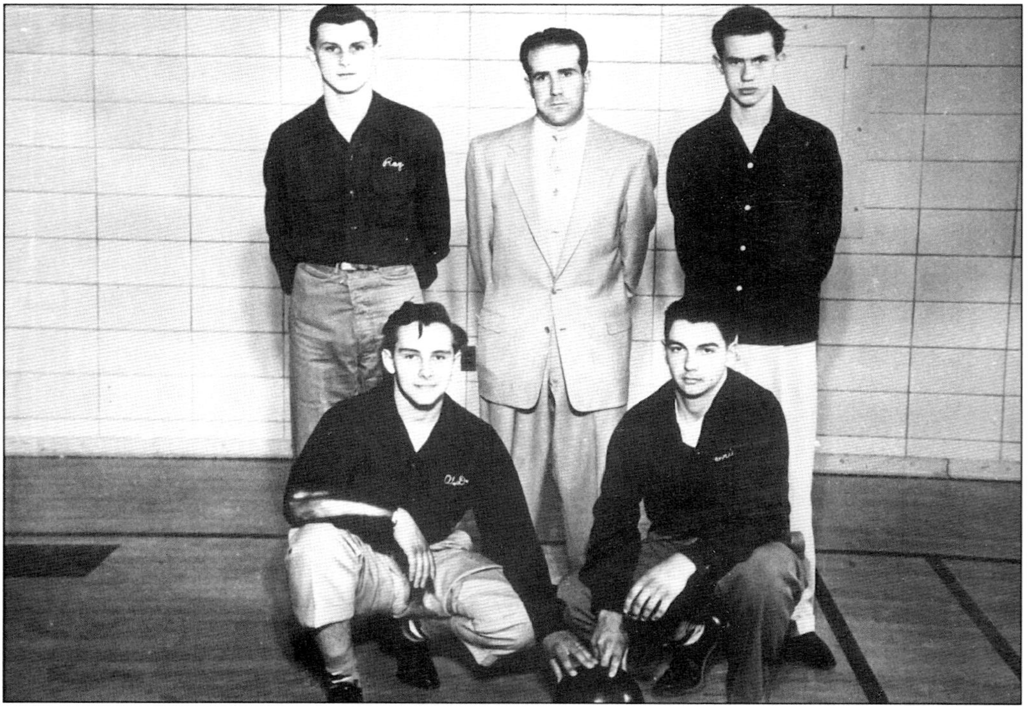

The bowling team poses for this photograph. (Collection of the Levittown Library.)

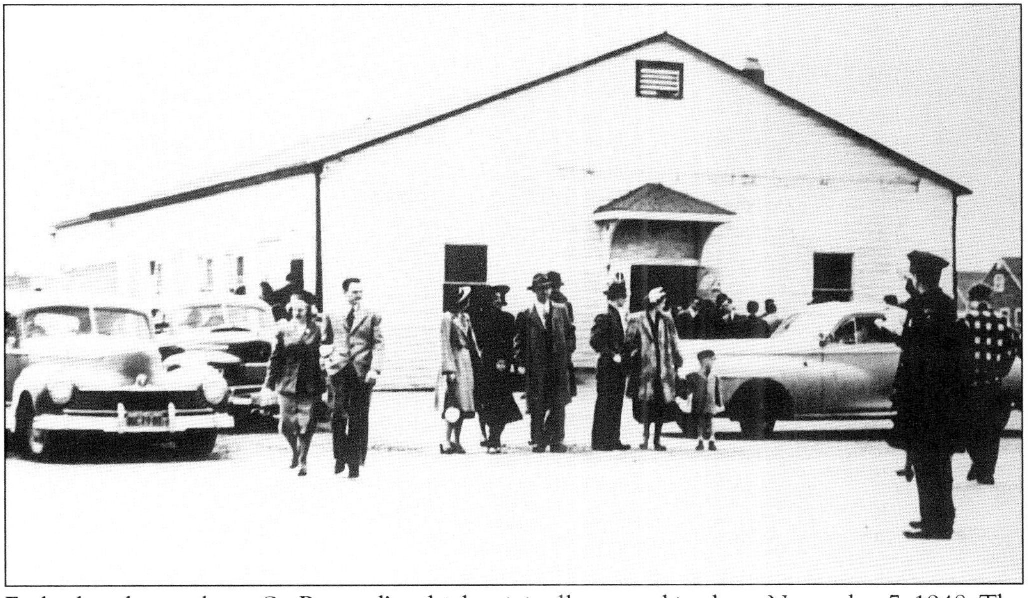

Early churchgoers leave St. Bernard's, which originally opened its doors November 7, 1948. The church building had previously served as a mess hall, garage, and airplane hangar. (Collection of the Levittown Library.)

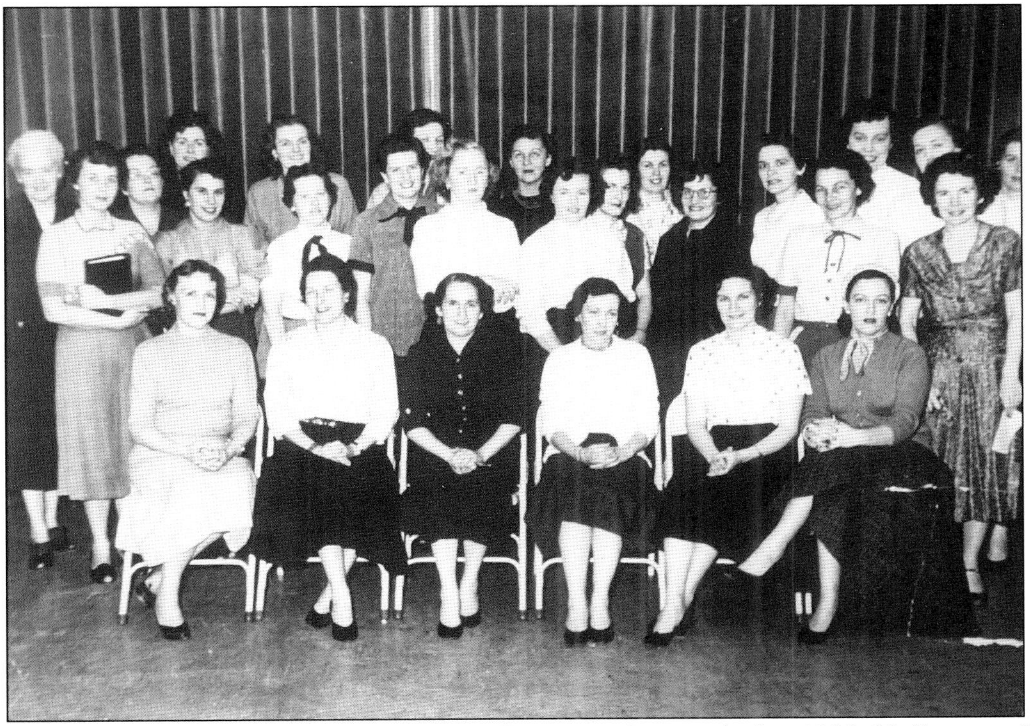

The St. Bernard's Rosary Society Board of Officers was photographed in 1955. (Collection of the Levittown Library.)

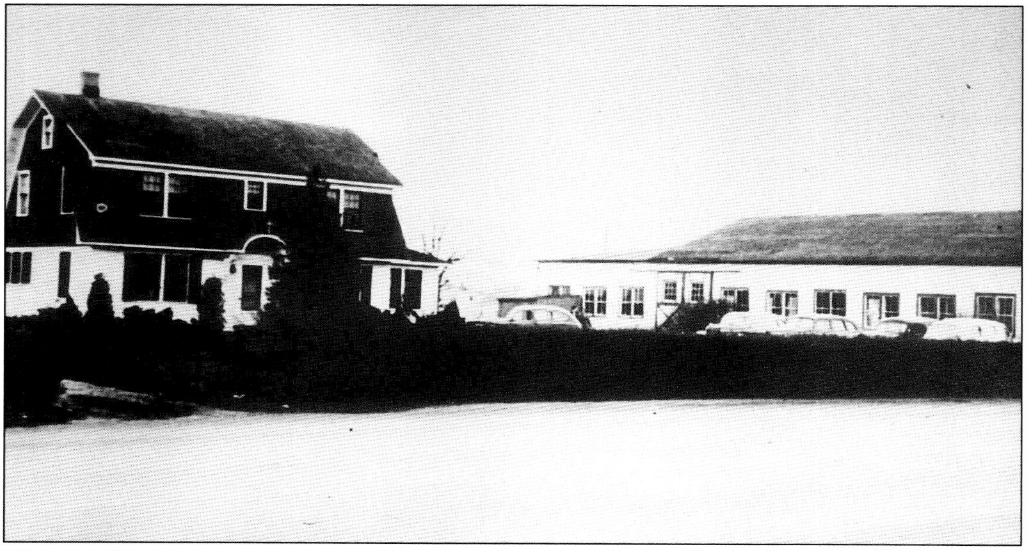

The church and rectory are captured in this photograph before their relocation. (Collection of the Levittown Library.)

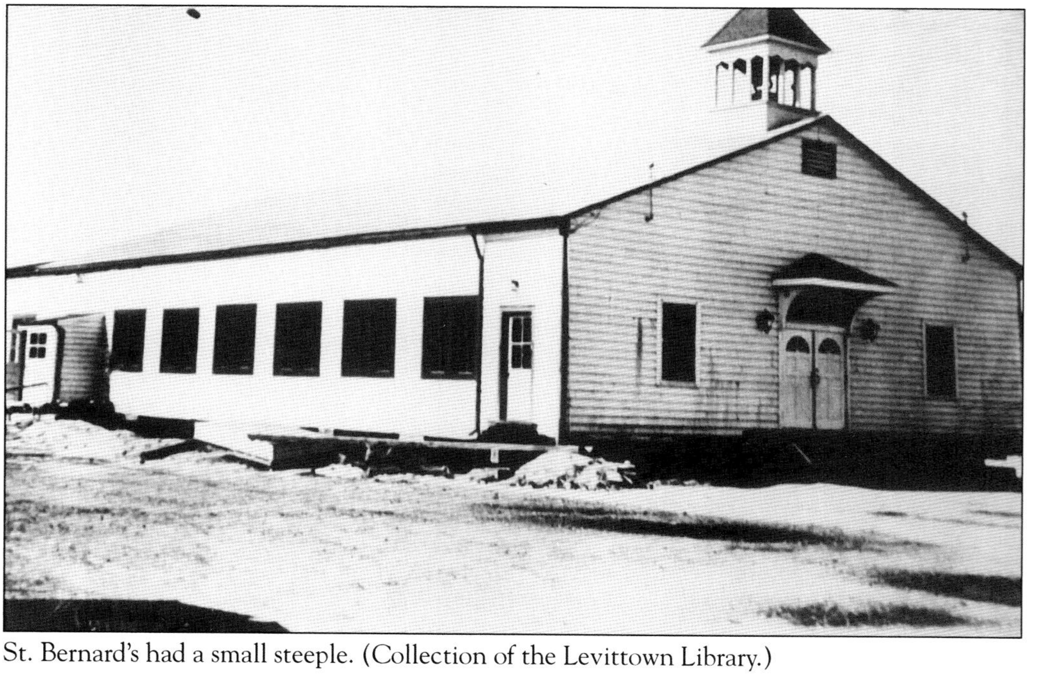

St. Bernard's had a small steeple. (Collection of the Levittown Library.)

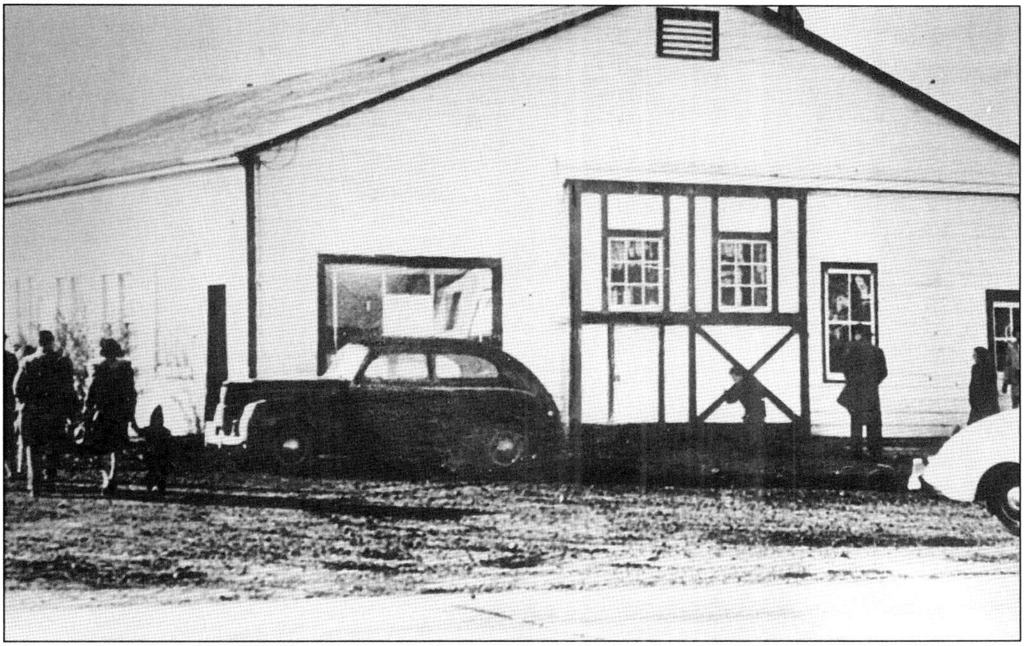

An old photograph shows St. Bernard's with its big doors. (Collection of the Levittown Library.)

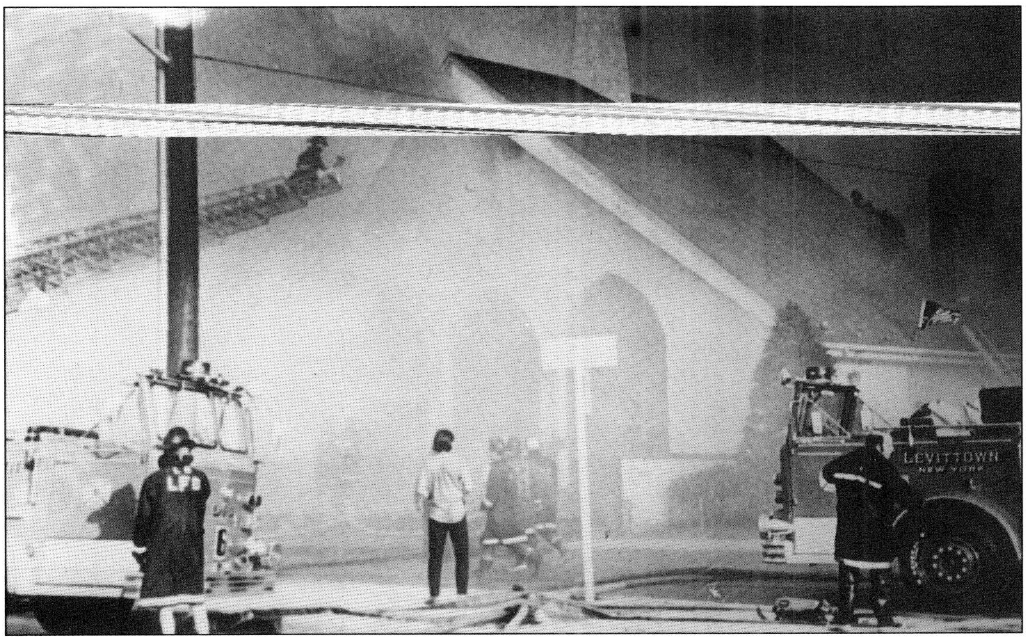

On May 31, 1970, St. Bernard's was engulfed in flames. The interior was destroyed. Fire companies from Levittown, Wantagh, East Meadow, and Bethpage battled the blaze. (Collection of Mary Ann and Tony Nuzzi.)

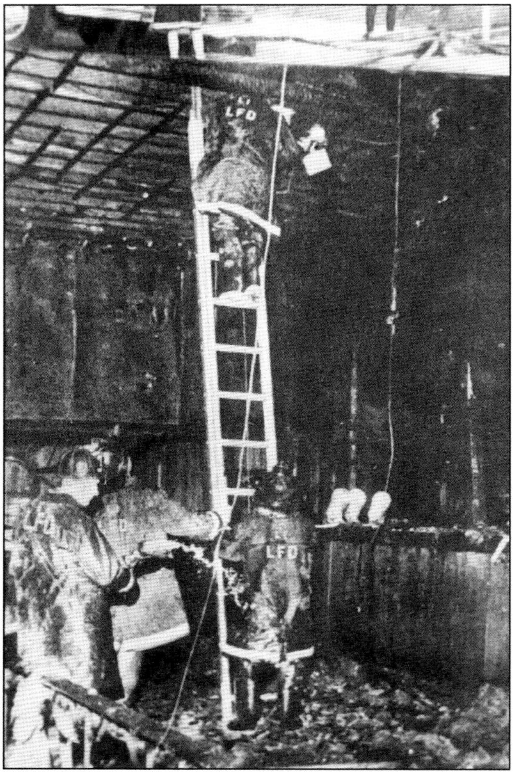

This interior shot of the church was taken after the devastating fire. (Collection of Mary Ann and Tony Nuzzi.)

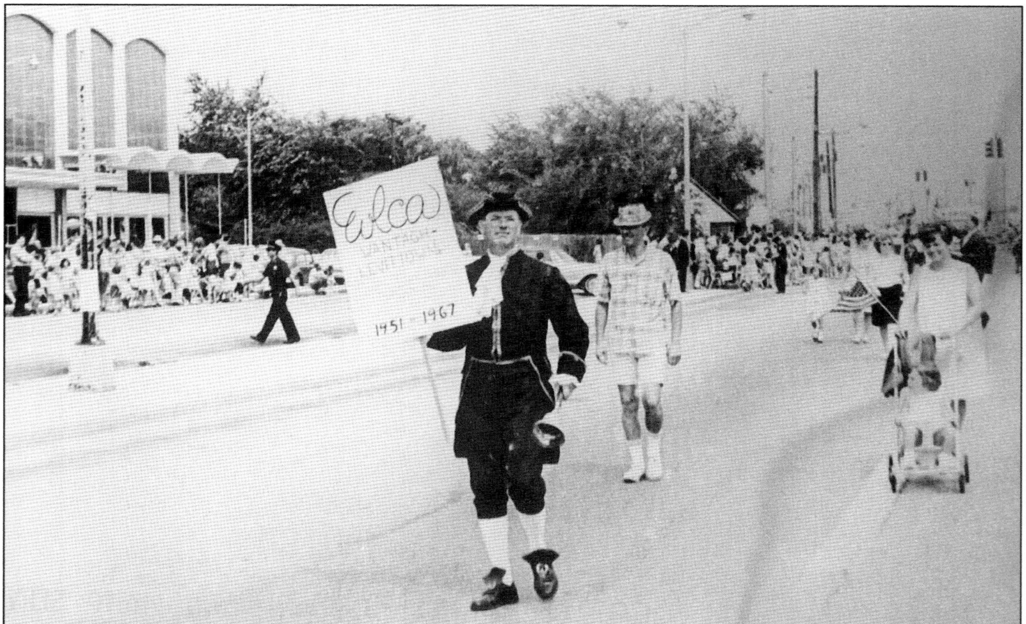

A marcher representing ELCA wears Revolutionary War garb during Levittown's 20th Anniversary Parade. (Collection of the Levittown Library.)

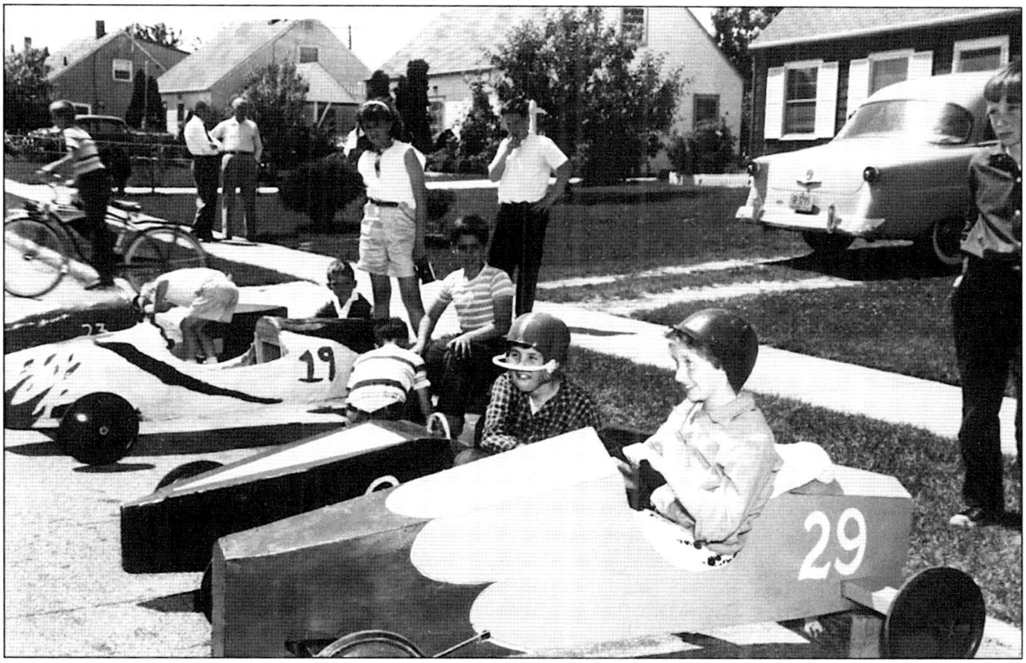

This photograph recalls a real piece of American memorabilia, the boxcar derby. These four-wheeled "chariots" were not a store-bought item, but usually the product of collaboration with an older relative. The designs were inventive, often constructed from salvaged odds and ends such as wheels from an old tricycle or baby carriage and scraps of lumber. The boxcars were obviously a source of pride. (Collection of the Levittown Library.)

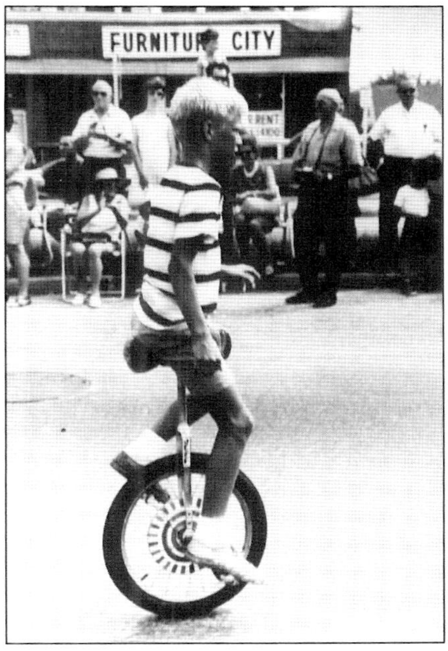

A young man on a unicycle in Levittown's 20th Anniversary Parade is immortalized in this photograph taken by Steve Kummerman. (Collection of the Levittown Library.)

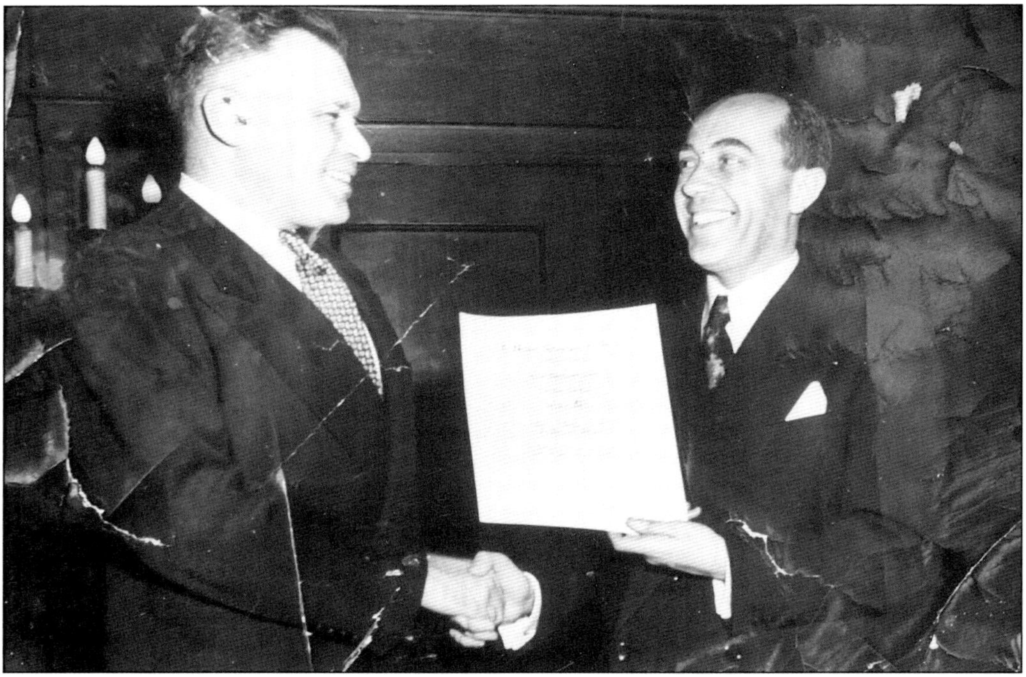

President of the Young Israel congregation, Abe Rosenblum accepts an award at the United Synagogue Convention in Washington, 1951. The award was given to Young Israel for the most membership advancement in one year. (Collection of Sybil Rosenblum.)

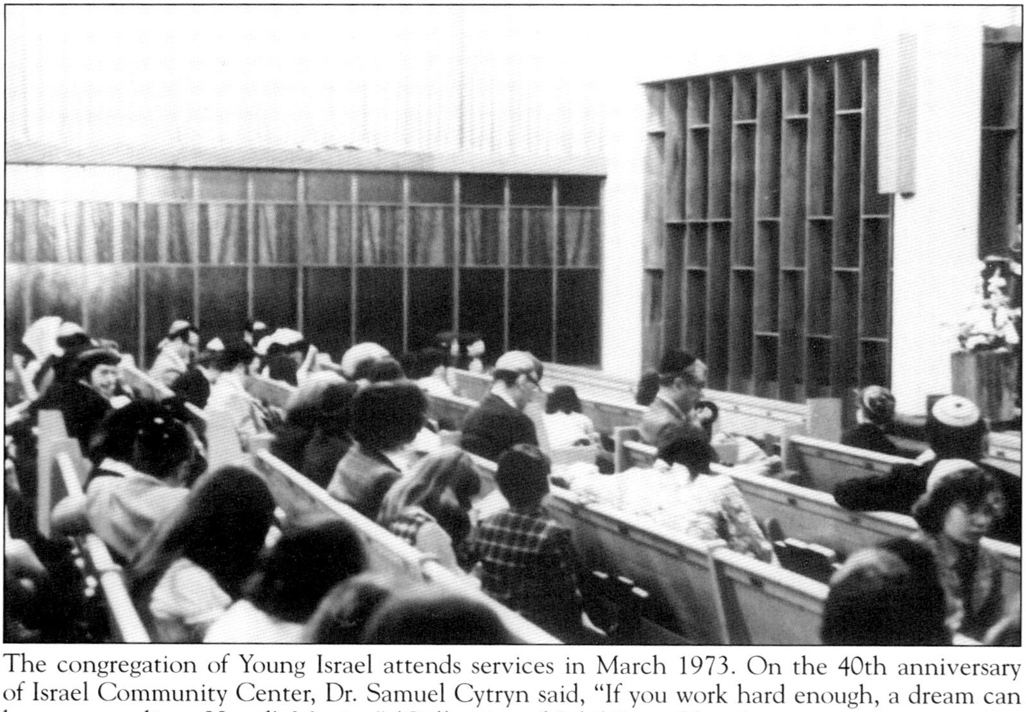

The congregation of Young Israel attends services in March 1973. On the 40th anniversary of Israel Community Center, Dr. Samuel Cytryn said, "If you work hard enough, a dream can become a reality—Hertzl's Maxim." (Collection of Sybil Rosenblum.)

Congressman John W. Wydler, of the 4th District, sent this card to Abraham Rosenblum after reading the following clipping: "Abraham Rosenblum of Long Lane has been appointed to serve on the cabinet of the newly formed Nassau-Suffolk Jewish National Fund Council on Long Island." Arthur V. Briskin, JNF president, stated that Rosenblum is one of a group of leaders in the Nassau-Suffolk area who have undertaken to help in the work of JNF on behalf of Israel. He is active in many local organizations. (Collection of Sybil Rosenblum.)

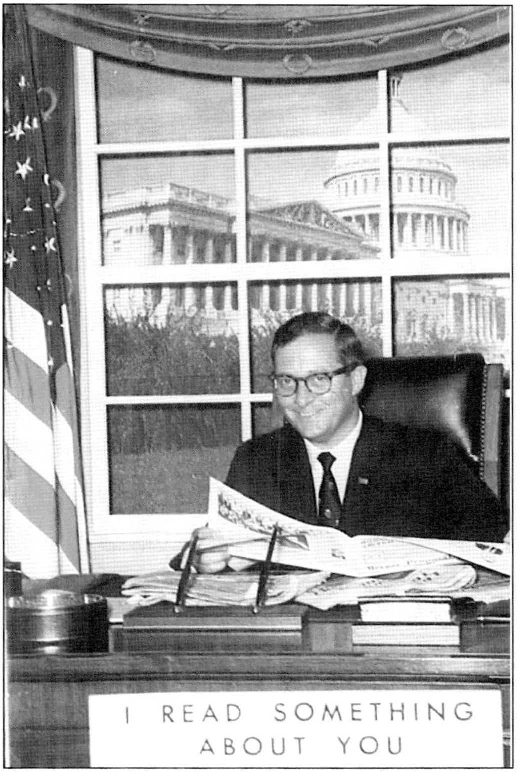

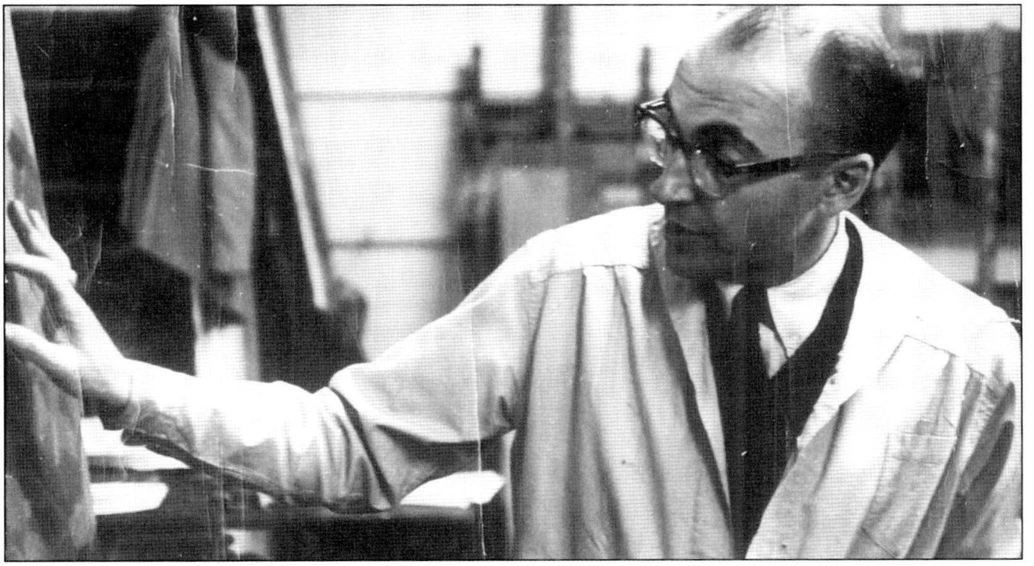

Sybil's brother Mort is the artist responsible for the beautiful mural in the chapel of Young Israel. He was a friend of the artist who did the mural in the Levittown Library. (Collection of Sybil Rosenblum.)

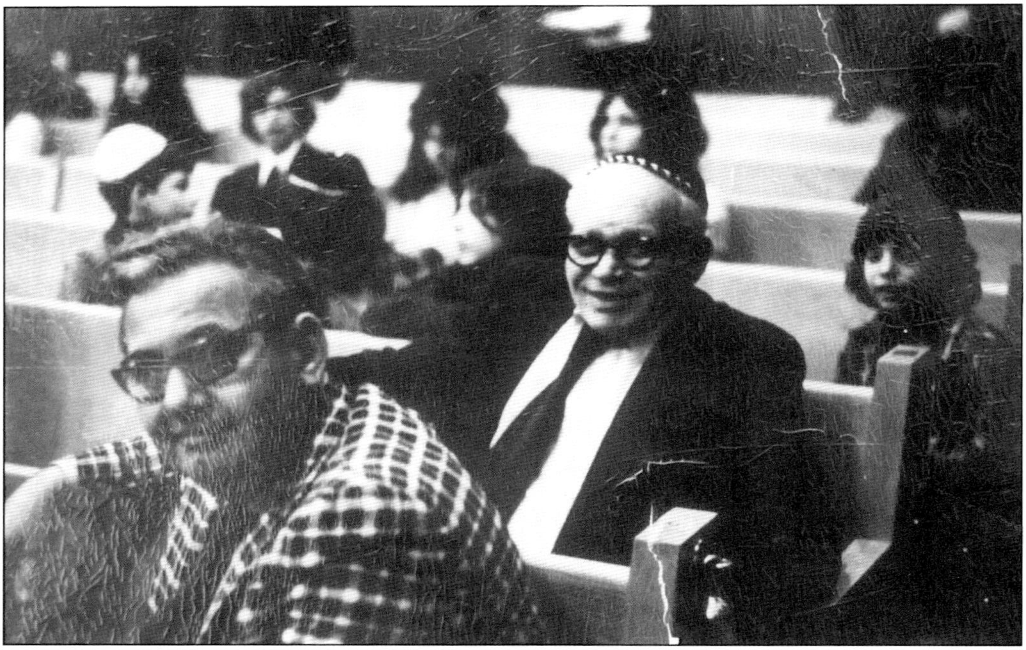

Longtime friends Dr. Samuel Cytryn (foreground) and Abe Rosenblum (directly behind him) were photographed at Kennedy International Airport. As part of a delegation from Young Israel called "Welcome to the Torah," they went to see a Torah that had survived Nazi Germany. The Torah, which is sacred in the Jewish faith, was then taken to its new home in the Young Israel chapel. Dr. Cytryn has been a highly regarded member of Young Israel and the Levittown community almost since its earliest days. He and his wife purchased two Capes, one as an office and the other as the family's home. Cytryn recently underwent back surgery and is recovering. (Collection of Sybil Rosenblum.)

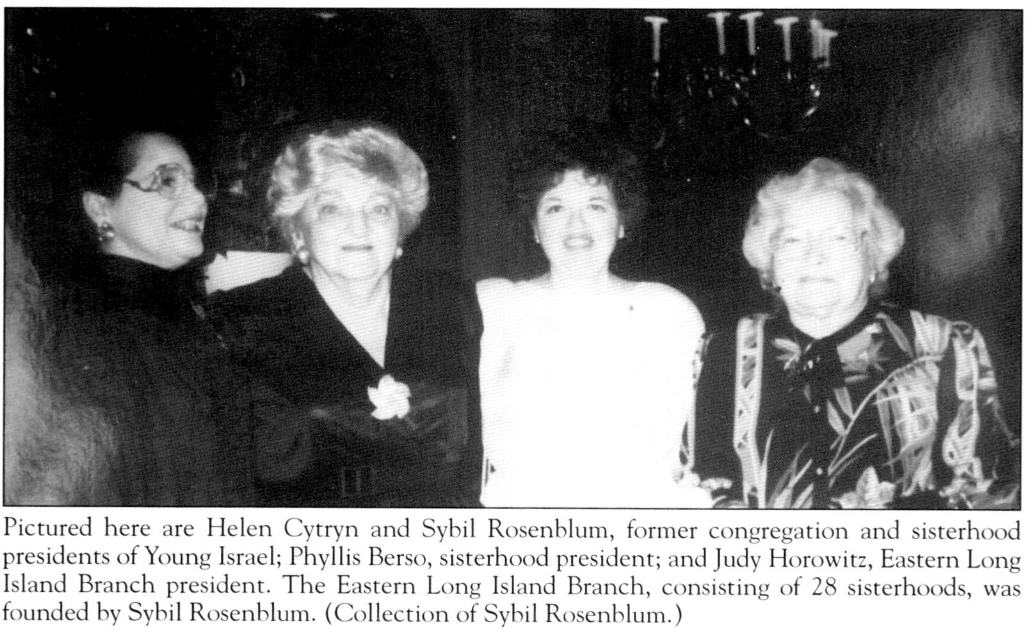

Pictured here are Helen Cytryn and Sybil Rosenblum, former congregation and sisterhood presidents of Young Israel; Phyllis Berso, sisterhood president; and Judy Horowitz, Eastern Long Island Branch president. The Eastern Long Island Branch, consisting of 28 sisterhoods, was founded by Sybil Rosenblum. (Collection of Sybil Rosenblum.)

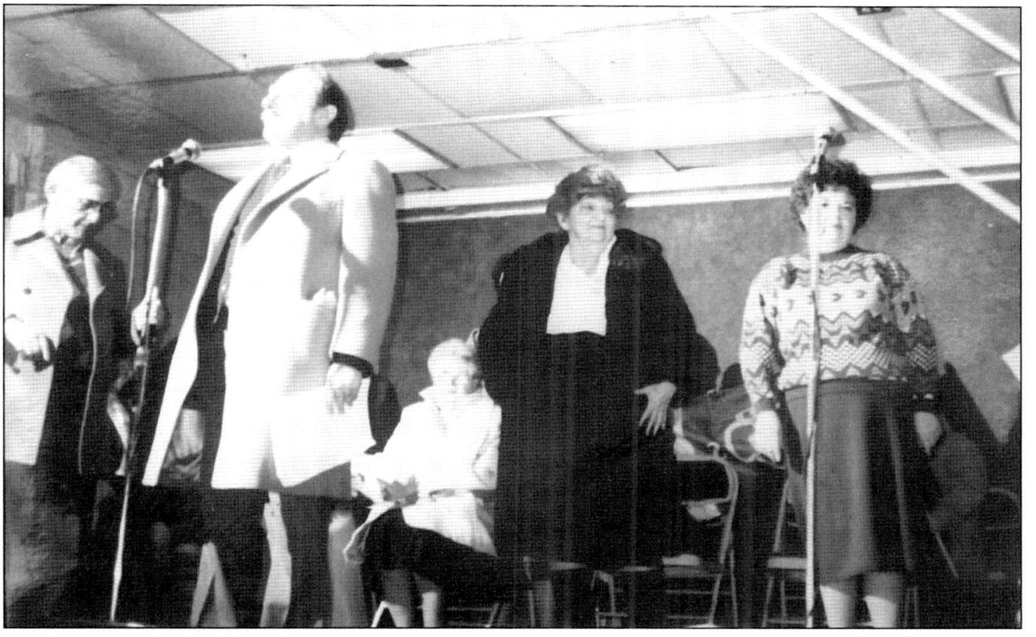

Rabbi Elster (Rabbi Pro Tem) is at the microphone at a special community Hanukkah party sponsored by the township of Hempstead. (Collection of Sybil Rosenblum.)

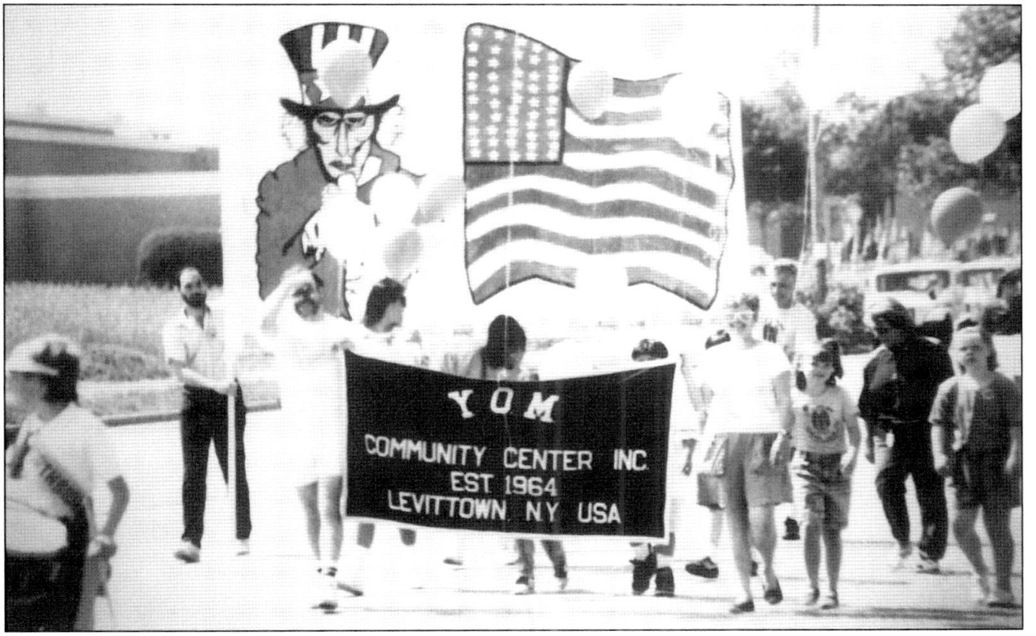

Members of YOM march in a Memorial Day parade. The colorful banner adorned with Uncle Sam and a large flag states "YOM wants you to remember our troops." YOM, which stands for Yours, Ours, and Mine, was founded in 1964 to reach out to teenagers who did not fit into many of the community-organized activities such as football and baseball leagues. Over the past years, YOM has greatly expanded its programs and services and today has a senior center, a day-care center, and many counseling services. (Courtesy of YOM.)

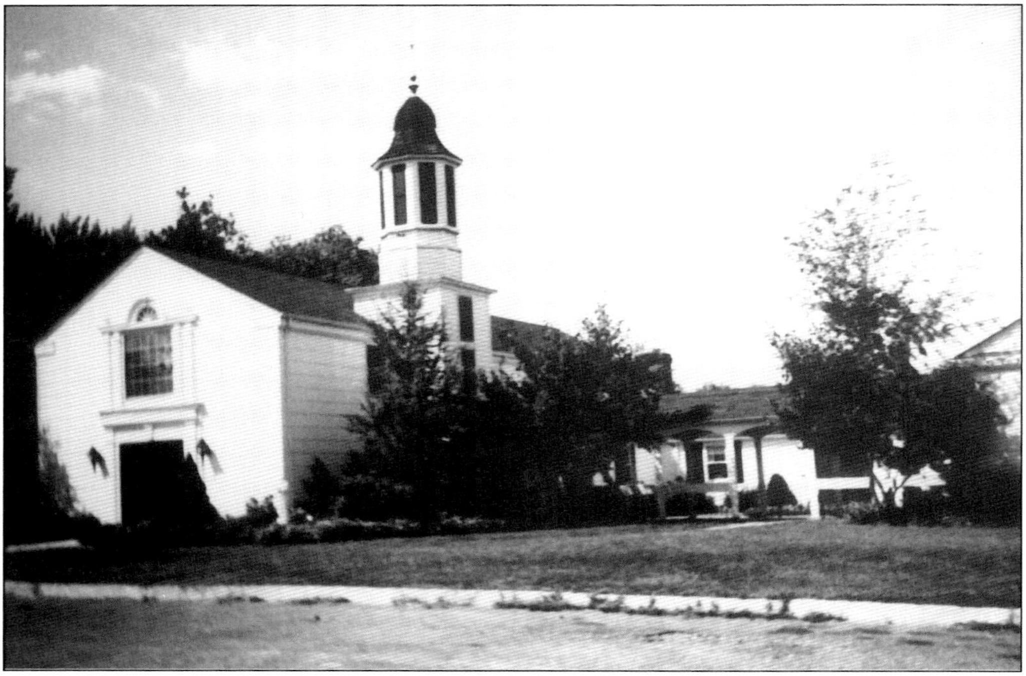

Pictured here is St. Francis Episcopal Church. (Collection of the Levittown Library.)

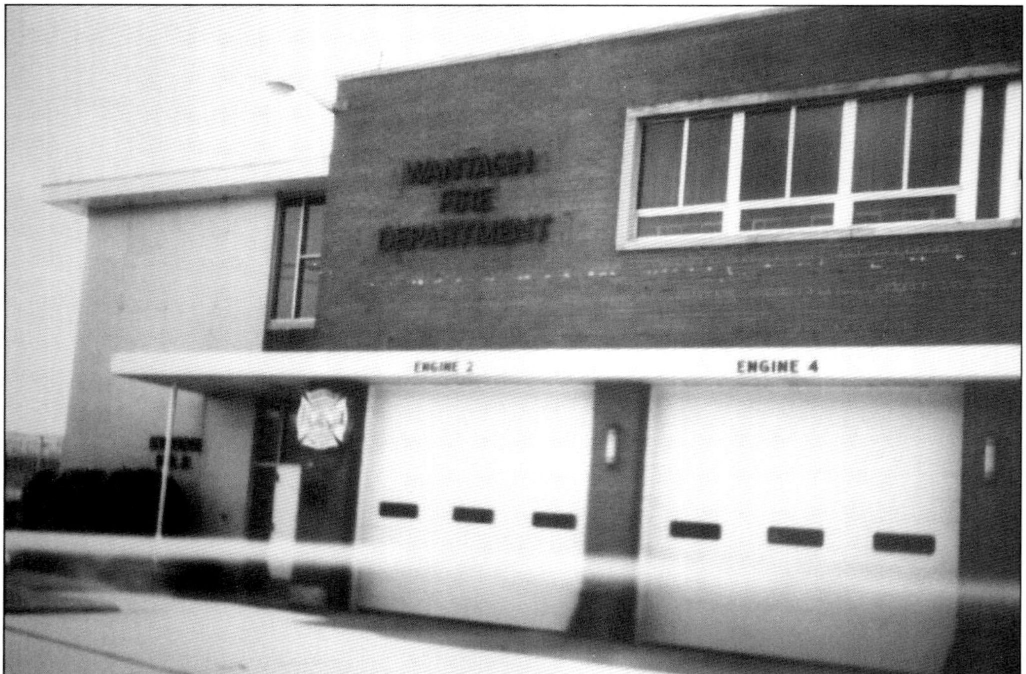

This photograph captures the Wantagh Fire Company.

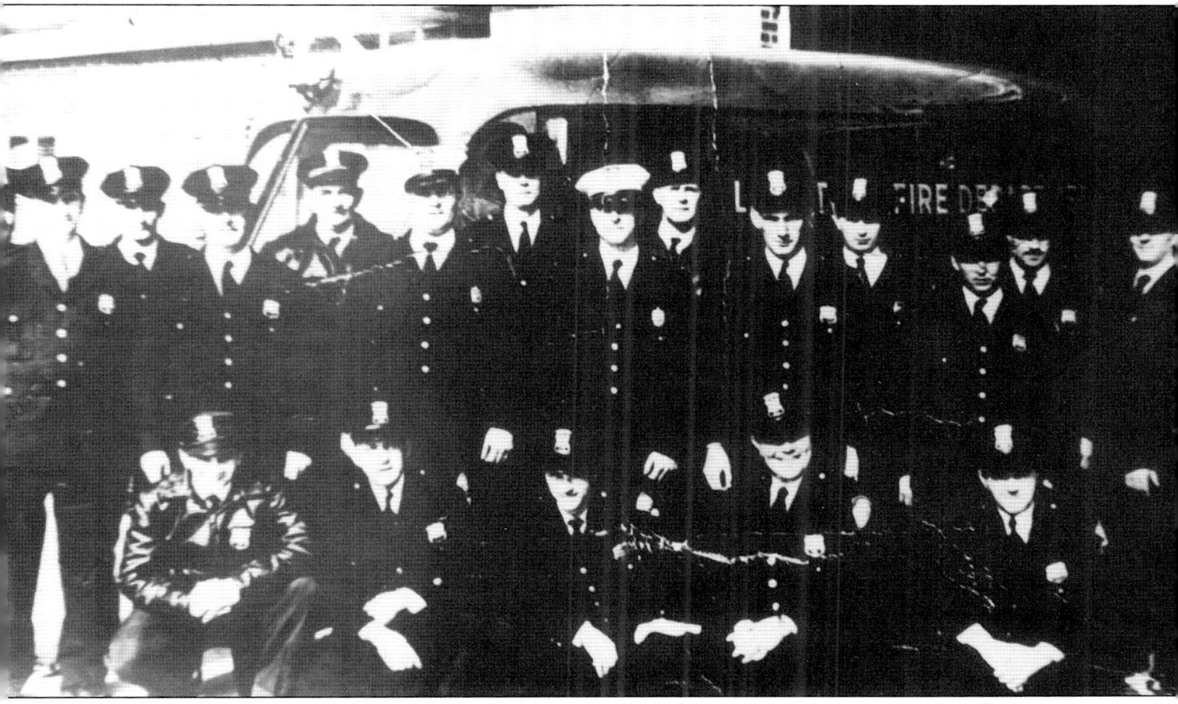

Levittown police and fire companies' officers are pictured here. The Levittown Fire Company was formed and went into operation in 1951 with John Cashman as its first chief. (Collection of the Levittown Library.)

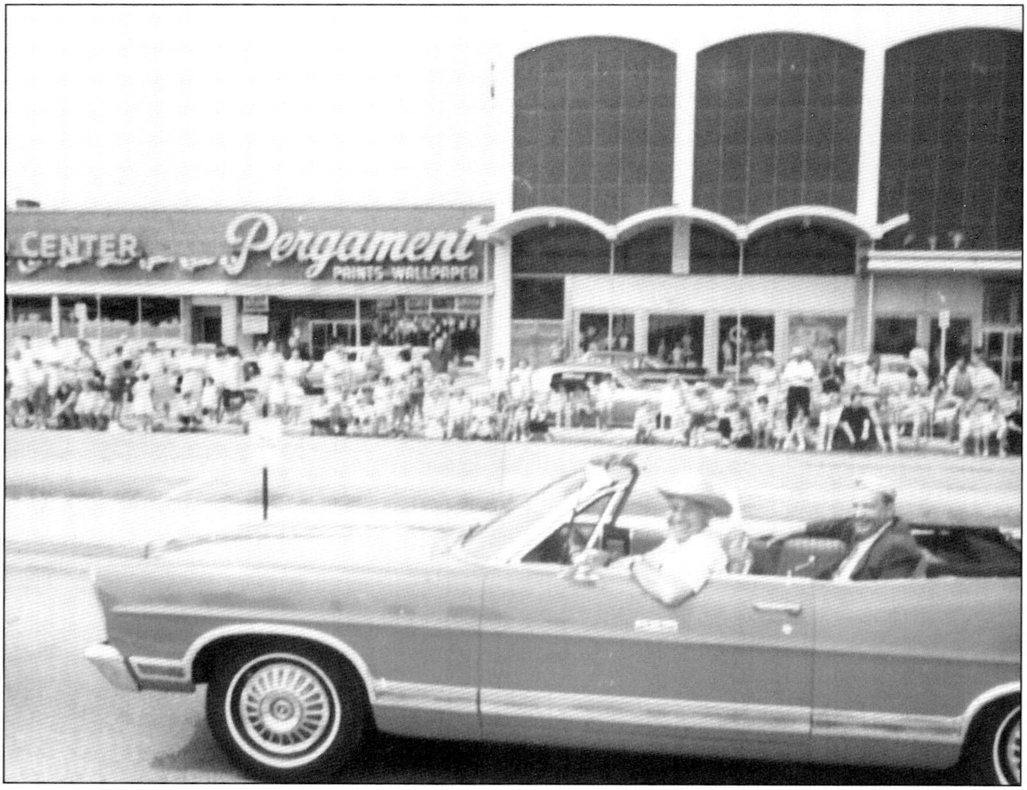

In a scene from the 20th Anniversary Parade, the man in the car is the owner of the first hardware store in Levittown. (Collection of Meta Smith.)

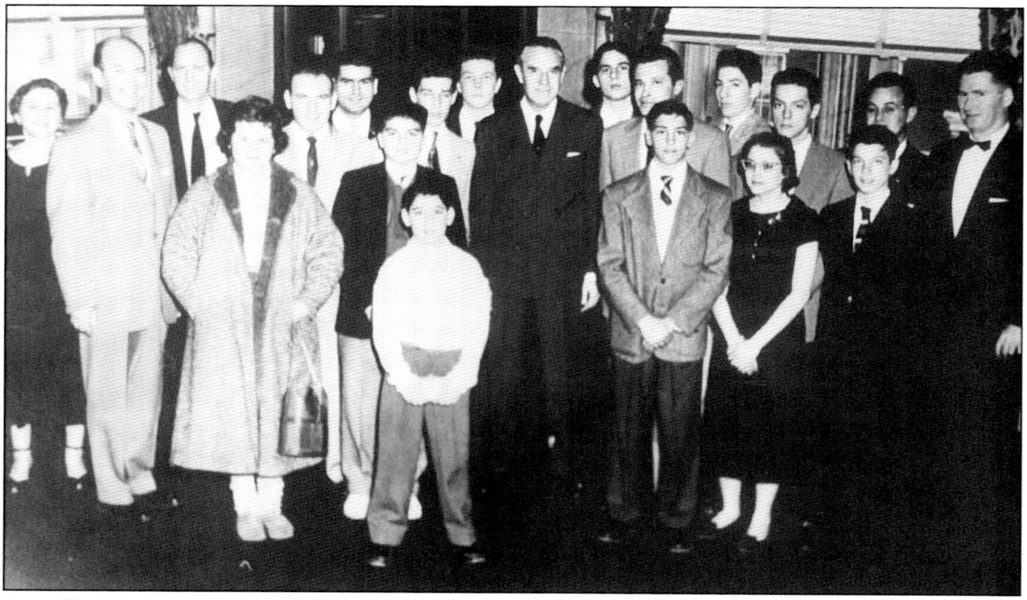
Averill Harriman and McCloskey are pictured here with a group. (Collection of the Levittown Library.)

Pictured here are shop students. (Collection of the Levittown Library.)

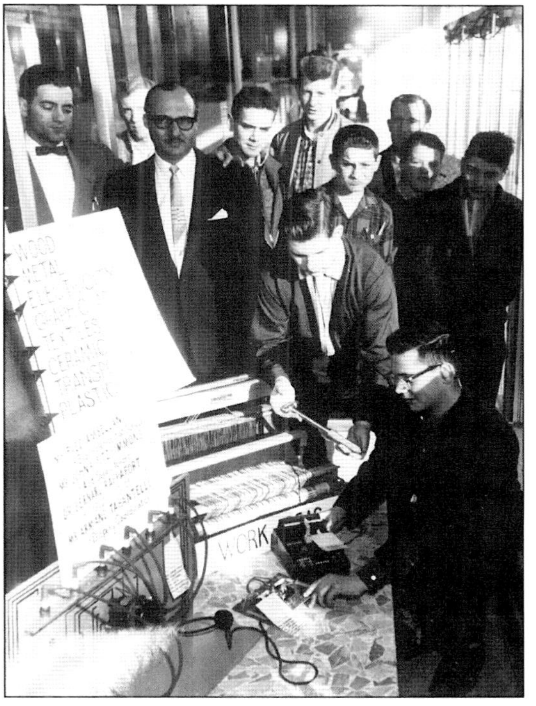

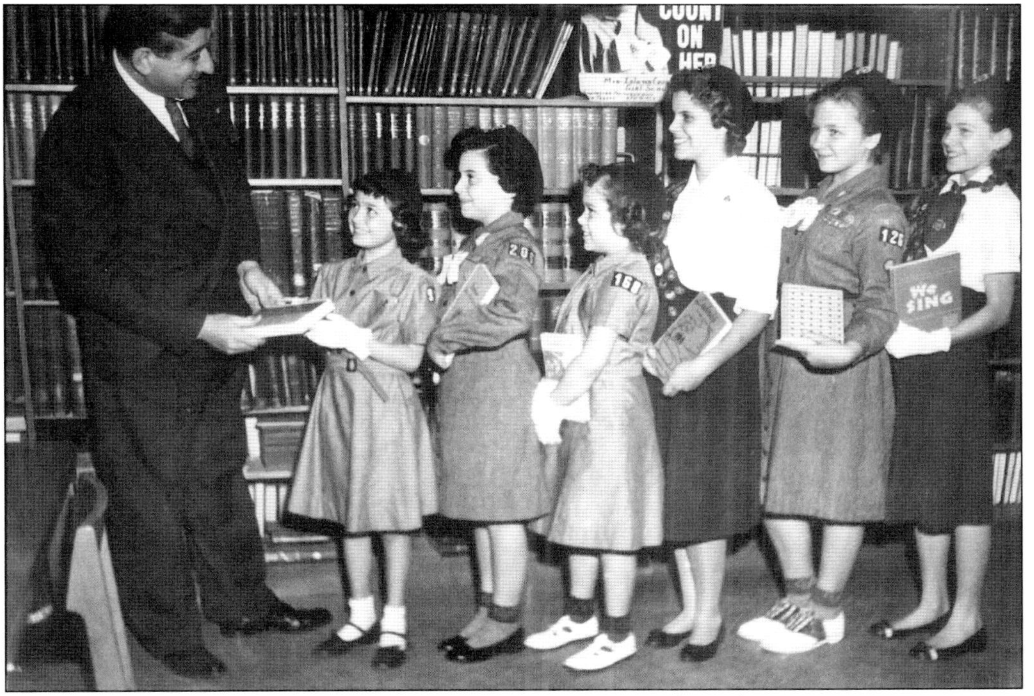

Girl Scouts present gift books. (Collection of the Levittown Library.)

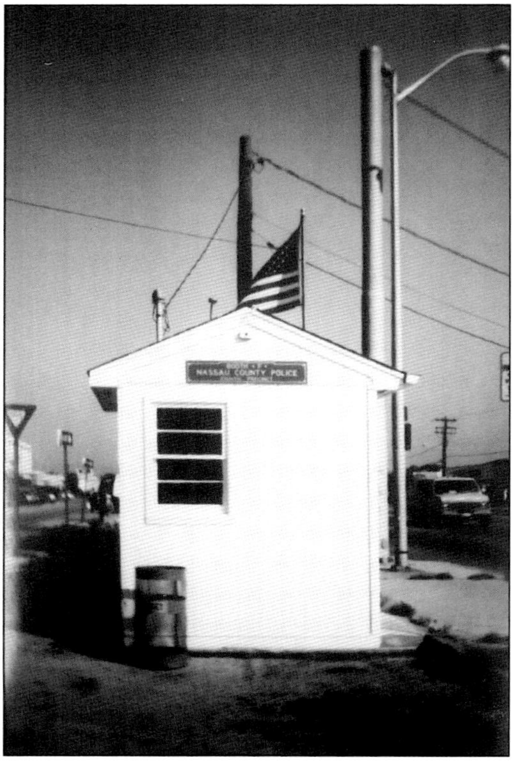

The Nassau County police booth is located in front of the Flea Market Shopping Center at the northwest corner of Hempstead Turnpike and Center Lane. (Collection of the Levittown Library.)

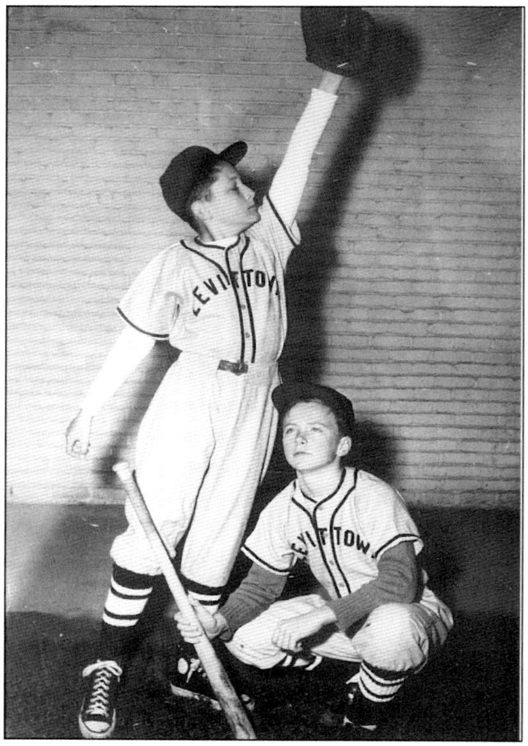

Two Levittown Little Leaguers strike a dramatic pose for this photograph. Organized sports were an important part of community life in Levittown. The first Little League began in 1951. (Collection of the Levittown Library.)

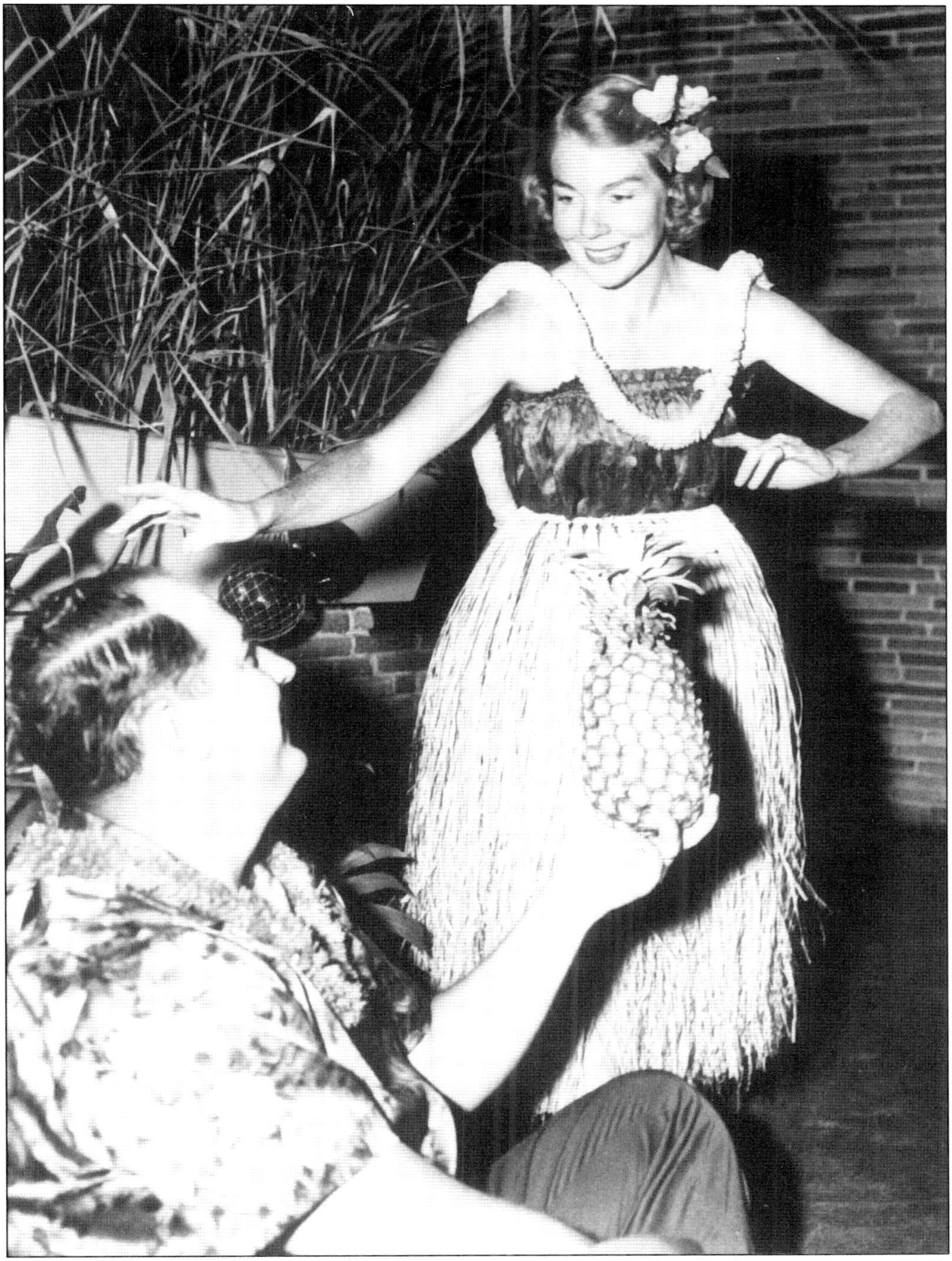

At a lively Hawaiian Party scene at Levittown Hall, Sylvia Ash does the hula. Levittown Hall, located on Levittown Parkway, was the scene of many community events. Designed by Alfred Levitt, the hall had an auditorium that could seat 500 and was built at a cost of $250,000. There were also smaller rooms in the complex. (Collection of the Levittown Library.)

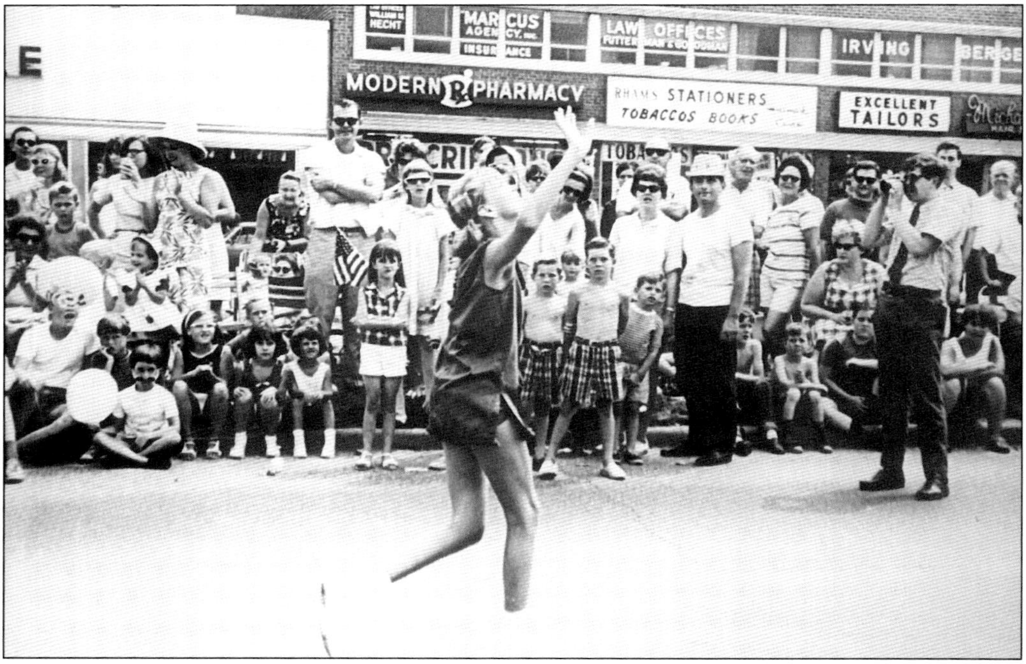

Everyone loves a parade, and what parade is complete without a baton twirler? Visible in the background is the Modern Pharmacy, Rhams Stationers, Marcus Insurance Agency, and Excellent Tailors. (Collection of the Levittown Library.)

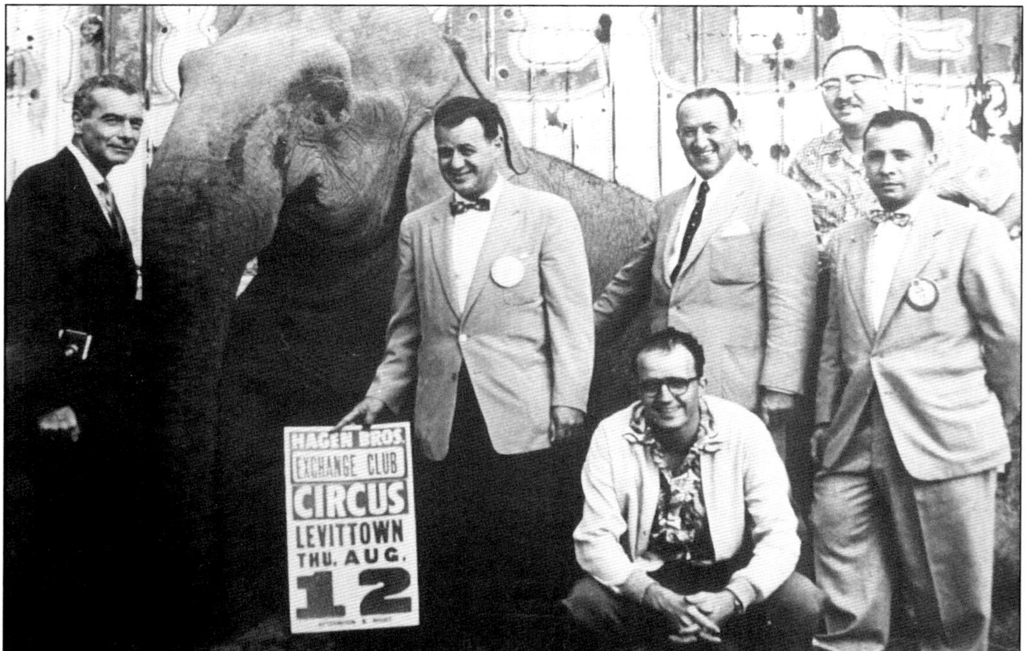

Hagen Brothers Circus came to town on August 12. Members of the Exchange Club pose with the circus elephant. (Collection of the Levittown Library.)

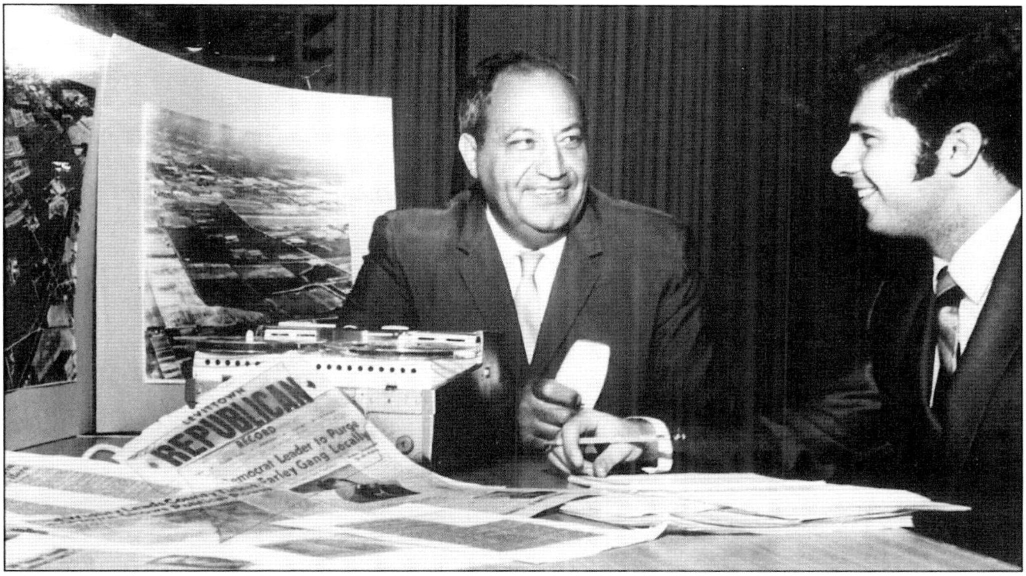

Judge Paul Widlitz shares memories with Library Cadet Joseph Spagnoli in 1967. At the time of the interview, Judge Widlitz had been on the trial bench longer than any judge in Nassau County. Widlitz contributed to many aspects of life in Levittown and was instrumental in procuring the land donated by Levitt for Young Israel. Mr. Spagnoli, a student at C.W. Post College, was part of a federally funded project aimed at recruiting college students to become librarians. Spagnoli is the author of the 70-page, annotated bibliography of Levittown, a tremendous resource for researchers. (Collection of the Levittown Library.)

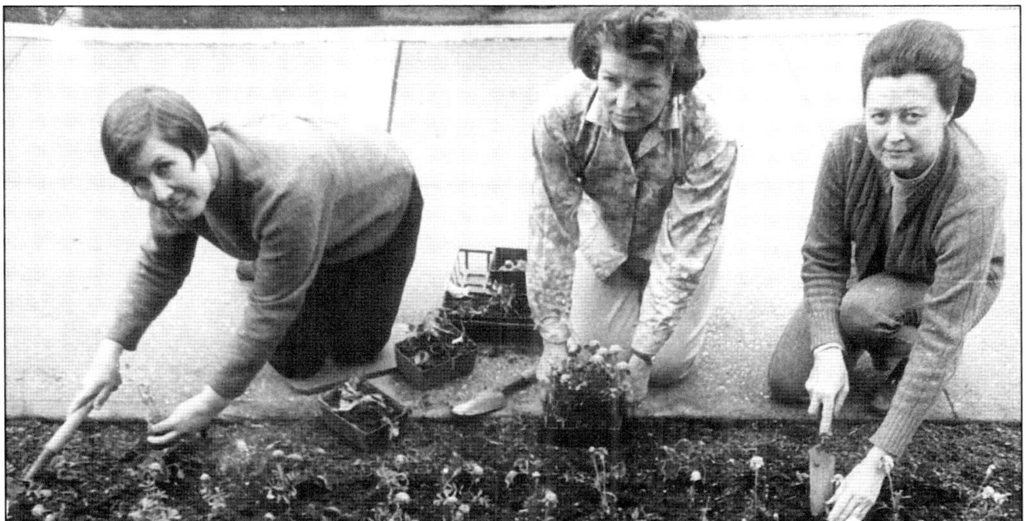

Levittown Garden Club ladies plant flowers at Levittown Public Library in May 1970. The press release from the library, dated May 8, reads, "As part of Community Beautification project, the Levittown Garden Club planted a colorful bed of marigolds and coleus at the entrance of the library. The garden club members who did the planting are from left to right, Mrs. Lorraine Warmuth, Mrs. Jean DeMeglia, Mrs. Donna Mould, and Mrs. Sadie Benza, all of Levittown." (Collection of the Levittown Library.)

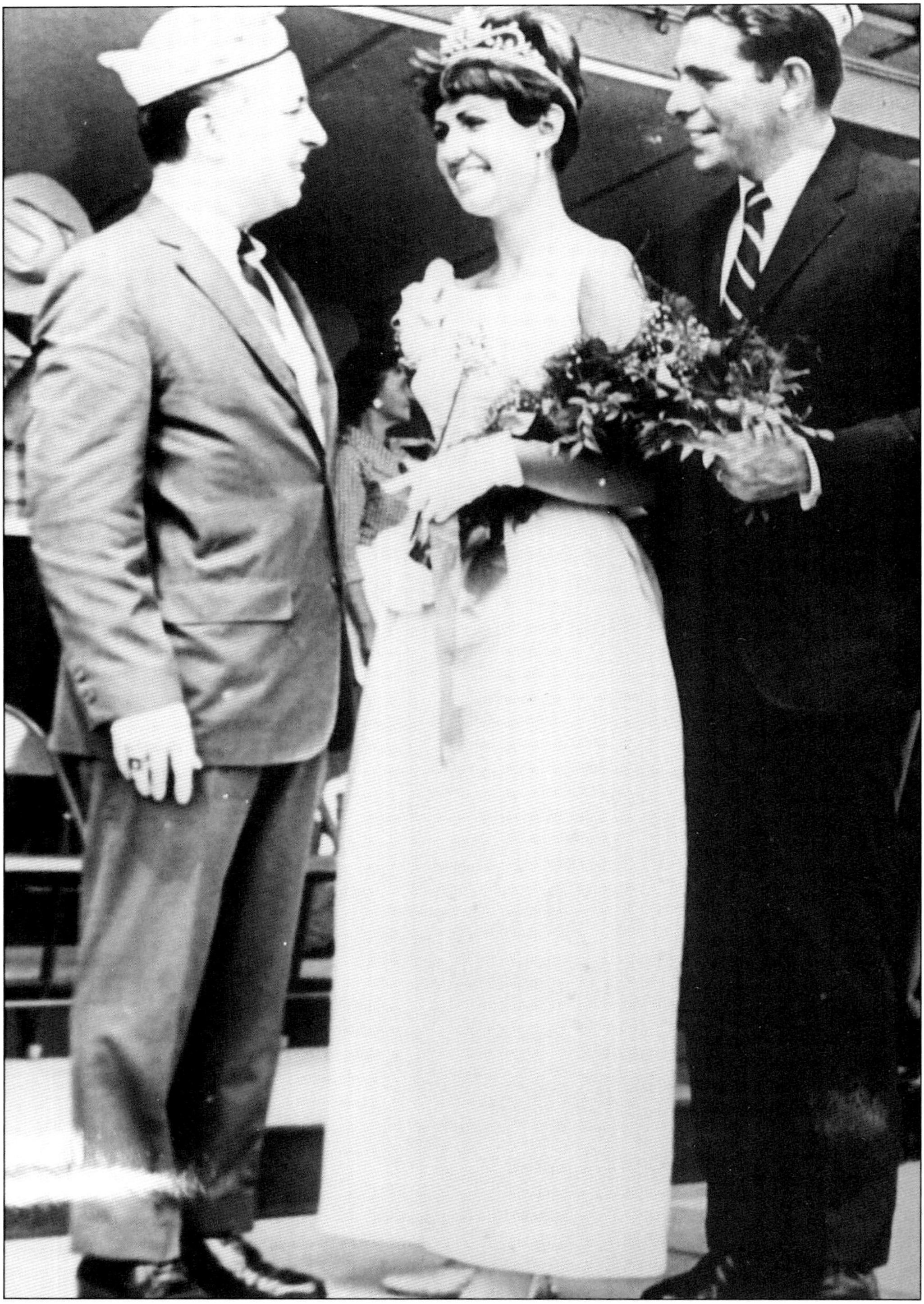

The queen of the 20th Anniversary Celebration is pictured here with Judge Sol Wachler. (Collection of the Levittown Library.)

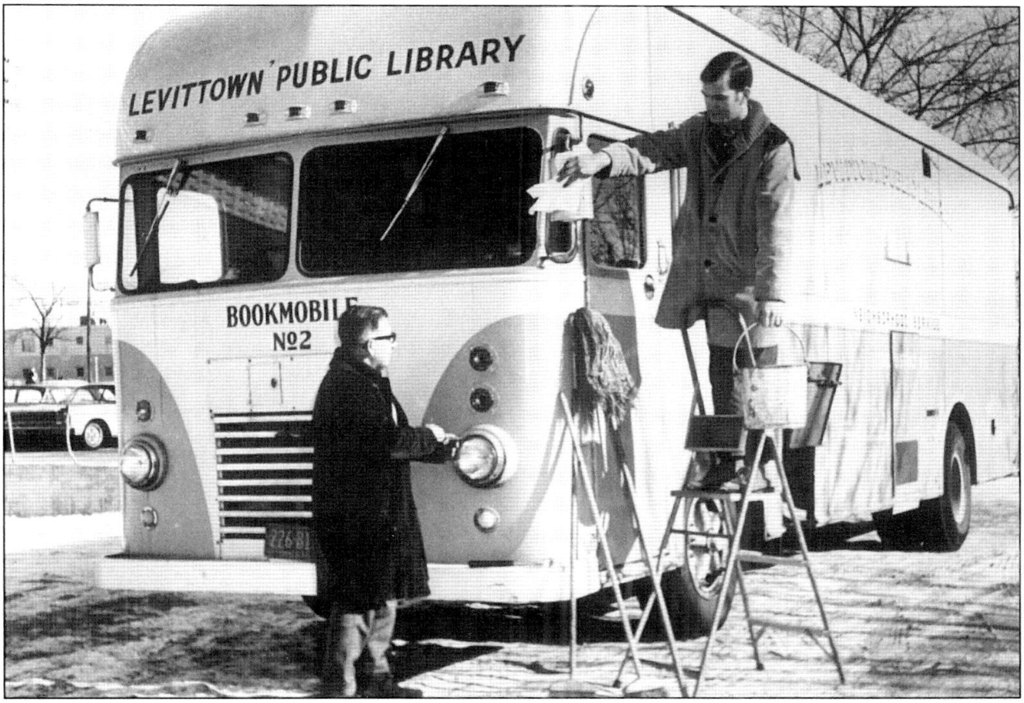

Levittown Library Bookmobile No. 2 gets spruced up. A large part of early library service was the bookmobiles that traveled through the community to bring books to the patrons. (Collection of the Levittown Library.)

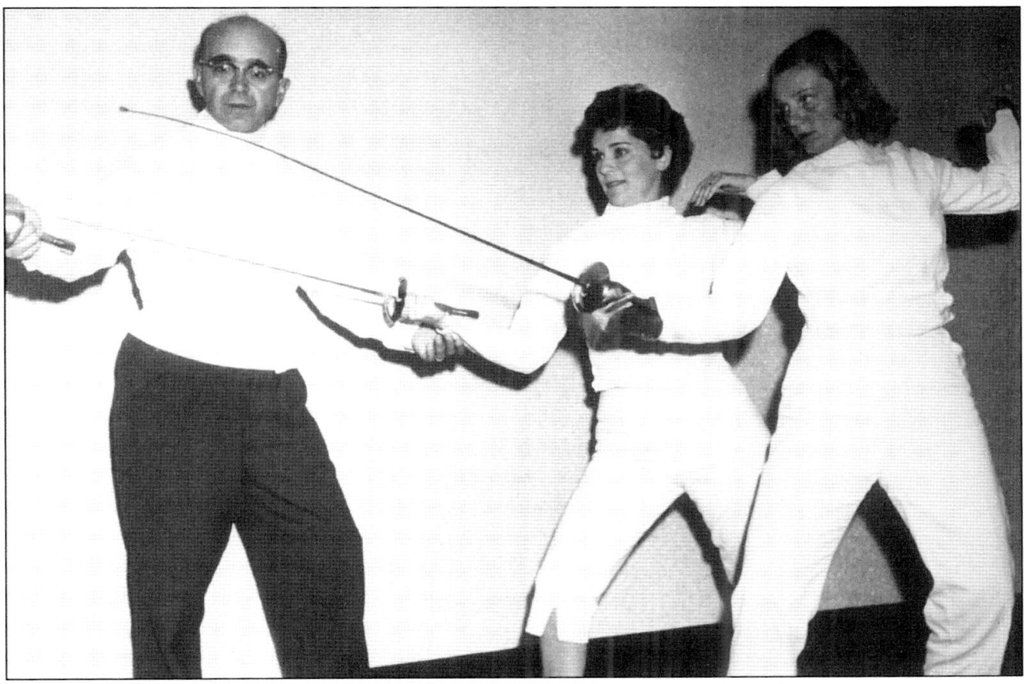

Adult fencers show off their skills. (Collection of the Levittown Library.)

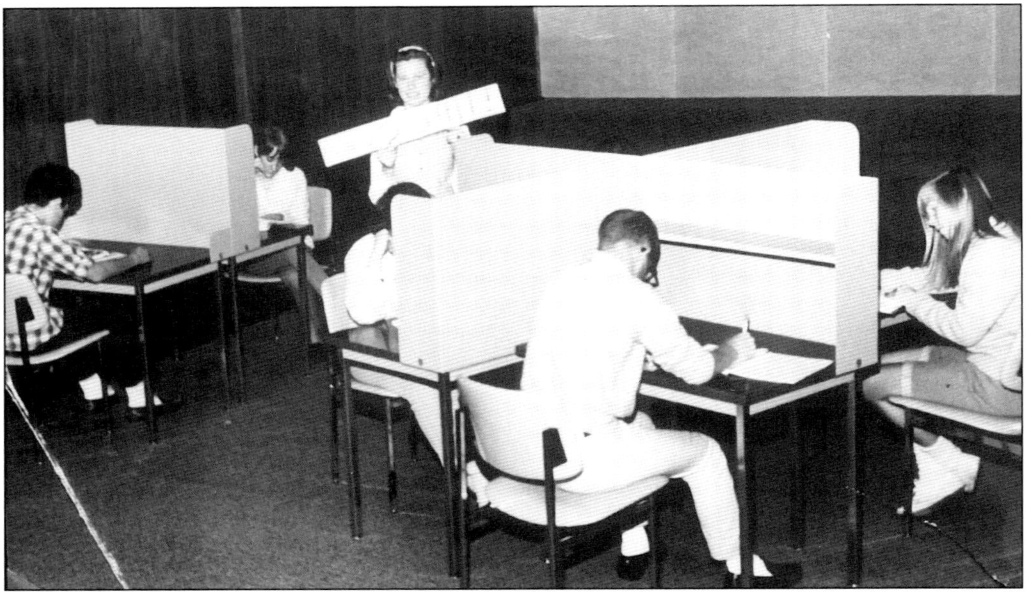

The Quiet Reading Room opened in Levittown Library in 1965. (Collection of the Levittown Library.)

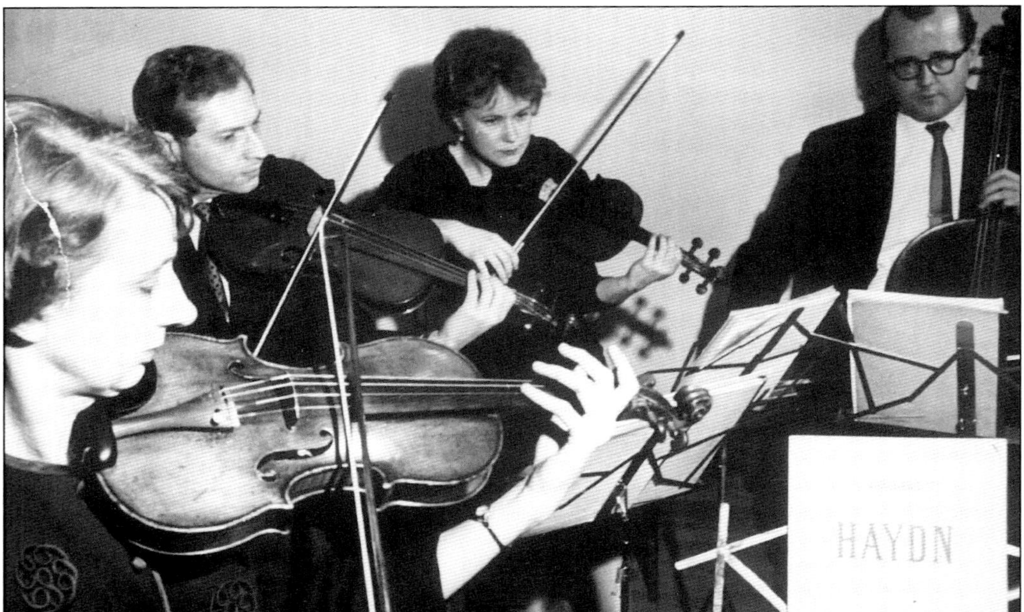

An evening of chamber music by the Ariosa String Quartet opened the Levittown Public Library's Spring Art Series. The quartet, led by Miss Mary Jane Metcalf, featured music by Haydn, Schubert, Stravinsky, and Beethoven. The performers are, from left to right, Mary Jane Metcalfe, first violin; Jack Katz, viola; Jerre Gibson, second violin; and Juri Taht, cello. Other programs in the series included an illustrated lecture on Pop Art with examples of local high school student art in this style, and a presentation by the Long Island Studio Theater. (Collection of the Levittown Library.)

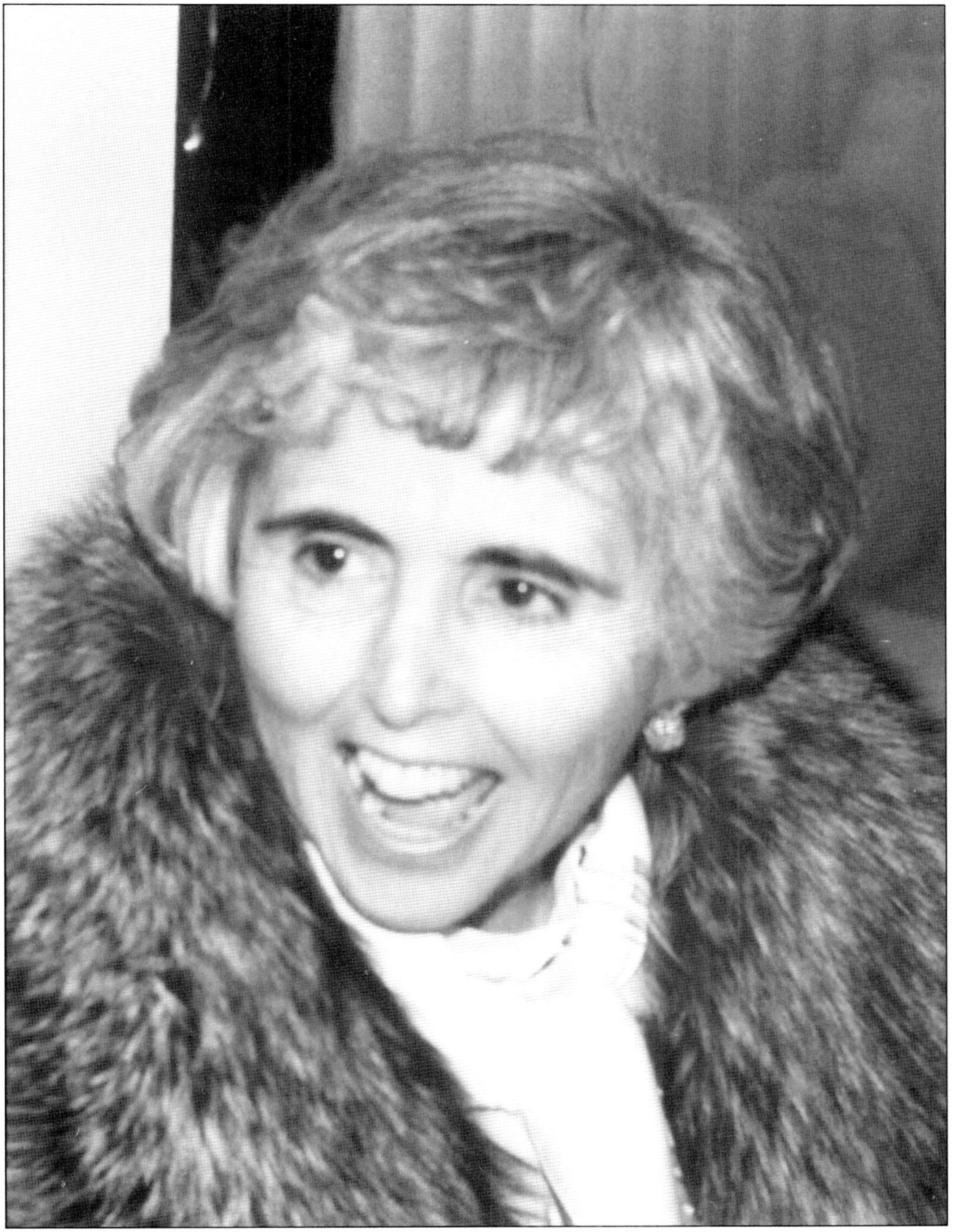

Janet Spar was the curator of the Levittown Library history collection for many years. Janet recalls as a young librarian being mentored by the late Ceil Roberts, a longtime Levittown resident and librarian. Their collaboration continued even after Mrs. Roberts's retirement, when she continued to volunteer her services. Throughout the production of both *Levittown* and *Levittown II*, Janet Spar has been an invaluable resource for her depth of knowledge and the fine spirit with which she gave the authors a great deal of help. (Courtesy of Janet Spar.)

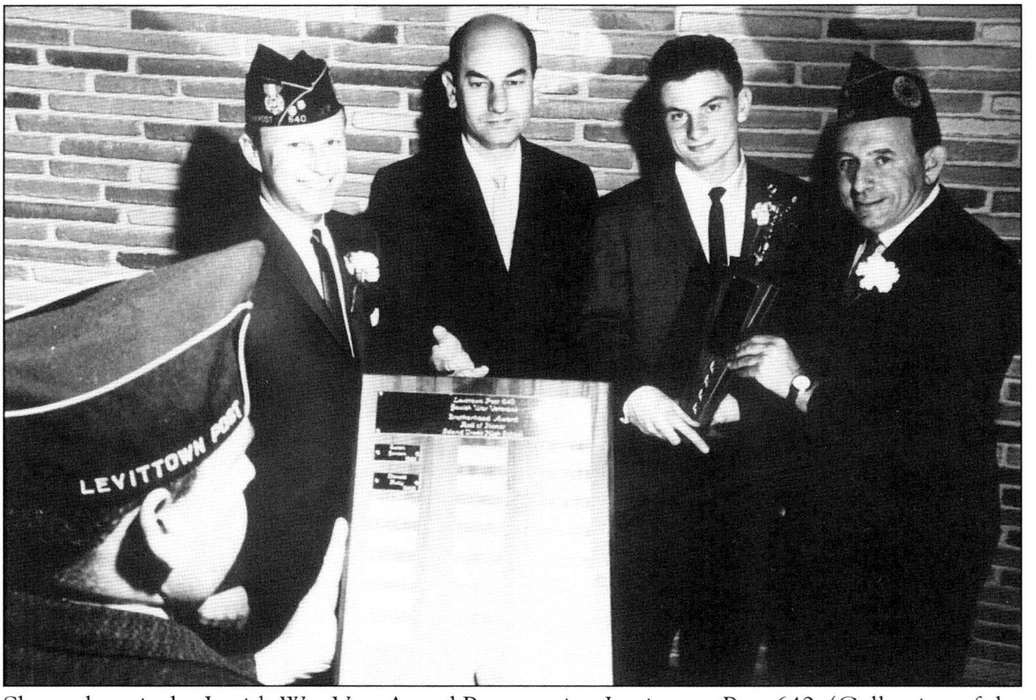

Shown here is the Jewish War Vets Award Presentation Levittown Post 640. (Collection of the Levittown Library.)

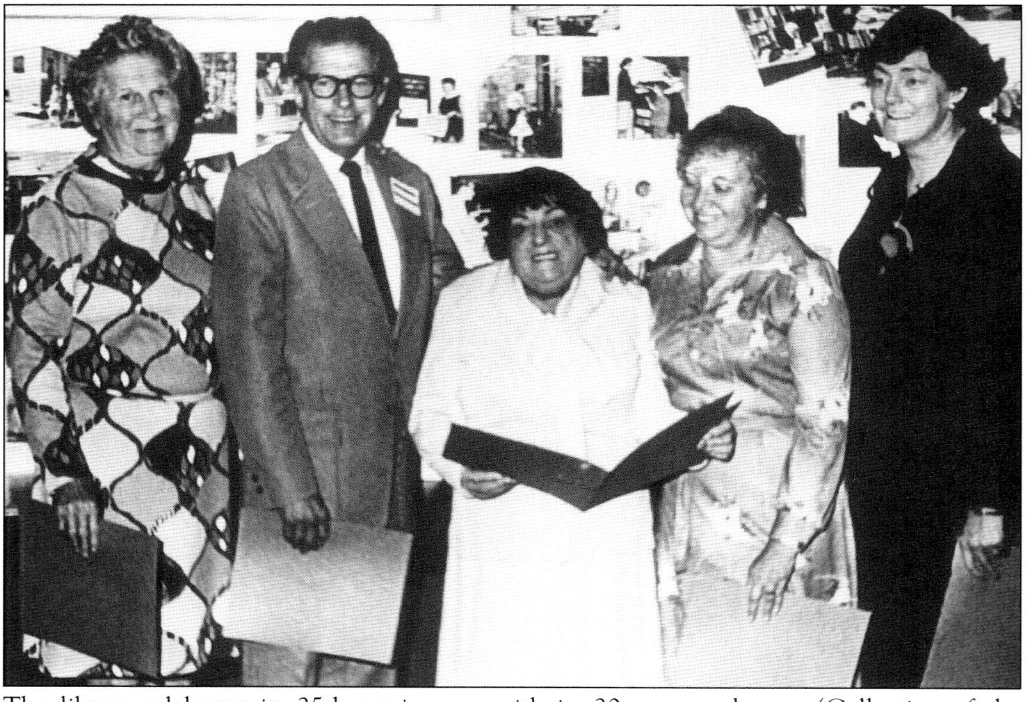

The library celebrates its 25th anniversary with its 20-year employees. (Collection of the Levittown Library.)

Cecile Roberts was both a revered librarian and an original resident of Levittown. She served in the library for 40 years, including as coordinator of the library's Senior Connection, a countywide self-help program for seniors. Director Pete Martin said, "Ceil was a super person, very much concerned with other people. She's going to be very much missed."

Mrs. Roberts died on July 22, 1996, at 71. The authors were very fond of Ceil and her enthusiasm and knowledge of her community.

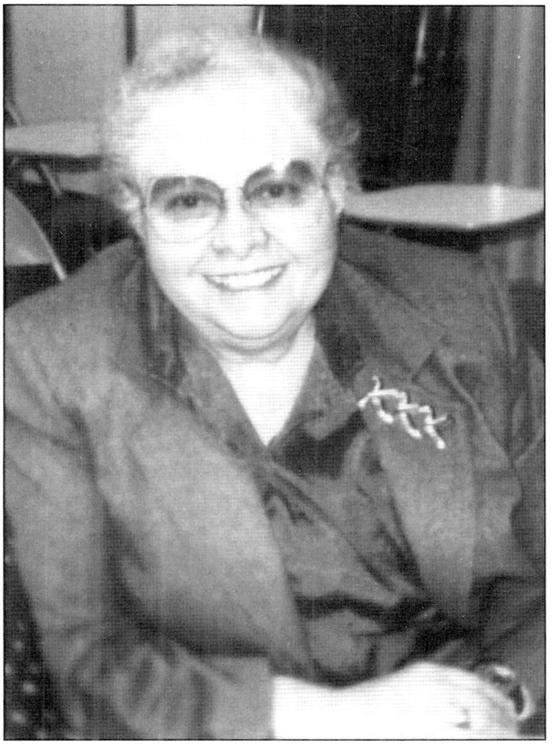

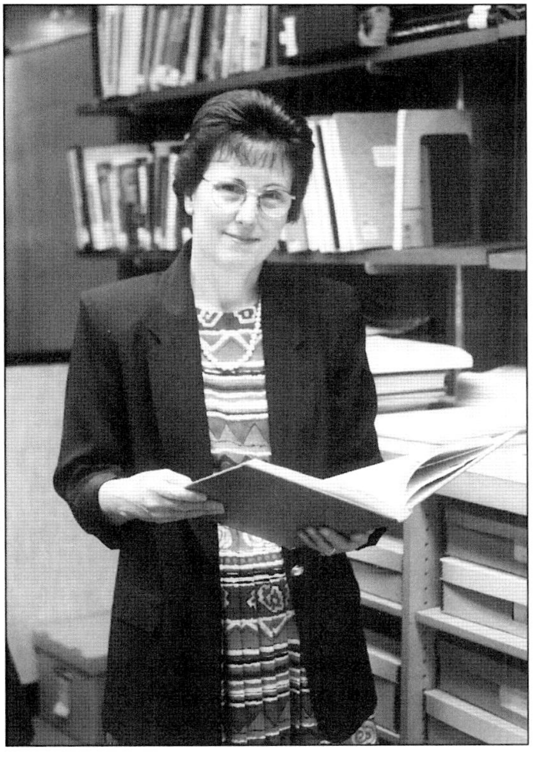

Ann Glorioso, curator of the Levittown history collection at the Levittown Library, took on the duty of preserving the history collection from Janet Spar. The collection contains 500 photographs relating to Levittown history and a 70-page annotated bibliography. (Photograph by Tova Navarra.)

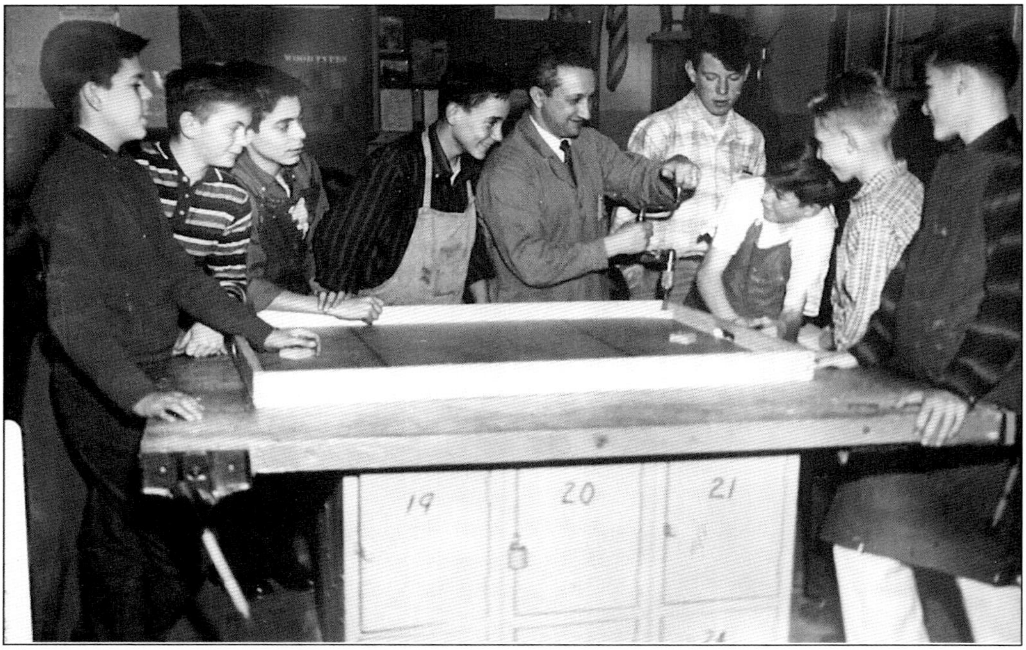

Shop students work on a table-hockey project. (Collection of the Levittown Library.)

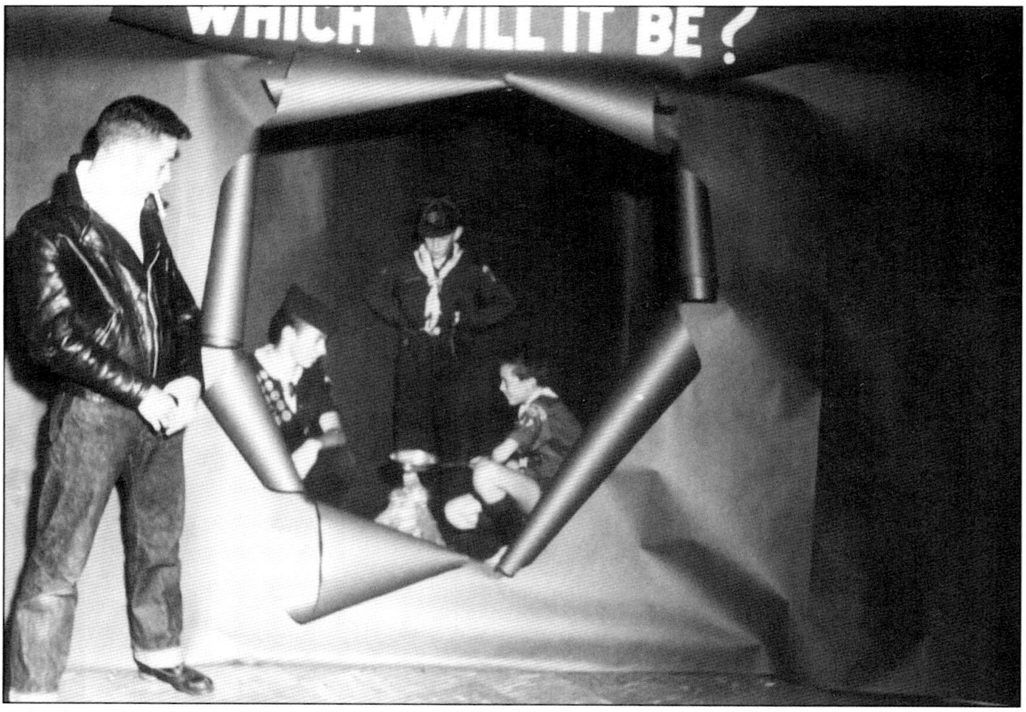

Which will it be? Boy Scouts engage in a wholesome activity, while the teen with slicked hair and leather jacket poses an ominous presence. Part of the Boy Scout code was aimed at averting antisocial behavior. (Collection of the Levittown Library.)

This sign commemorates Levittown's first schoolhouse. (Collection of the Levittown Library.)

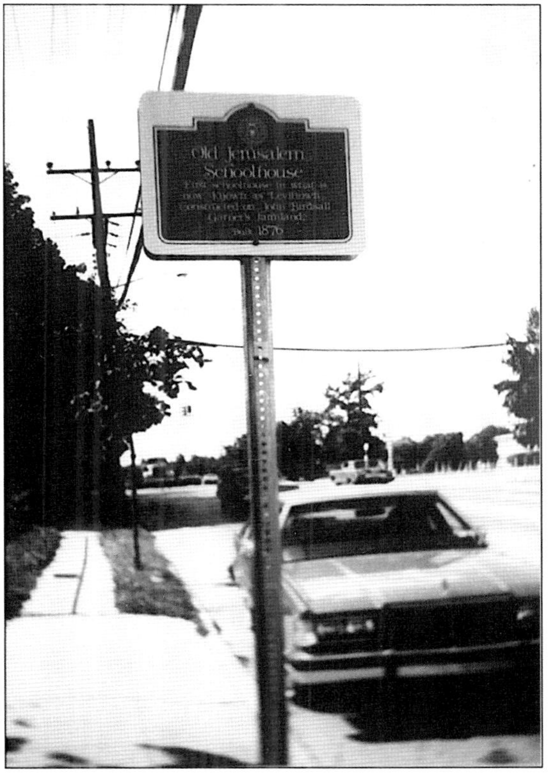

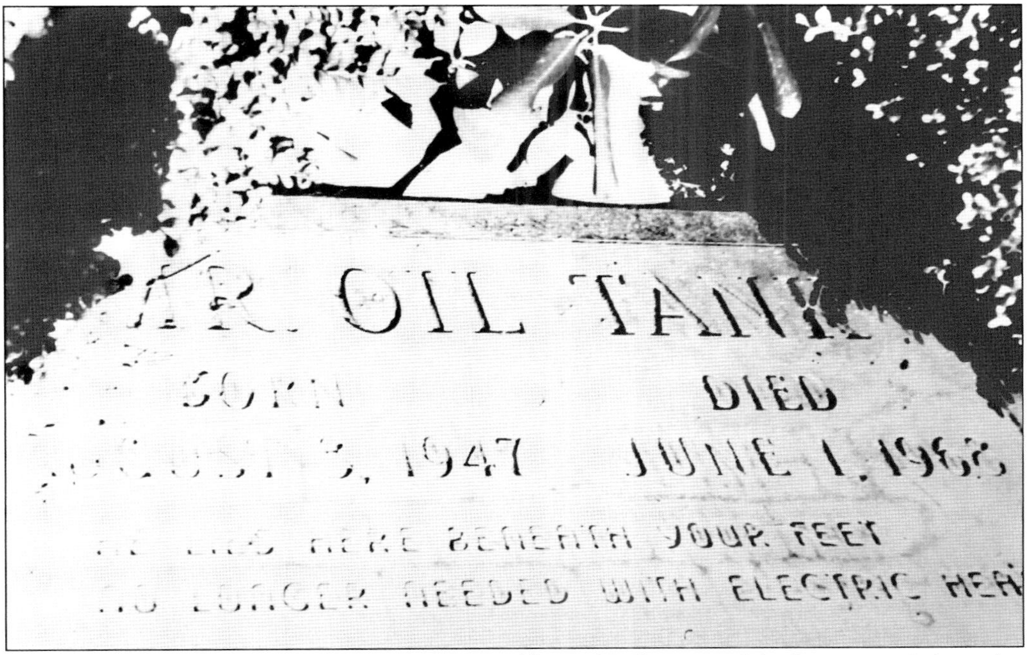

The "Mr. Oil Tank" mock gravestone is pictured here. (Collection of the Levittown Library.)

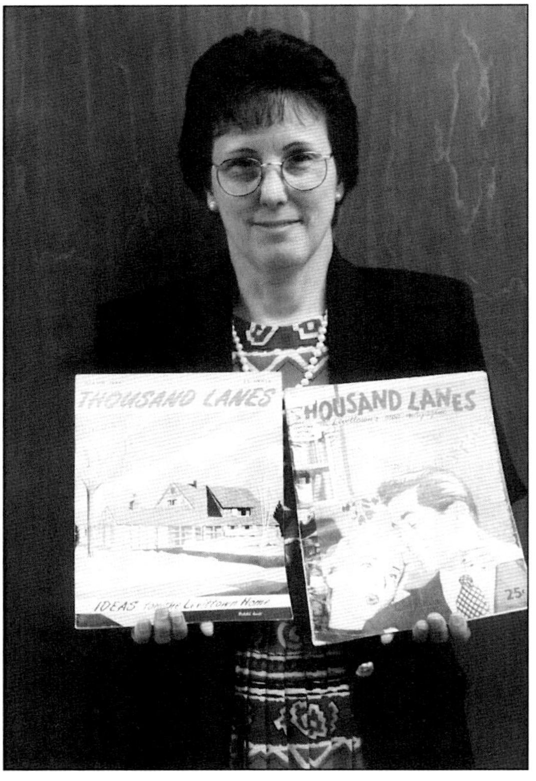

Levittown librarian Ann Glorioso holds two copies of *Thousand Lanes* magazine. The immensely popular *Thousand Lanes* began in November 1951. Betty and Bill Wannen were the publishers, and John Pergola was circulation manager. The magazine hooked into the favorite Levittown pastime of improving and possibly "stamping" the homes as the owners' individual creation. Initially the magazine dealt with topics of concern for Levittowners, but eventually evolved into dealing solely with various aspects of home ownership and improvement. One of the authors' favorites is a cartoon published in *Thousand Lanes* that reveals the professional's price as more if the homeowner helps with the renovation. (Collection of the Levittown Library.)

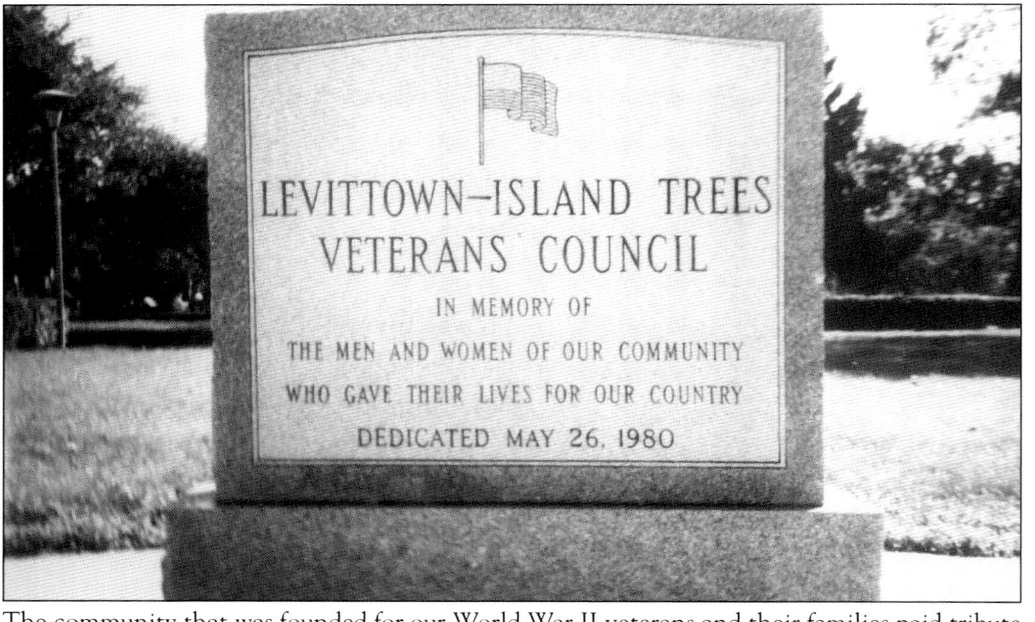

The community that was founded for our World War II veterans and their families paid tribute to those who died in service to their country with this monument. The monument, dedicated on May 26, 1980, was sponsored by the Levittown-Island Trees Veterans Council. (Collection of the Levittown Library.)

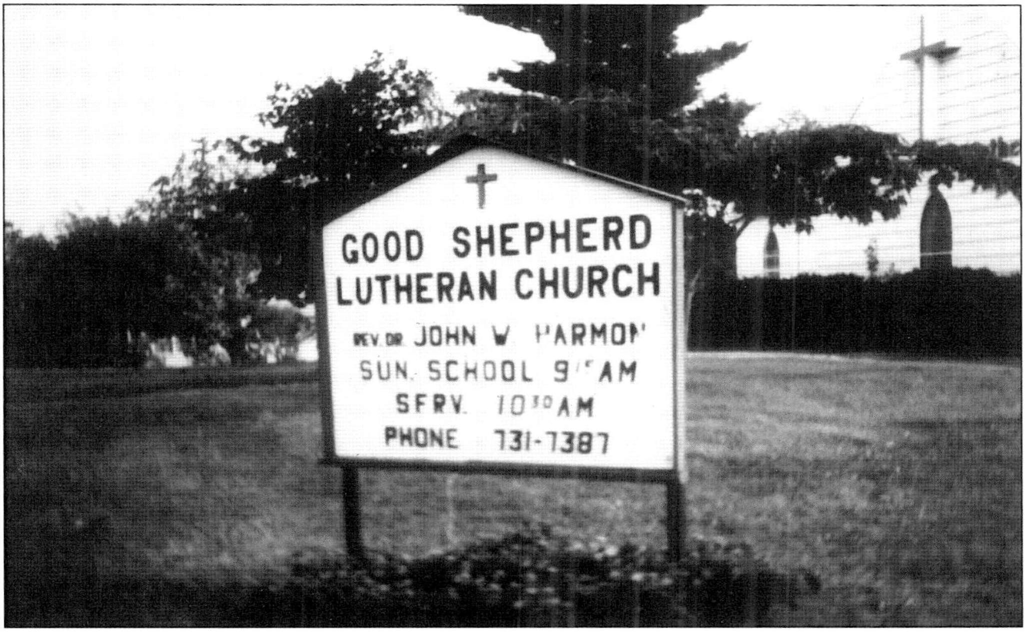

Pictured here is the Good Shepherd Lutheran Church on Hempstead Turnpike. (Collection of the Levittown Library.)

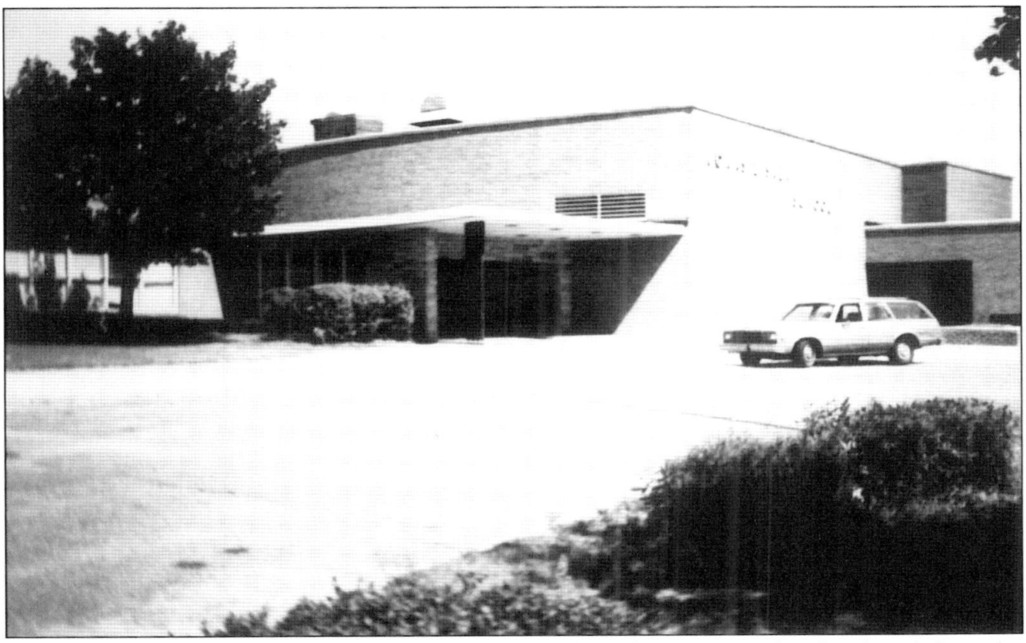

The Jonas Salk School on Jerusalem Road was named for the scientist who developed the polio vaccine. (Collection of the Levittown Library.)

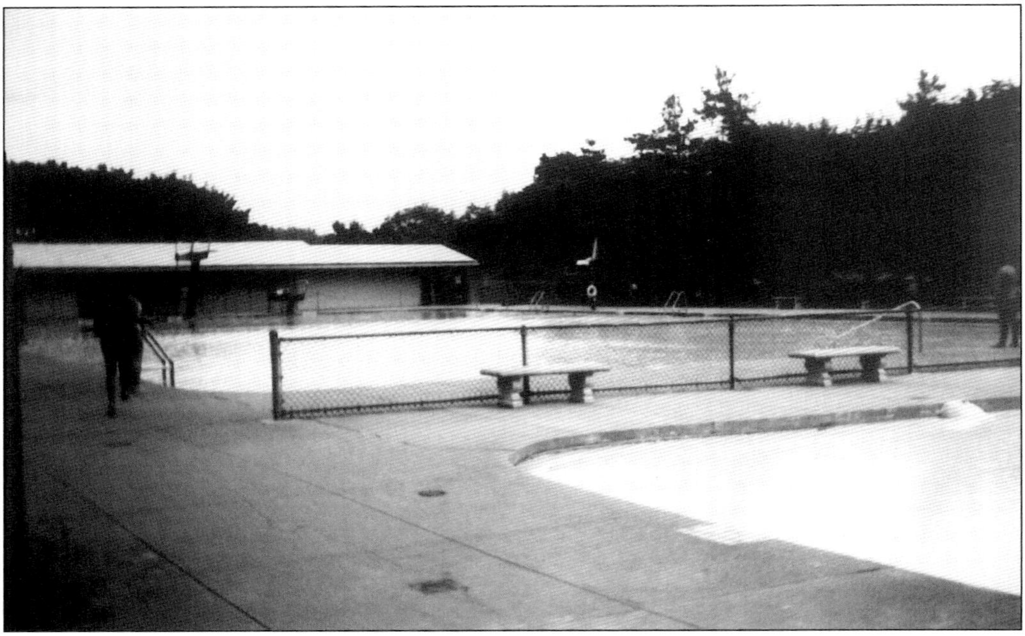

The Levitts donated several swimming pools to the community, one of which is pictured here.

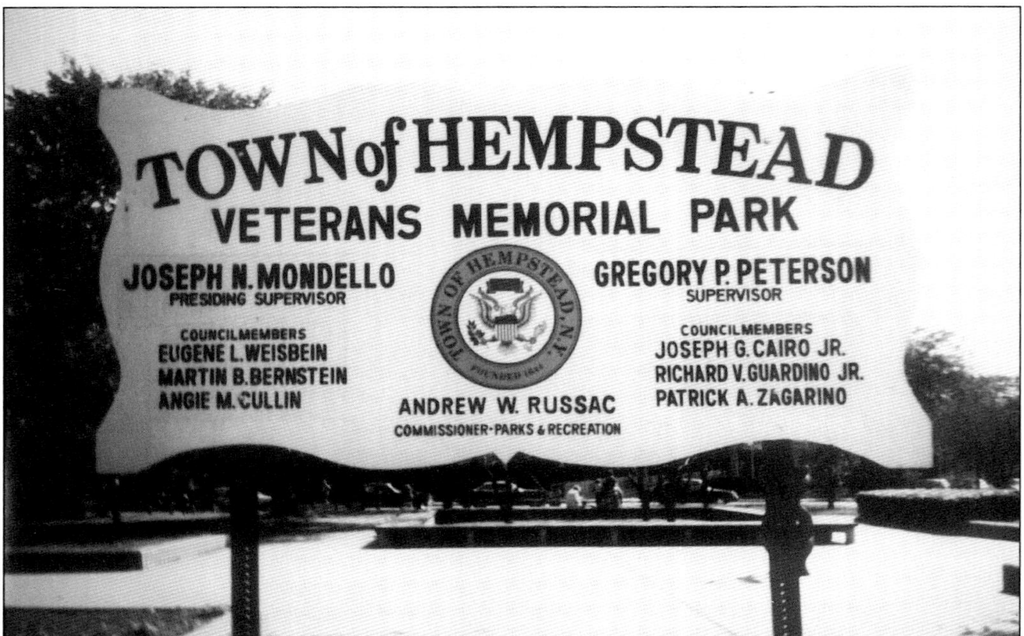

This "gateway" sign is hard to miss. (Collection of the Levittown Library.)

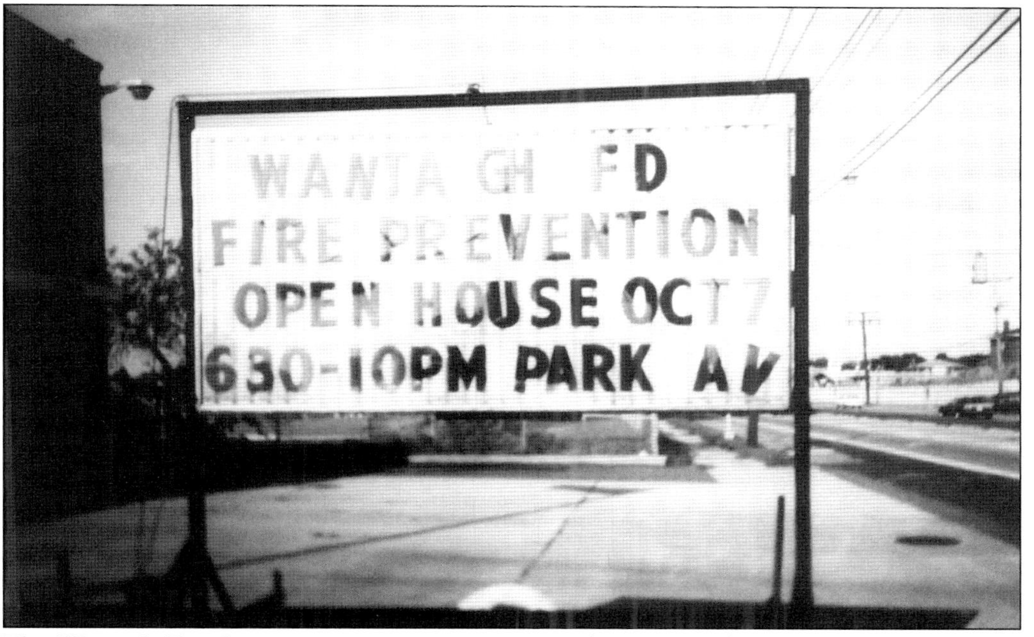

The Wantagh Fire Department announces an open house at Park Avenue in honor of fire prevention. (Collection of the Levittown Library.)

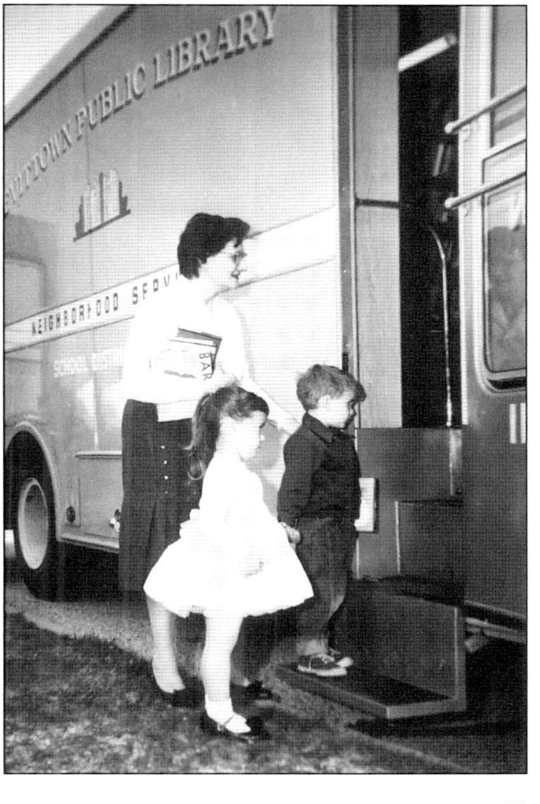

Children get ready to board the local bookmobile. (Collection of the Levittown Library.)

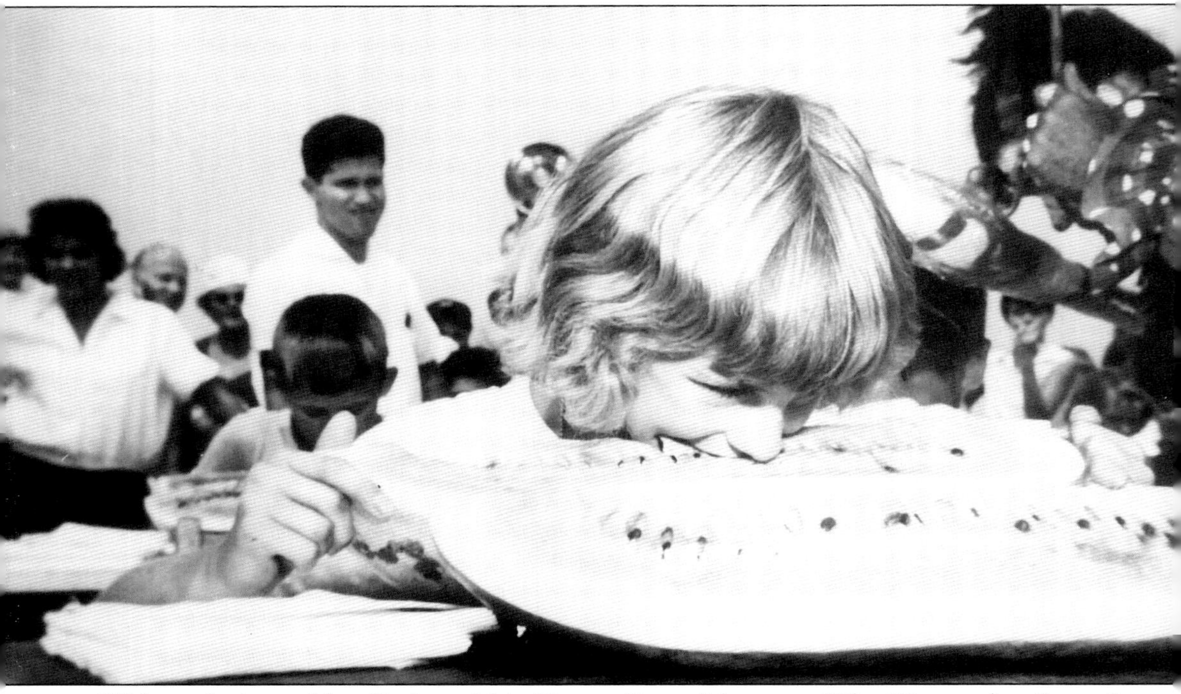

With apologies to Van Gogh and his "Potato Eaters," here are "The Watermelon Eaters." (Collection of the Levittown Library.)

Here is an interesting shot of a Levittown family. The composition places particular emphasis on the two children in the foreground, perhaps a tribute to Levittown's devotion to its younger generations. (Collection of the Levittown Library.)

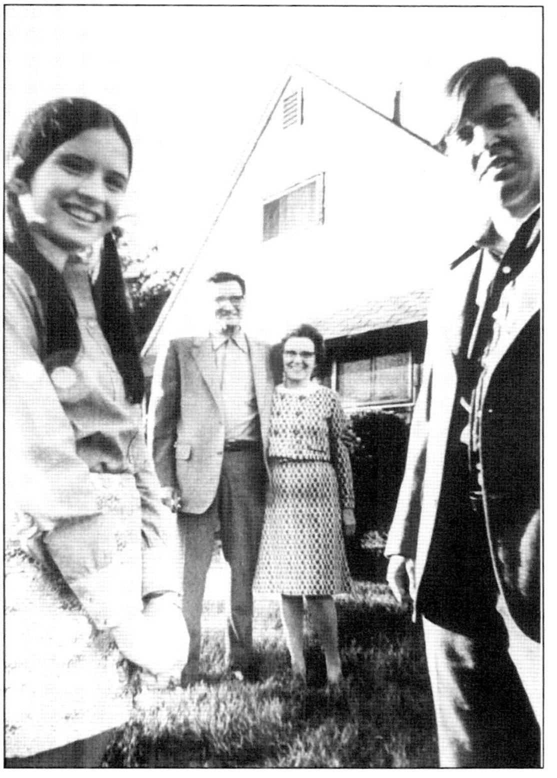

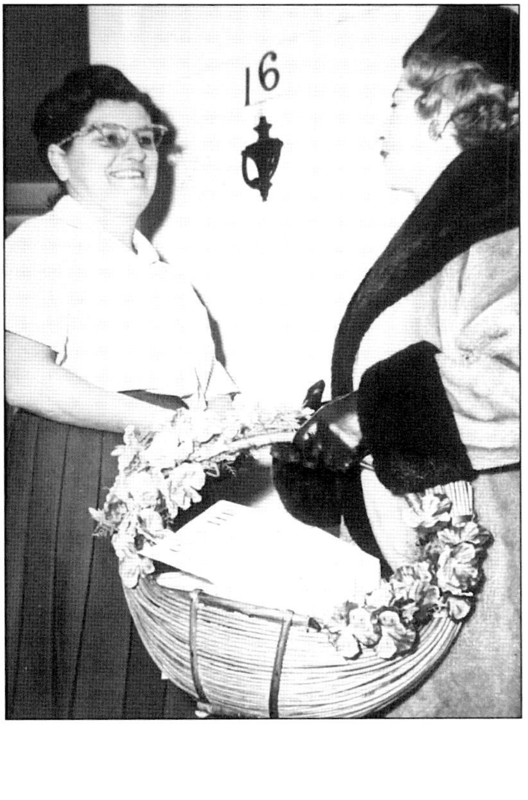

A custom that has for the most part escaped this generation is the "welcome wagon." A "welcome wagon" lady greets new residents with a basket of gifts from participating merchants and community organizations. (Collection of the Levittown Library.)

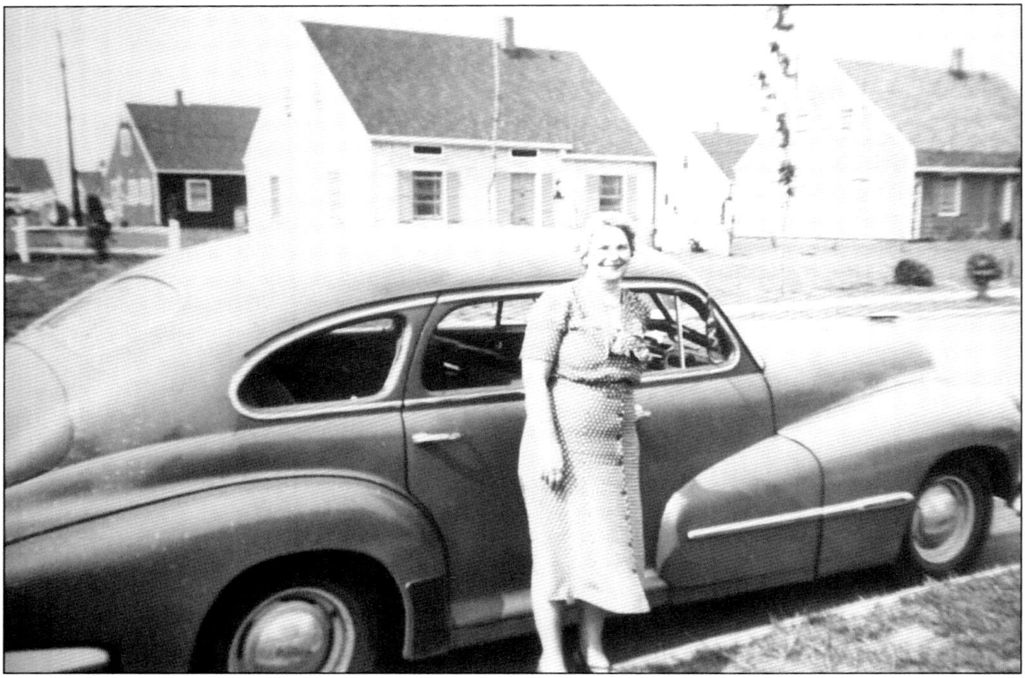

Original Levittowner Clare Worthing's mother stands in front of the family car in the development of Capes. (Collection of Clare and Jerry Worthing.)

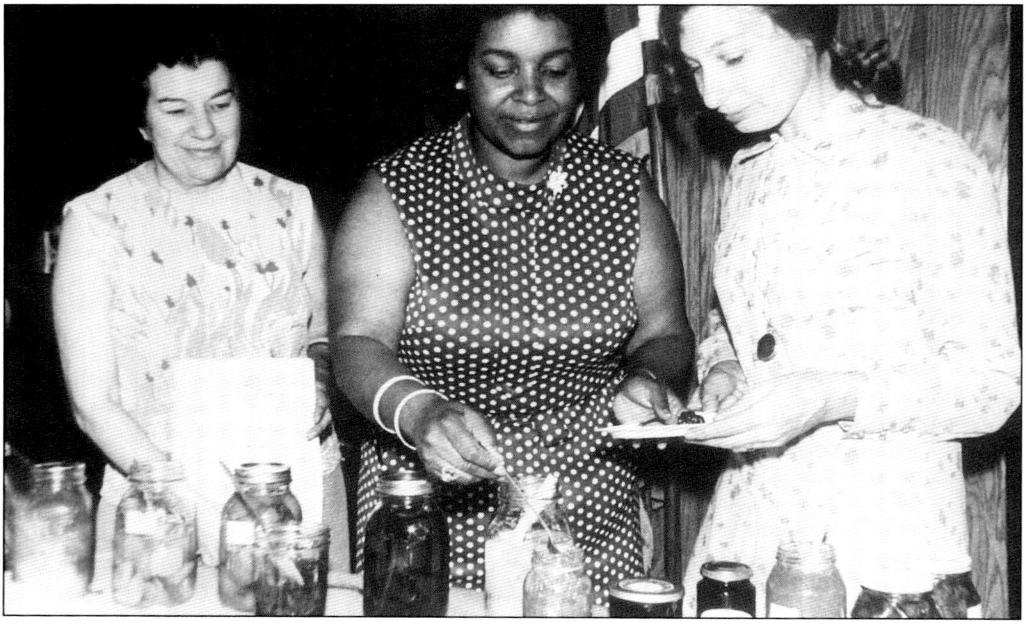

One of the many programs presented by the Levittown Public Library was entitled "Canning, Preserving, and Freezing," and was presented by Mrs. Vera Rivers (center) of the Nassau County Extension Service. There was a recipe book and a tasting table of gourmet treats donated by library staff. Mrs. Rivers serves Mrs. Feldman, while Mrs. Helen Crisafulli holds one of the recipe books. (Collection of the Levittown Library.)

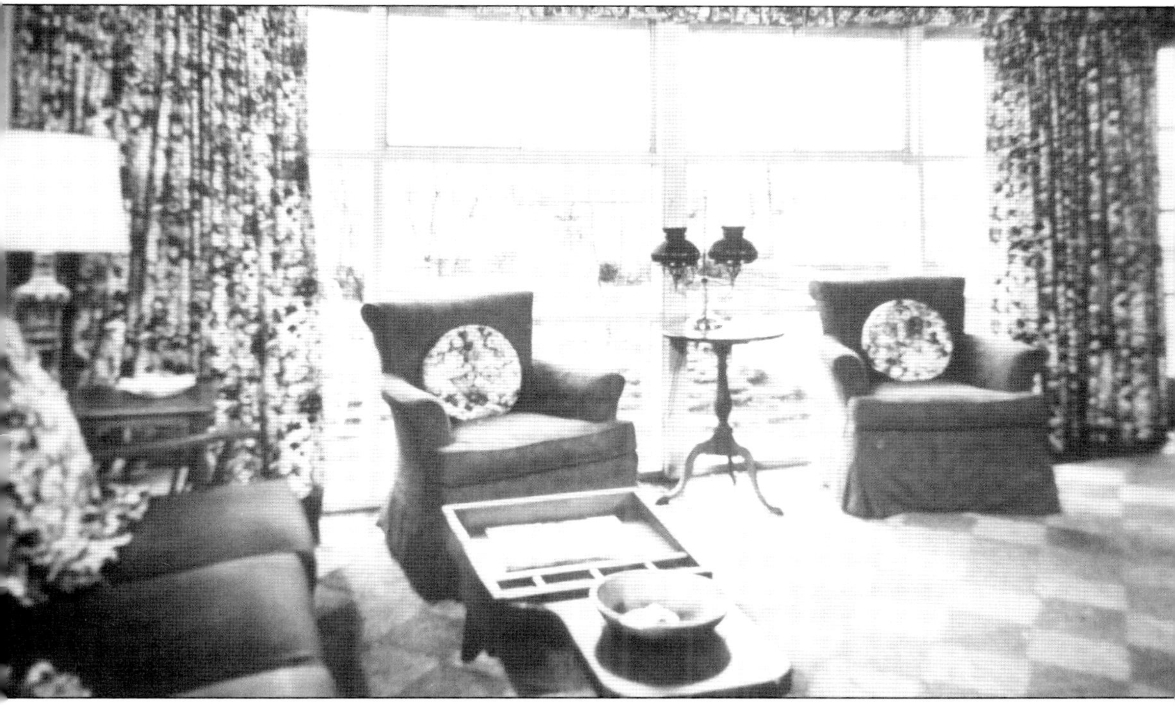

This tastefully decorated living room belongs to a Levitt home on Bluegrass Lane and Hempstead Turnpike. (Collection of the Levittown Library.)

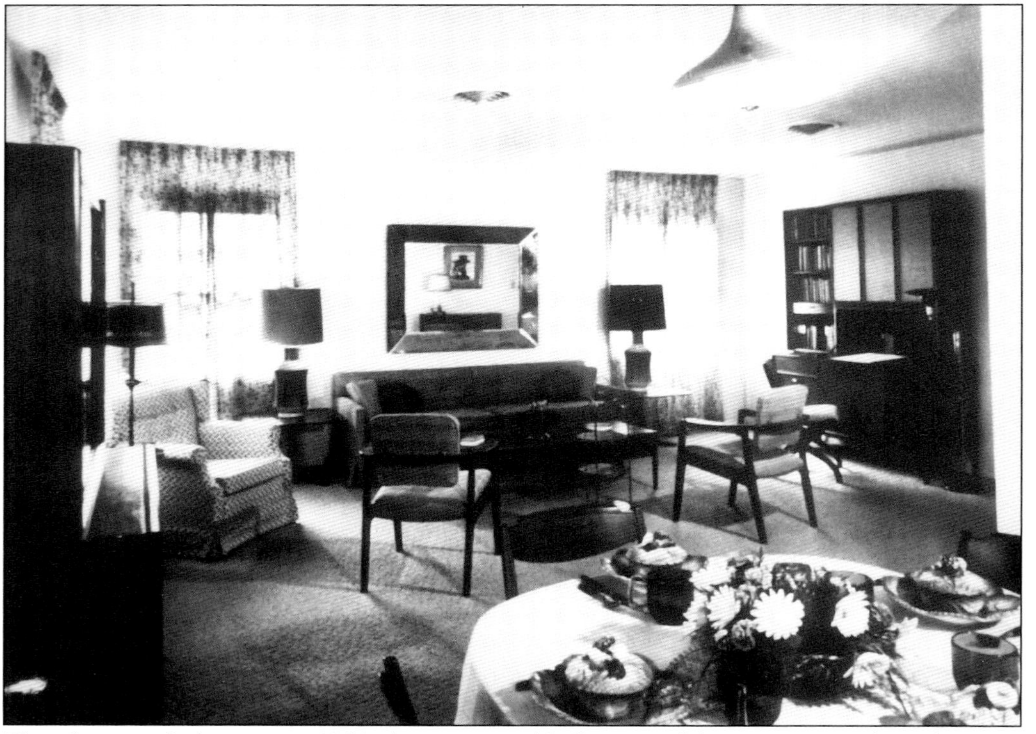

This photograph depicts a *c.* 1950s dining room. (Collection of the Levittown Library.)

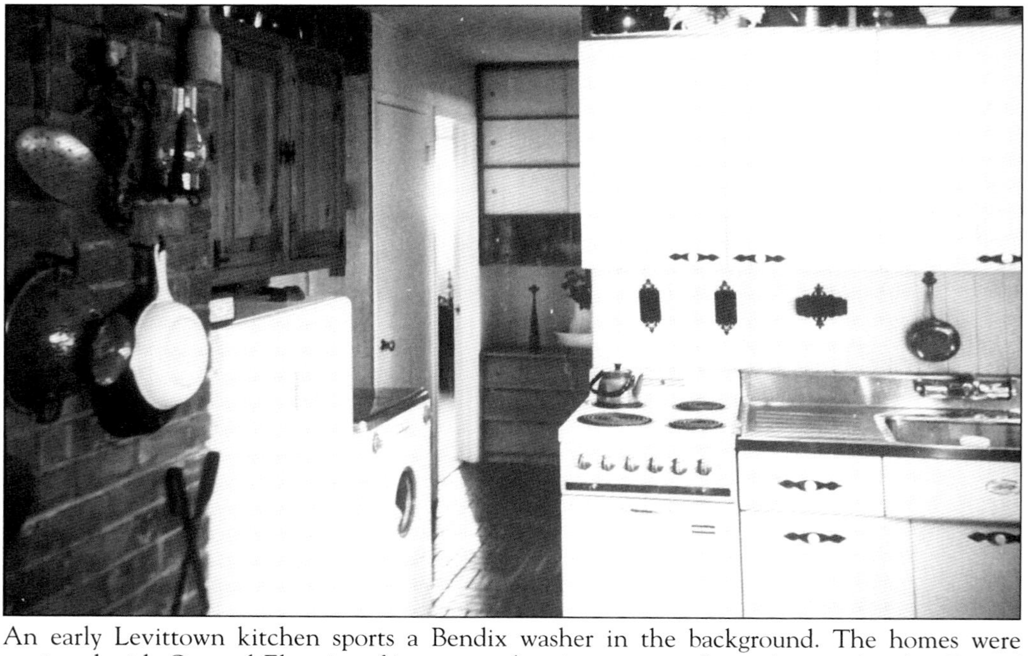

An early Levittown kitchen sports a Bendix washer in the background. The homes were equipped with General Electric refrigerators, electric stoves, and stainless-steel sinks. One of the selling points of the homes was the high quality of appliances that were included in the price. (Collection of the Levittown Library.)

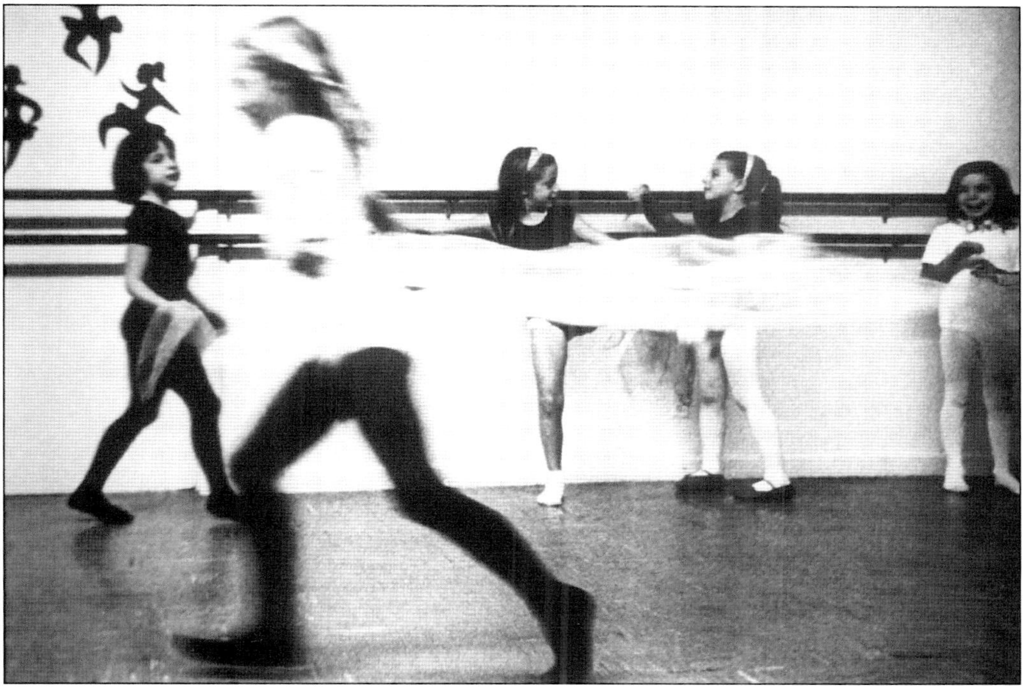

A local school of dance creates a joyful environment for young ballerinas both at barre and "on the fly!"

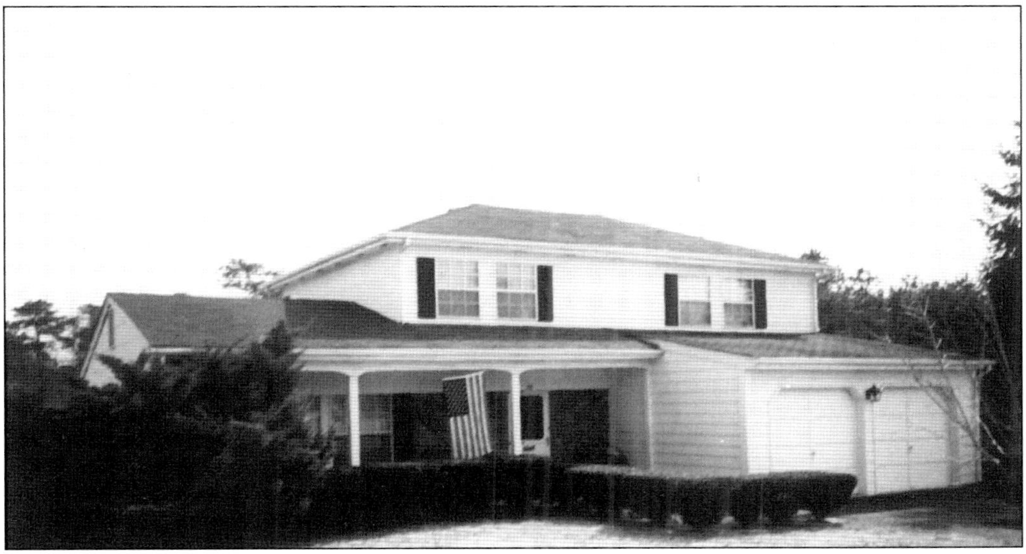

One of the last Levitt developments built in New Jersey was in the town of Toms River. This hip-roofed, center-hall Colonial seems rather luxurious compared to the early Cape. The home also boasted a two-car garage. (Collection of Barbara Pepe.)

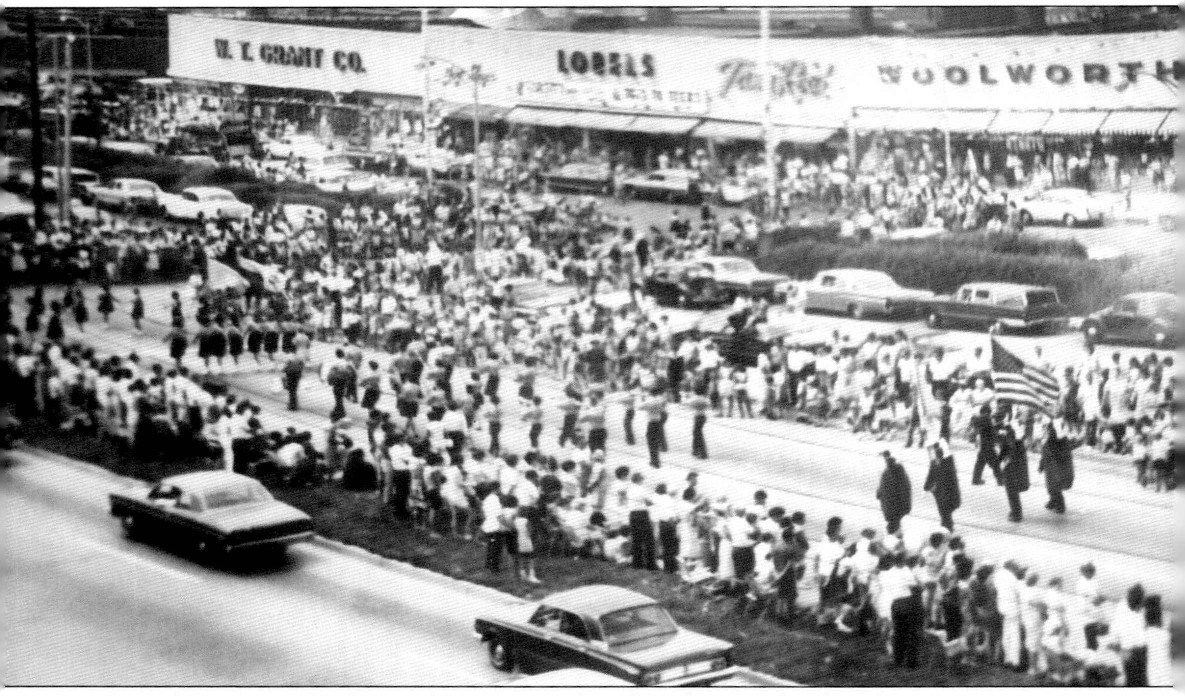

One of Levittown's early parades is captured in this photograph taken by Steve Kummerman on July 23, 1967. Visible in the background are the W.T. Grant Company, Lobel's, and Woolworth's. These stores were part of a series of stores in a complex known as the Levittown Center. (Collection of the Levittown Library.)

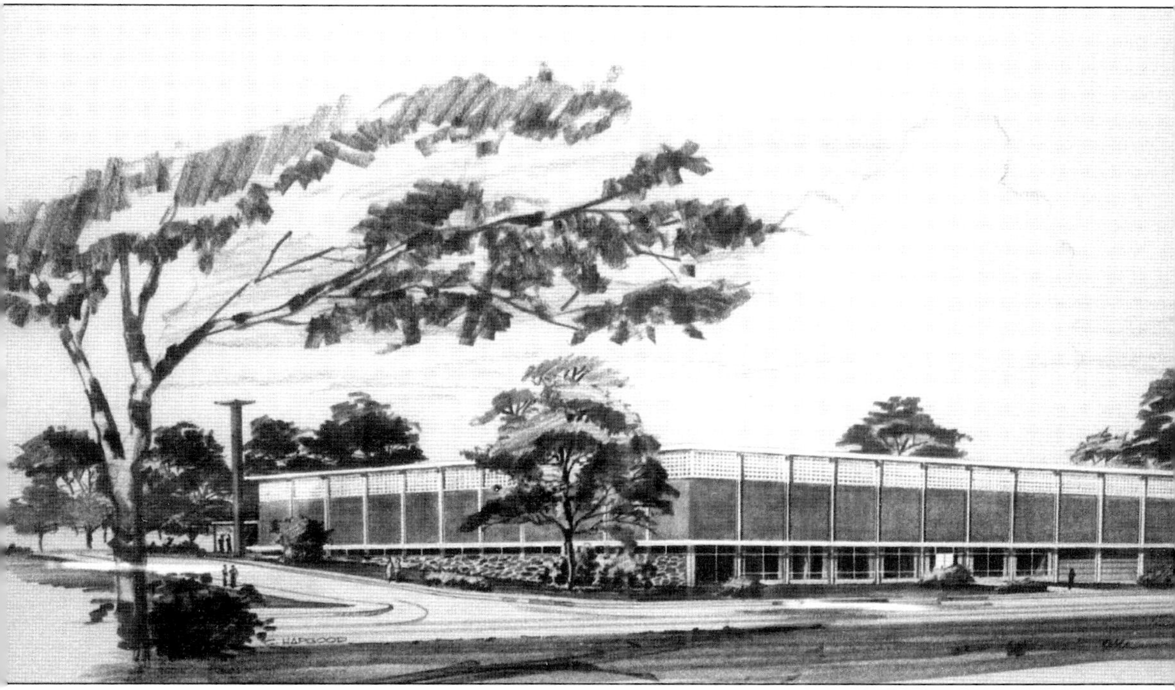

This is an artist's rendering of the Levittown Library on Bluegrass Lane. The library was a dream many years in the making until it finally became a reality on June 23, 1963. The library was a source of controversy in the early days of Levittown because of the taxes needed to support it. Designed by architect Allardt, it first opened in 1951 and was housed in a store donated by the Levitts in the South Village Green. (Collection of the Levittown Library.)

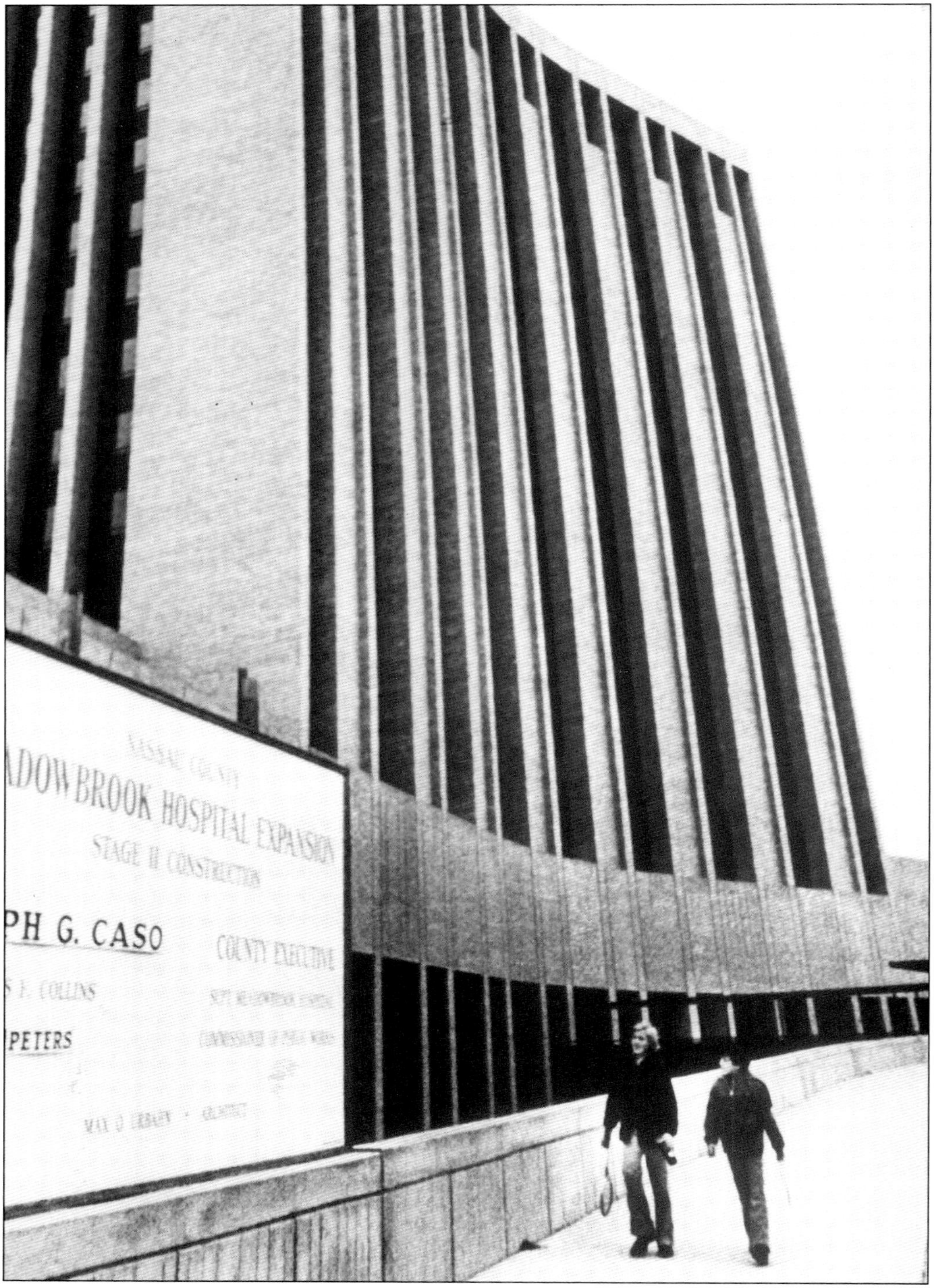

Pictured here is the Nassau County Medical Center on Hempstead Turnpike in East Meadow. The 19-story dynamic-care building opened in 1973 when Meadowbrook Hospital became Nassau County Medical Center. (Collection of the Levittown Library.)

One of the new laws was the "Pooper Scooper" law that required dog owners to pick up after their pets. As the sign states, there was a fine of $25 for noncompliance. (Collection of the Levittown Library.)

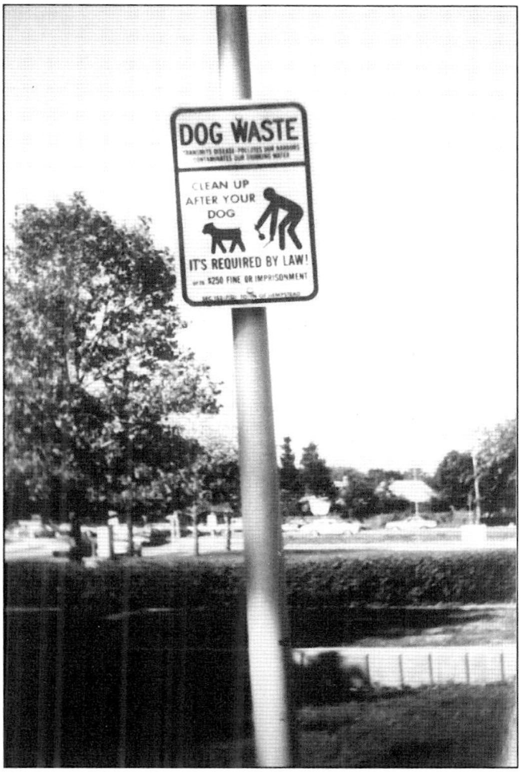

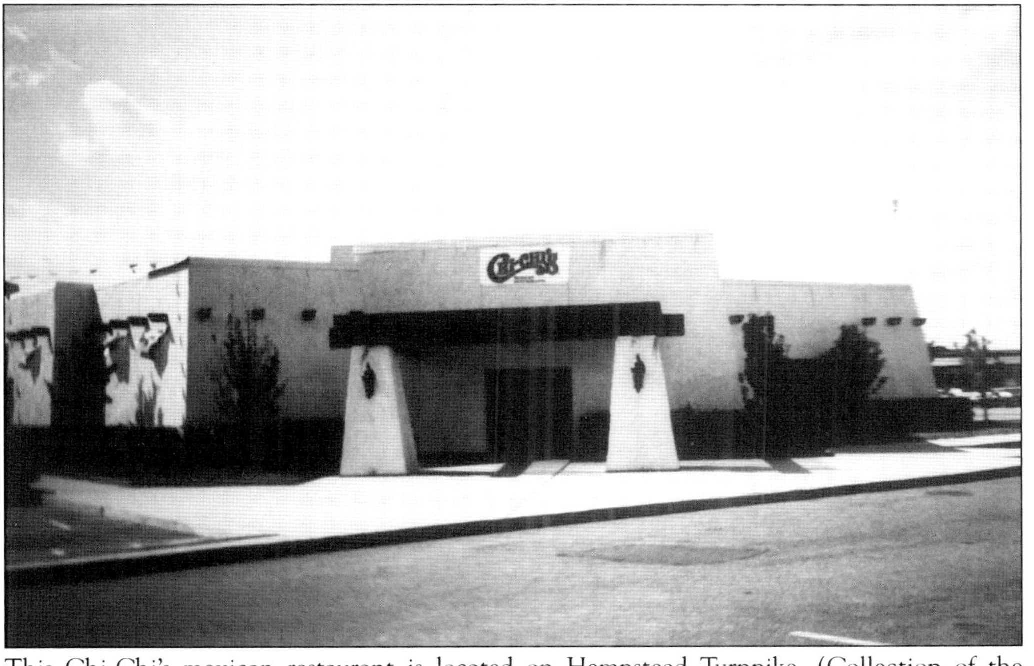

This Chi-Chi's mexican restaurant is located on Hempstead Turnpike. (Collection of the Levittown Library.)

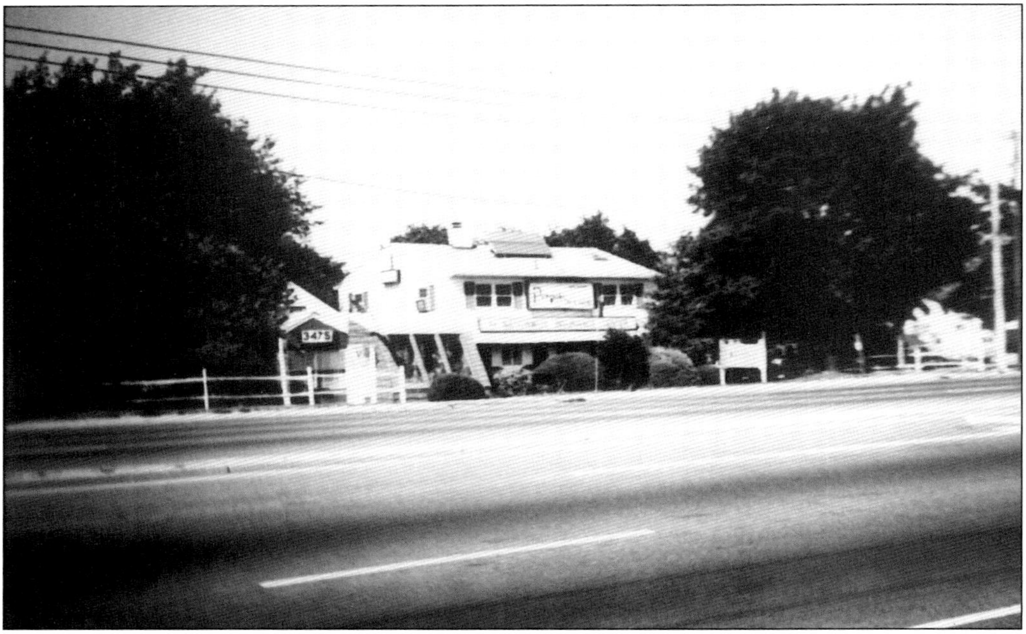

Pergola Real Estate is situated on Hempstead Turnpike. John Pergola has been active in Levittown community affairs for many years. In addition to owning a real estate business, Pergola was the circulation manager for the popular Levittown magazine *Thousand Lanes*. (Collection of the Levittown Library.)

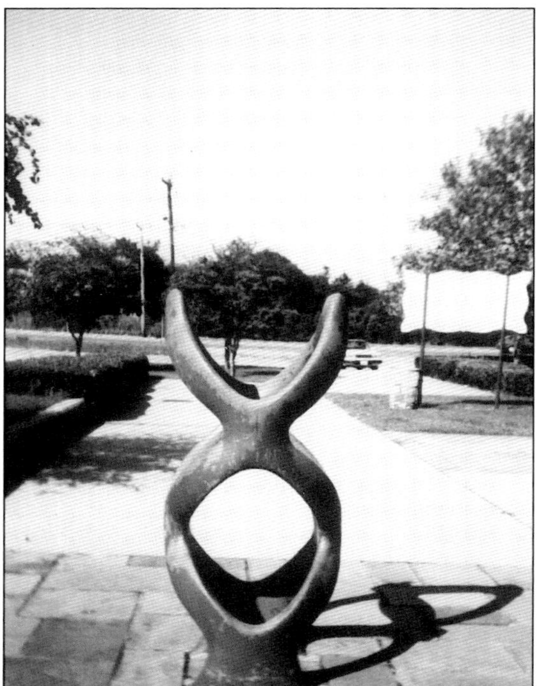

This modern sculpture can be seen in the park outside the library. (Collection of the Levittown Library.)

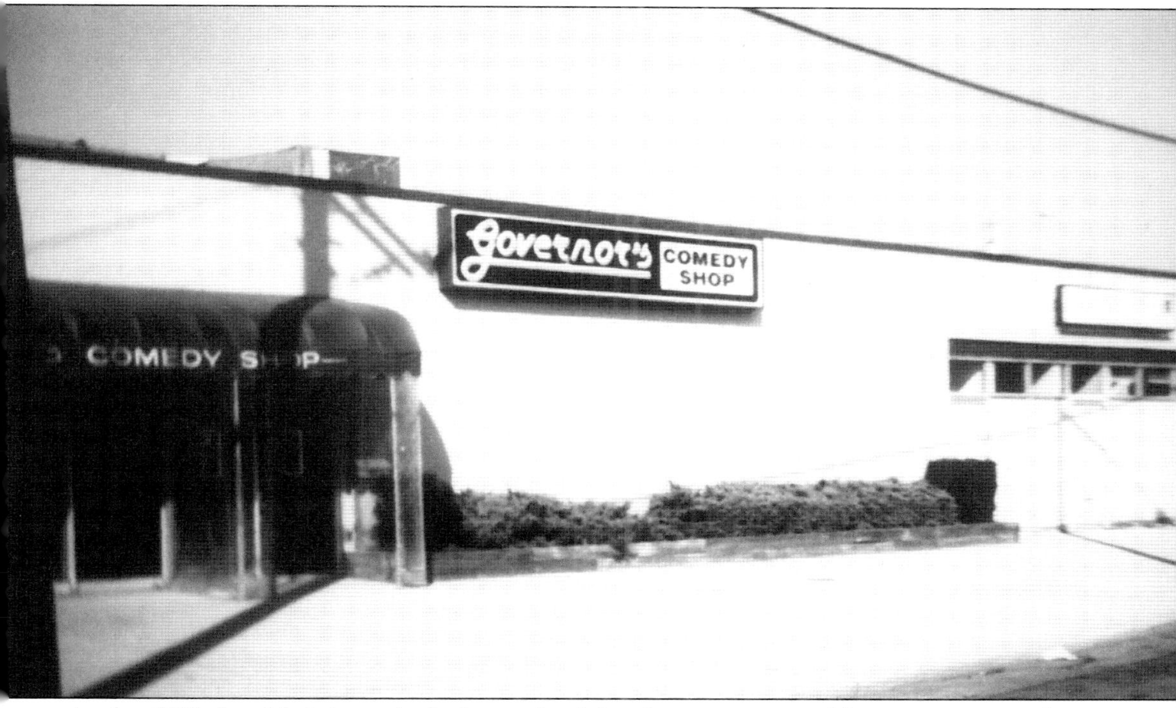

As the 1980s heralded the arrival of comedy clubs where patrons could go to enjoy stand-up comedians, Levittown became the home of the Governor's Comedy Shop. (Collection of the Levittown Library.)

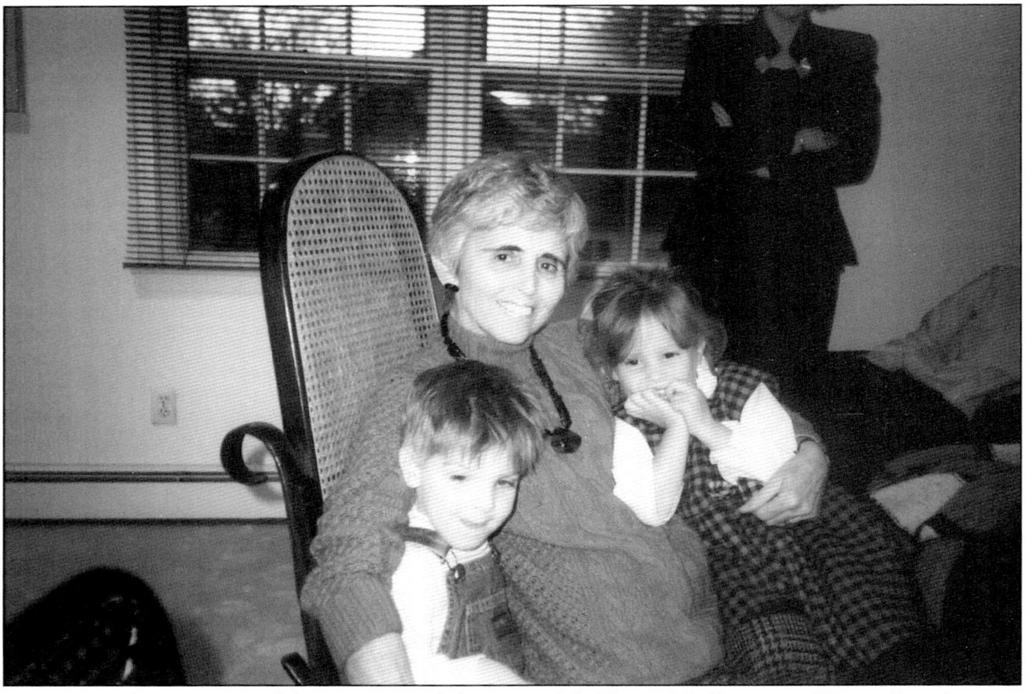

Janet Spar shares a peaceful moment with her grandchildren. (Collection of Janet Spar.)

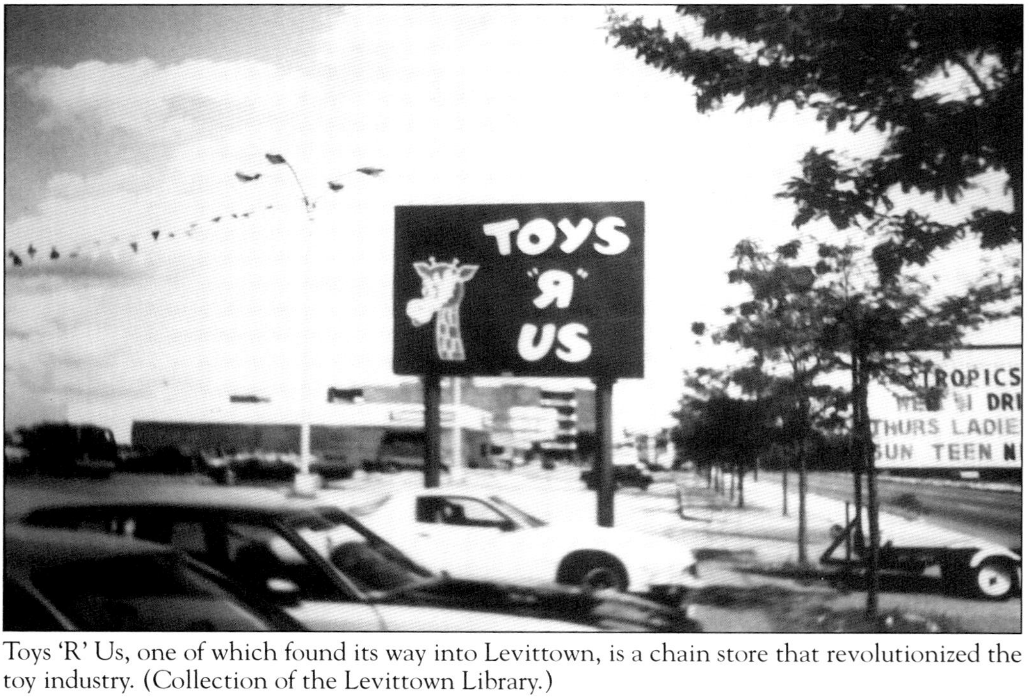

Toys 'R' Us, one of which found its way into Levittown, is a chain store that revolutionized the toy industry. (Collection of the Levittown Library.)

Five

Bon Anniversaire, Levittown

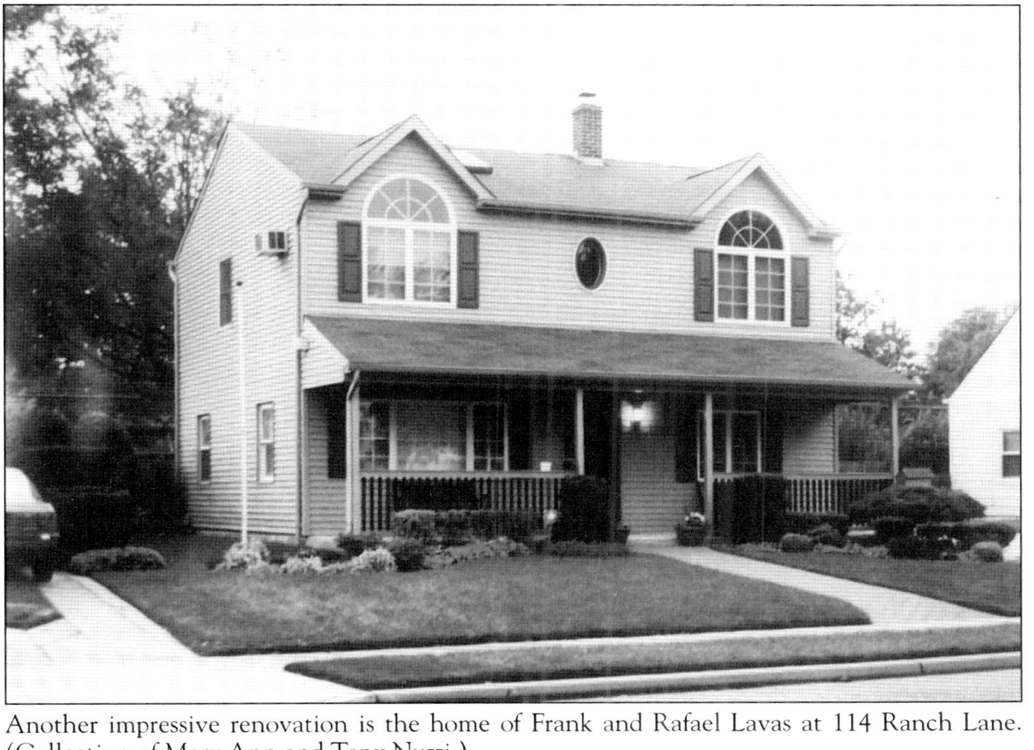

Another impressive renovation is the home of Frank and Rafael Lavas at 114 Ranch Lane. (Collection of Mary Ann and Tony Nuzzi.)

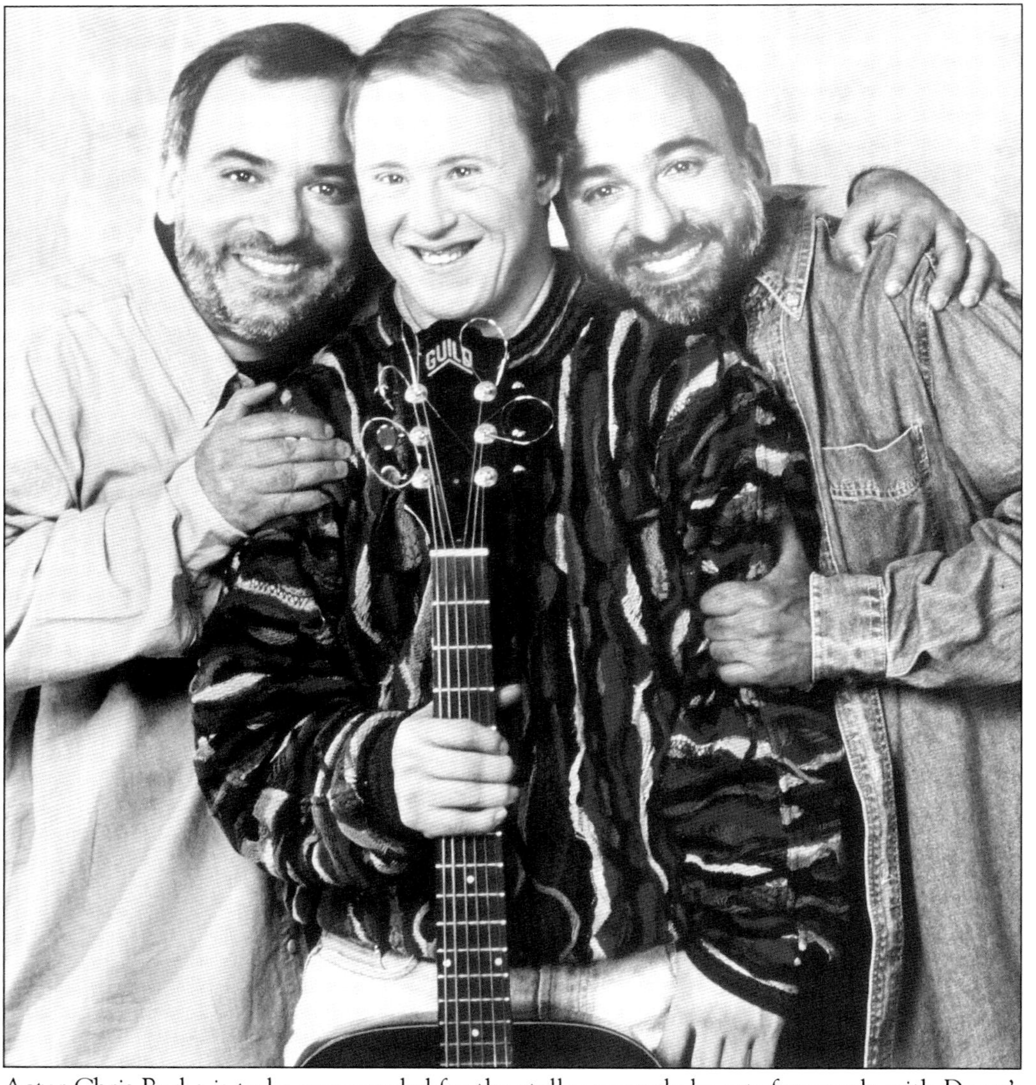

Actor Chris Burke is to be commended for the stellar example he sets for people with Down's syndrome and for his inspiration to everyone. He is flanked by fellow band members Joe and John DeMasi, who had been Chris's music counselors many years before at a summer camp for the disabled. Chris, known for his role as Corky on the television hit series *Life Goes On*, exhibits such a strong sense of self-worth by calling Down's syndrome "up syndrome." The authors (who double as an R.N. and an M.S.N.) celebrate Chris, Joe, and John's fine contributions to our diverse culture. Their office is in Levittown. (Courtesy of Chris Burke.)

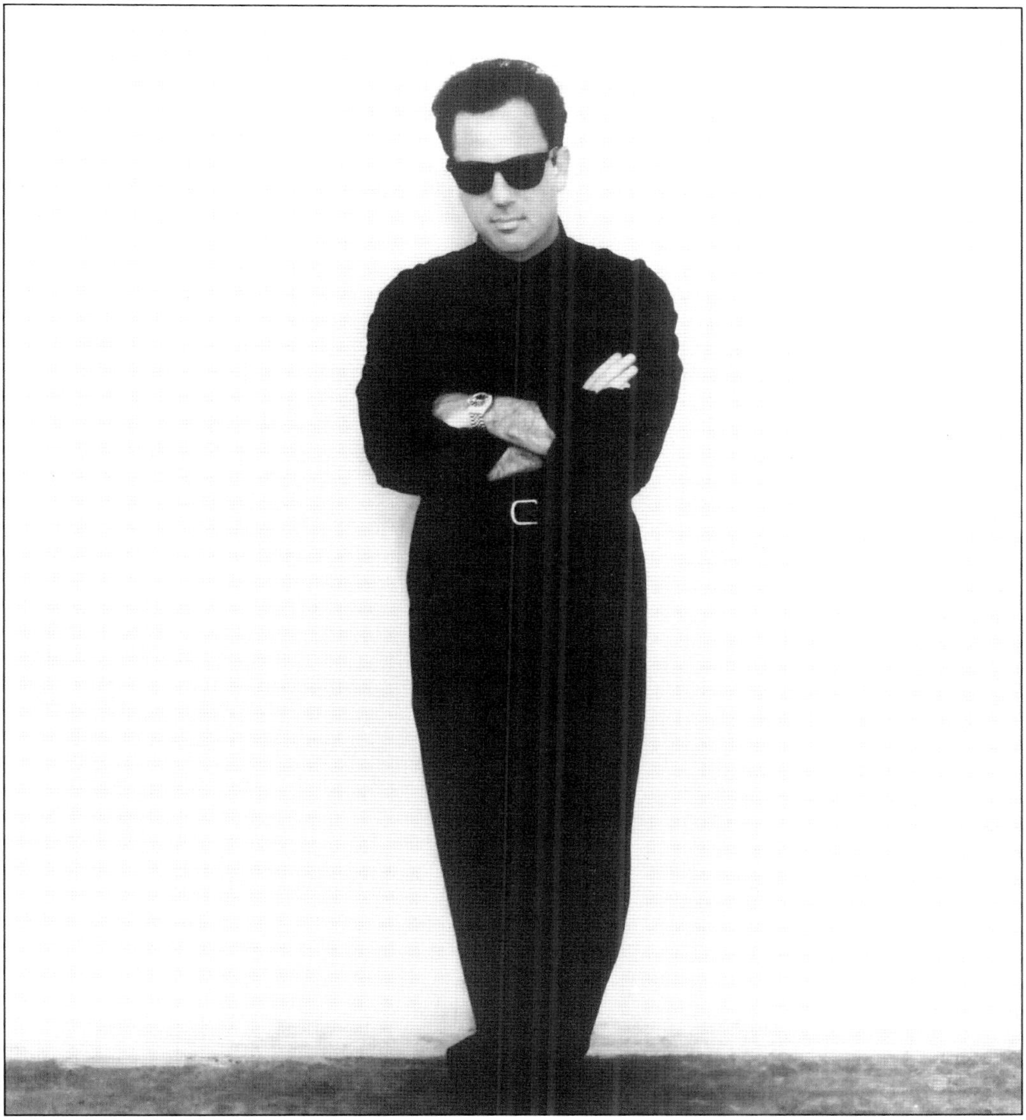

Singer Billy Joel, who grew up in a Levitt home, is pictured here. (Courtesy of Maritime Music, Inc. Photo by Mark Hannauer.)

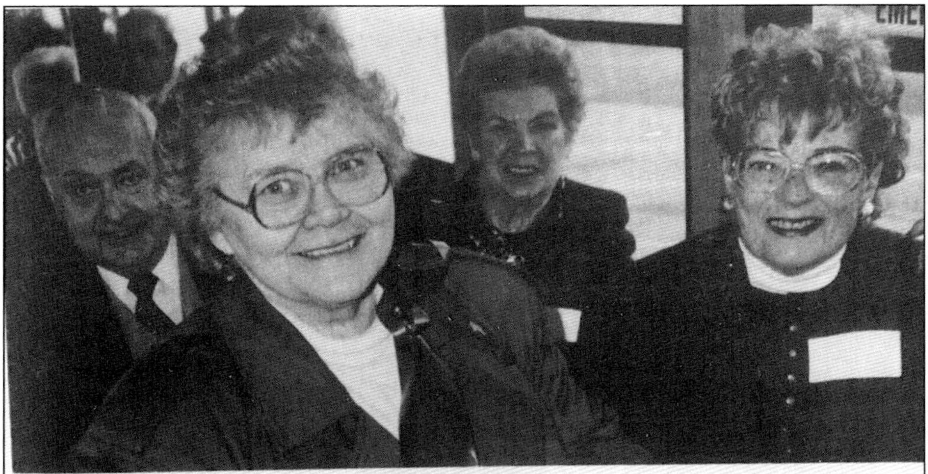

Helen Kelly

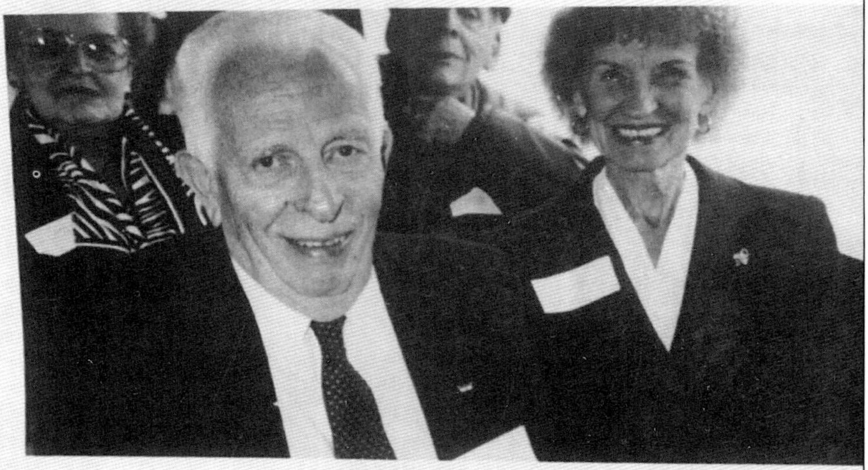

Warren & Mary Smith

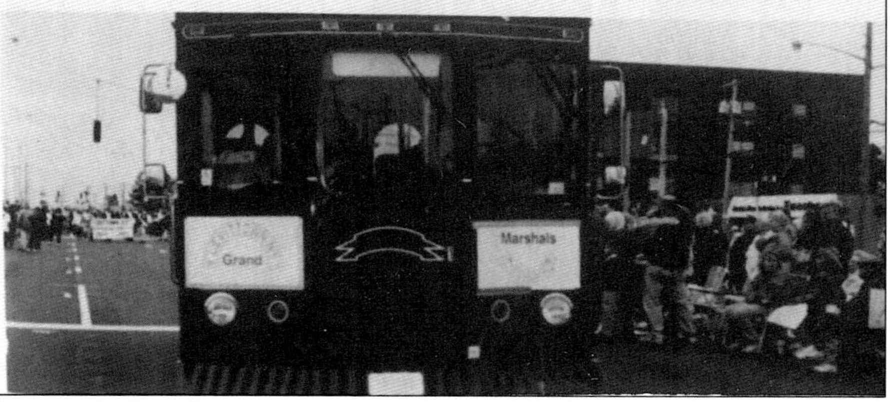

These photographs from the 50th anniversary celebration show the exuberance and sense of fun that characterize many original Levittowners and those who loyally call Levittown home.

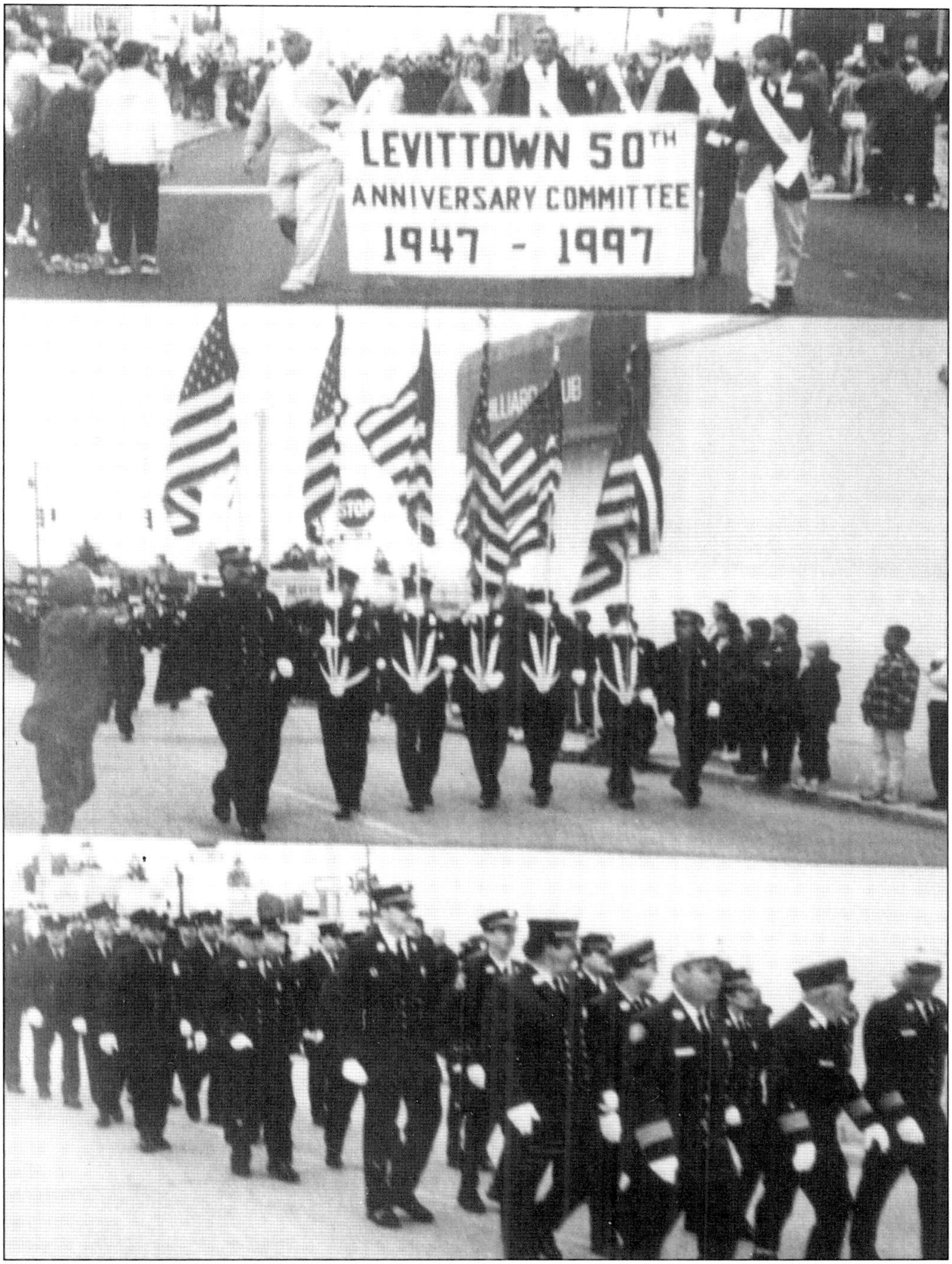

These photographs show the 50th anniversary committee marching. Some of the members of the 50th anniversary Steering Committee included Beth Dalton Costello, of Dalton Funeral Homes; Polly Dwyer of the Levittown Historical Society; Maurice and Louise Cassano; Kevin Regan; John Rotondo; Joshua Soren, Levittown historian; Mike Santorello; Donna and Pete Ryan; Diane Shapiro; and Dr. Herman Sirois, Levittown superintendent of schools.

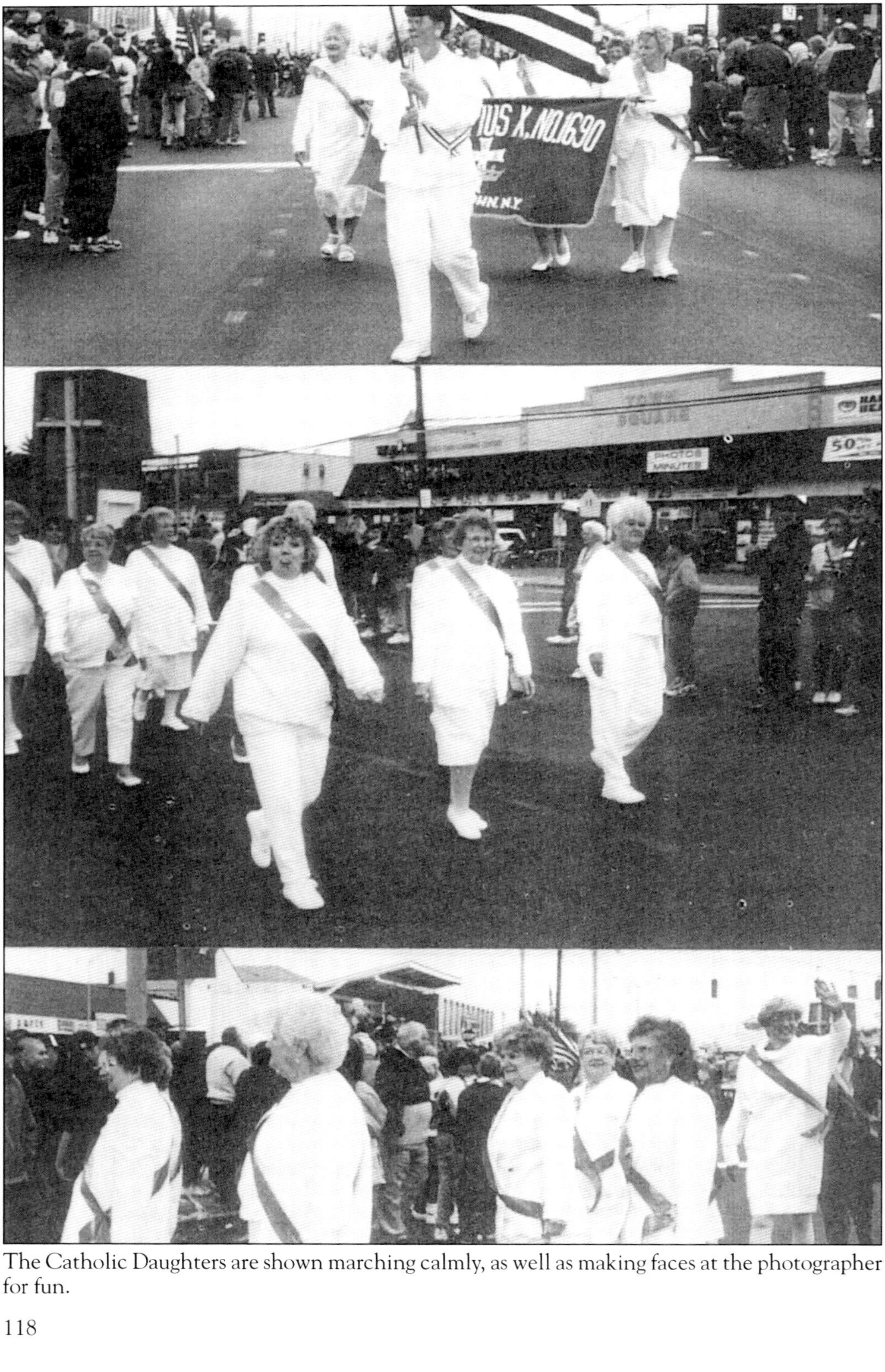

The Catholic Daughters are shown marching calmly, as well as making faces at the photographer for fun.

Louise Cassano, one of the co-chairpersons of the Levittown 50th Anniversary Celebration, speaks at the Levittown Library at the dedication of the time capsule to be opened in the year 2047. In one of the final activities of the 50th anniversary celebration, community members were given an opportunity to sign the capsule. The capsule is to be opened at the Levittown Centennial Celebration. Until 2047, the capsule, made of 4 feet of PVC pipe, will be housed at the Levittown Library with the library's historical collection. (Photograph by Tova Navarra.)

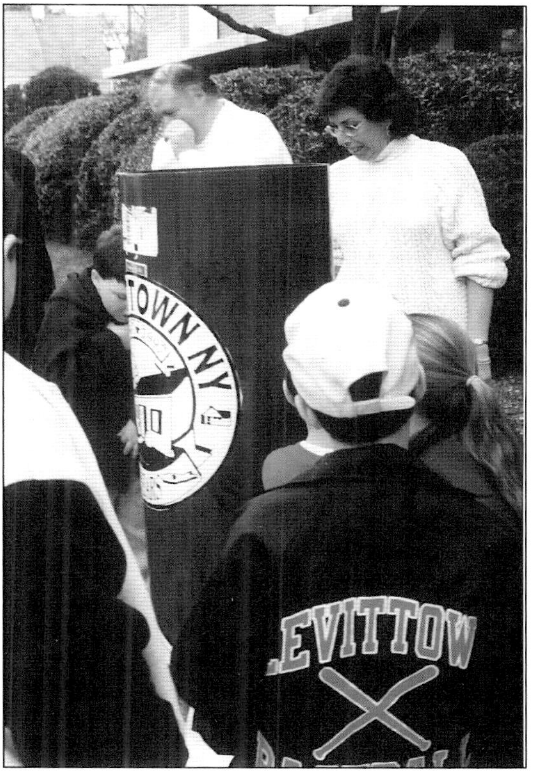

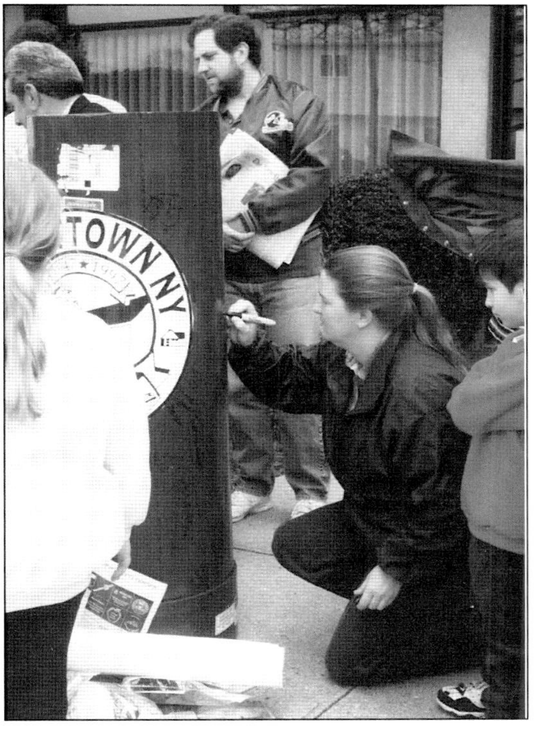

Signing the capsule seems a bit like putting your "John Hancock" on the Declaration of Independence. (Photograph by Tova Navarra.)

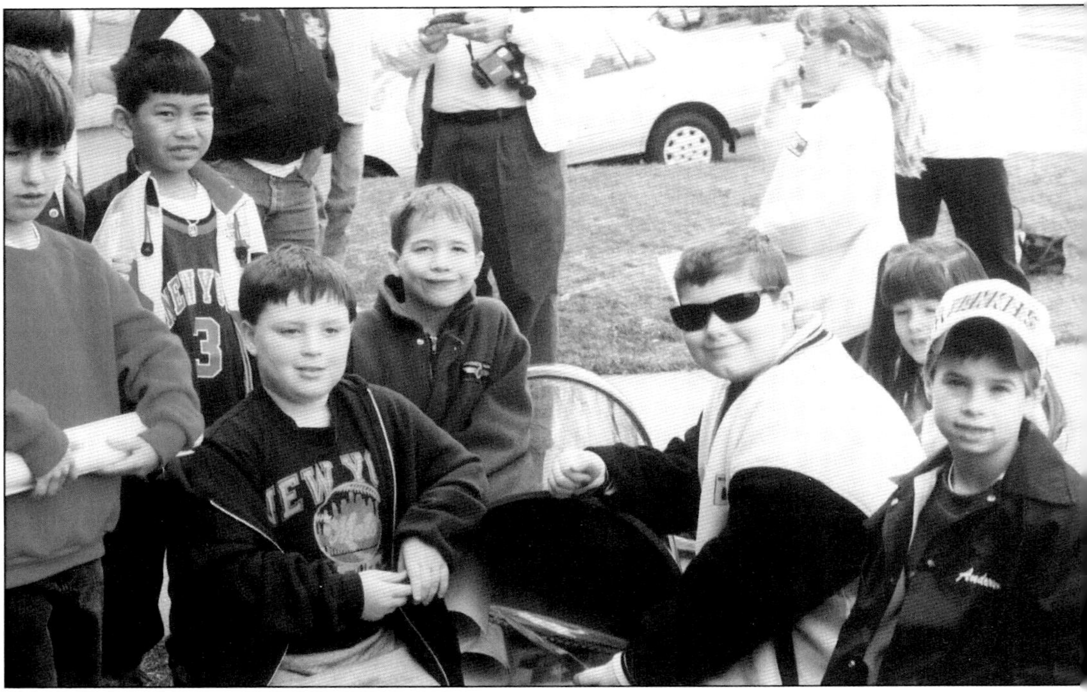

Local Levittowners gather around the time capsule. Items in it include: samples of 50th anniversary momentos; flyers from each of the anniversary events; a 50th anniversary calendar; 50th anniversary stationery; a copy of an original Levitt house deed; an example of an elementary student's work; a directory of community celebrations; videotapes of the 50th parade and the reunion for the classes of 1954–59; a Levittown Historical Society postcard; an endorsement stamp from the committee checking account; Newsday's Long Island History Project; Anton Publications' *Levittown's 50th Anniversary*; one of each coin from 1997; a Beanie Baby; and copies of *The History of Levittown, New York* by Lynn Matarrese, *Levittown, The First 50 Years* by Margaret Lundrigan and Tova Navarra, and *A Legacy for Levittown* by Clare T. Ellis. (Photograph by Tova Navarra.)

Timelines: The global Perspective

1930–1939 The Depression

Levitt & Sons building contractors celebrate their first year in business, 1930
Constantinople renamed Istanbul, 1930
Premier Hamaguchi of Japan assassinated, 1930
Sinclair Lewis wins Nobel Prize for Literature with *Babbit*, 1930
The planet Pluto discovered by C.W. Tombaugh at the Lowell Observatory, 1930
Jehovah's Witnesses established, 1931
"The Star-Spangled Banner," with lyrics by Francis Scott Key, established as the U.S. national anthem, 1931
The Empire State Building and the George Washington Bridge completed, 1931
Franklin D. Roosevelt elected 32nd U.S. President, 1932, creates the "New Deal"
The Depression, with 15 million people out of work, 1932
The Lindbergh baby kidnapped and murdered, 1932
Adolf Hitler appointed German Chancellor, granted dictatorial powers, and creates the first concentration camps, 1933
King Kong among the popular films released, and the Chicago World's Fair opens, 1933
Prohibition repealed in 21st Amendment to U.S. Constitution, 1933
Hicksville, Long Island farmer discovers that the golden nematode (identified as the culprit in 1941) was damaging his potato crops, 1934
Alcoholics Anonymous founded in New York City, 1935
George Gershwin's opera *Porgy and Bess* opens in New York City, 1935
U.S. Social Security Act signed by President Franklin Roosevelt, 1935
FDR reelected U.S. President, Spanish Civil War begins, Abyssinian War ends, 1936
King Edward VIII abdicates his throne to wed American divorcee Wallis Simpson, and the two become the Duke and Duchess of Windsor, 1936
King Farouk succeeds his father, King Fuad of Egypt, 1936

War on Japan declared by Chiang Kai-shek, 1936
Margaret Mitchell wins Pulitzer Prize for *Gone with the Wind*, and Eugene O'Neill wins Nobel Prize for Literature, 1936
Baseball Hall of Fame founded at Cooperstown, NY, 1936
Amelia Earhart lost on Pacific flight, and the dirigible Hindenburg crashes in Lakehurst, NJ, 1937
The first jet engine built by Frank Whittle, and insulin first used as treatment of diabetes, 1937
Minimum wage law for women set forth by U.S. Supreme Court, 1937
Public panic caused by Orson Welles's radio program of H.G. Wells's "War of the Worlds," 1938

1939–1949 The Gathering Storm

The Lascaux caves, known for prehistoric wall paintings *c.* 20,000 B.C., discovered in France, 1940
FDR reelected to third term as President, 1940
Penicillin developed as an antibiotic of choice by Howard Florey, 1940
United States declares war on Germany and Italy, World War II continues, and Japanese attack Pearl Harbor December 7, 1941
Enrico Fermi splits the atom, and the first electronic "brain" (computer) developed in New York, 1942
Poliomyelitis, a virus that attacks the central nervous system through the blood, killed nearly 1,200 and leaves thousands more, mostly children, crippled in the United States, 1943
FDR wins fourth term as President, with Harry S. Truman as vice president, 1944
D-Day landings made in Normandy as World War II continues and Battle of the Bulge at Ardennes begins, 1944
United States drops atomic bombs on Hiroshima and Nagasaki, 1945
"V.E. Day" marks end of war in Europe, 1945
World War II ends after Japanese surrender, August 14, 1945
Juan Peron elected president of Argentina, 1946
British Prime Minister Winston Churchill gives the "Iron Curtain" speech, 1946
Chilean poet Gabriela Mistral wins the Nobel Prize for Literature, 1946
Dr. Benjamin Spock writes *Baby and Child Care*, 1946
R.E. Byrd conducts the South Pole expedition, 1946
The Diary of Anne Frank published, 1947
Abraham Levitt and sons Alfred and William help solve the GI's housing problem by creating Levittown, the American prototype suburb in Long Island, NY, 1947
The transistor invented by Bell Laboratories scientists, 1947
The Dead Sea Scrolls (*c.* 22 B.C.–100 A.D.) discovered, 1947
Jackie Robinson becomes first black in Major League baseball, 1947
Tennessee Williams wins Pulitzer Prize for *A Streetcar Named Desire*, 1948
Mohandas Gandhi, known as the "Mahatma," shot and killed, 1948
Israel declared a state, 1948
Harry S. Truman elected president, 1948
Sexual Behavior in the Human Male written by Alfred C. Kinsey, 1948
Apartheid established in South Africa, 1949; United Nations warned of imminent civil war in Korea, 1949
The 1949 ranch, priced at $7,990, was the first Levitt & Sons home built for sale in Levittown.

1950–1959 The Fast-Changing Fifties, From The Baby Boom to the Beatniks

U.S. State Department official Alger Hiss convicted of perjury, 1950
Korean Conflict begins, 1950
Antihistamines emerge as treatment of colds and allergies, 1950
King Abdullah of Jordan assassinated in Jerusalem, 1951
Julius and Ethel Rosenberg convicted of espionage and sentenced to death, 1951
Color television introduced in America, 1951
The last Levitt ranch built was sold to Mr. and Mrs. Ernest Southard, 161 Tardy Lane, November 1951
Dwight D. Eisenhower elected U.S. President, 1952
Albert Schweitzer wins Nobel Peace Prize, 1952
Sen. Joseph McCarthy "witch-hunt" hearings conducted from 1952 to 1954
USSR explodes the hydrogen bomb, and lung cancer first attributed to cigarette smoking, 1953
Dr. Jonas E. Salk develops polio vaccine, begins inoculating children in Pittsburgh, PA, 1954
Billy Graham conducts evangelistic meetings in New York, London, and Berlin, 1954
Supreme Court bans segregation by color in public schools, 1954
Italian liner Andrea Doria sinks off Nantucket Island after collision with Stockholm, 1956
American actress Grace Kelly weds Prince Rainier of Monaco, 1956
Eisenhower wins second term as U.S. President, and Fidel Castro arrives in Cuba to overthrow dictator Fulgencio Batista, 1956
John F. Kennedy wins Pulitzer Prize for *Profiles in Courage*, 1957
Soprano Maria Callas makes her New York debut in Bellini's opera Norma, and Elvis Presley becomes popular rock 'n' roll star, 1956
Sir Laurence Olivier receives honorary doctorate from Oxford University, and Dr. Seuss writes *The Cat in the Hat*, 1957
The Common Market formed after "The Six" signs Rome Treaty, 1957
USSR launches the first earth satellites, Sputnik I and II, 1957
Thirteen-year-old Bobby Fischer becomes chess champion, 1957
Alaska becomes 49th state of the U.S., 1958
Charles De Gaulle elected president of France, Ayub Khan elected prime minister of Pakistan, and Nelson A. Rockefeller elected governor of New York, 1958
Boris Pasternak wins Nobel Prize for Literature, 1958
American golfer Arnold Palmer wins his first Masters tournament, 1958
National Aeronautics and Space Administration (NASA) established, 1958
The "Beatnik" movement spreads from California throughout the United States and Europe, 1958
Hawaii becomes 50th state of the United States, and James Michener writes *Hawaii*, 1959
Pope John XXIII calls first Ecumenical Council since 1870, 1959
USSR launches rocket carrying two monkeys, 1959
"Nutcracker Man" skull, approximately dated 600,000 B.C., found in Tanganyika by Louis S.B. Leakey, 1959

1960–1969 The "Give-A-Damn" Years, The Great Society, and Back to Basics

John F. Kennedy elected U.S. President, 1960
Three women become ministers of the Swedish Lutheran Church, 1960

Optical microwave laser built, 1960
Harper Lee wins Pulitzer Prize for *To Kill a Mockingbird*, 1961
Dag Hammarskjold wins Nobel Peace Prize, 1961
U.S. severs diplomatic relations with Cuba, and Moscow synagogues close, 1961
The last journey of the Orient Express travels from Paris to Bucharest, 1961
Cuban Missile Crisis: the U.S. blockade of Cuba, 1962, Adolf Eichmann hanged, 1962
Abraham Levitt dies, 1962
The drug thalidomide causes serious birth defects, 1962
John Steinbeck wins Nobel Prize for Literature, 1962
President John F. Kennedy assassinated by Lee Harvey Oswald; Vice President Lyndon B. Johnson sworn in as President, 1963
Civil Rights march on Washington, D.C., Dr. Martin Luther King Jr. gives his "I have a dream" speech, 1963
Earthquake in Yugoslavia claims about 1,100 victims, 1963
Incumbent Lyndon Johnson beats Barry Goldwater in U.S. presidential race, 1964
The Verrazano-Narrows Bridge opened, 1964
Riots at soccer match in Lima, Peru, leave 300 spectators dead, 1964
Malta becomes independent within Commonwealth, 1964
The Great Blackout in New York City affects 30 million people, 1965
Malcolm X shot in New York, 1965
Alfred Levitt dies at 54, 1966
Miniskirts become fashionable, 1966
Pope Paul VI issues encyclical on the Vietnamese War, 1966
Mitch Leigh's "Man of La Mancha" opens as Broadway musical, 1966
Six-Day War between Israel and Arab nations begins, 1967
New York Yankee Mickey Mantle hits his 500th home run, 1967
Dr. Christiaan Barnard performs the world's first human heart transplantation, 1967
Singer Barbra Streisand gives concert to 135,000 in Central Park, 1967
Violent crime in America increases 57 percent since 1960, 1968
Dr. Martin Luther King Jr. slain April 5, and Senator Robert F. Kennedy assassinated June 6, 1968
Jacqueline Kennedy weds Aristotle Onassis, 1968
Richard M. Nixon elected president, 1968
Astronaut Neil Armstrong "dances" on the moon, July 21, 1969
300,000 hippies and others attend Woodstock Music and Art Fair in New York, 1969

1970–1979 The "Me" Generation, From Hippies to Yuppies

National Guard kills four Kent State University students protesting Vietnam War, 1970
Alexander Solzhenitsyn wins Nobel Prize for Literature, 1970
Israel's fourth Prime Minister, Golda Meir, visits London, 1970
Biafra capitulates to federal government of Nigeria and ends the civil war between the nations, 1970
U.S. bombs North Vietnam and Vietcong supply routes in Cambodia; fighting in Indochina spreads to Laos and Cambodia, 1971
"Fiddler on the Roof" becomes the longest running Broadway musical, 1971
TV advertisements for cigarettes banned in America, 1971
American 18 year olds get the right to vote as 26th Amendment to the Constitution ratified, 1971
"The Jesus Movement" publicized in America, 1971
The five-day uprising at Attica prison leaves ten guards and 32 prisoners dead, 1971

Five men arrested by Washington, D.C. police in Watergate affair, 1972
Richard Nixon defeats George McGovern in presidential race, 1972
Billie Jean King defeats Bobby Riggs in tennis match, 1973
Liza Minnelli and Marlon Brando receive Academy Awards as Best Actress (*Cabaret*) and Best Actor (*The Godfather*), 1973
U.S. Supreme Court rules against individual states prohibiting abortion during the first six months of pregnancy, and pornographic film *Deep Throat* ruled "irredeemably obscene" by New York Criminal Court, 1973
President Richard Nixon resigns, August 9, 1974
Nine Israeli athletes killed in Olympic Village, Sept. 6, 1972
President Gerald Ford pardons Nixon, Sept. 9, 1974
Smallpox epidemic in India kills 10,000 to 20,000, 1974
Elizabeth Ann Bayley Seton canonized as first American saint, 1975
International Brotherhood of Teamsters President James R. Hoffa disappears, 1975
Linus Pauling receives the U.S. National Medal of Honor, 1975
Mauna Loa volcano erupts for first time since 1950 in Hawaii, 1976
The bicentennial of the United States celebrated, July 4, 1976
Rev. Sun Myung Moon's Unification Church rejected by New York City
Council of Churches, and parents protest against "brainwashing" of Moon's followers, called "Moonies," 1976
Aerosol spray cans reported damaging to the atmosphere's ozone layer, 1976
July 14, 1977: another great New York black-out caused by lightning bolts that hit Consolidated Edison Company's two largest generating facilities
U.S. President Jimmy Carter pardons nearly all American draft dodgers of the Vietnam War era, 1977
Jonestown mass suicide, 400 people die, 1978
A Gutenberg Bible sells for $2 million at a New York auction, highest price ever paid for a book, 1978
In England, Lesley Brown gives birth to her daughter, the "test-tube baby," first child conceived outside a woman's body, 1978
Israel Premier Menahem Begin and Egyptian President Anwar Sadat receive the Nobel Peace Prize, 1978
Longest American coal-miners' strike ends after 110th day, 1978
Margaret Thatcher becomes conservative prime minister of Britain, 1979
John Cheever wins Pulitzer Prize and National Book Critics Circle Award for *The Stories of John Cheever*, 1979
Egypt and Israel signs peace treaty, March 27, 1979
Three Mile Island, Pennsylvania, nuclear catastrophe averted, March 30, 1979

1980–1989 Introducing the Information Age

John Lennon shot to death by Mark Chapman in New York, 1980
U.S. population reported to be 226,504,825, 1980 Census
Mount St. Helens volcano in Washington State erupts, May 20, 1980
Ronald Reagan elected 40th U.S. President, 1980
Polish radio broadcasts a Mass for first time under Polish communist rule, 1980
First giant panda cub born in captivity in Mexico, 1980
President Reagan shot and wounded by John Hinckley, March 20, 1981
Sandra Day O'Connor becomes first woman Justice of the Supreme Court, 1981
Anwar Sadat assassinated, Oct. 6, 1981, and Indira Gandhi slain, Oct. 31, 1984
Iran releases all 52 hostages, 1981

Prince Charles and Lady Diana Spencer wed July 29, 1981
I.B.M. introduces the personal computer (PC), 1981
USA Today daily newspaper first published, 1982
Gabriel Garcia Marquez of Colombia wins Nobel Prize for Literature, 1982
Futurist theme park EPCOT opened by Disneyworld in Florida, 1982
Alice Walker wins Pulitzer Prize for *The Color Purple*, 1983
AIDS virus discovered independently by American and French research teams, 1984
PG-13 film rating established by The Motion Picture Association of America, 1984
Standard Oil of California buys and merges with Gulf for $13.2 million, resulting in world's largest corporate merger, 1984
Terrorists kill 13 people at Leonardo da Vinci Airport in Rome, Italy, Dec. 27, 1985
Space shuttle Challenger exploded moments after take-off, killing seven crew members including Christa McAuliffe, the first "teacher in space," 1986
133,000 evacuated after reactor explodes at Chernobyl (nuclear) Power Station in Kiev, USSR, 1986
Desmond Tutu becomes the first black Archbishop of Cape Town, South Africa, 1986
The 100th anniversary of the Statue of Liberty celebrated, July 4, 1986
Black Monday, stocks falls 508 points, Oct. 19, 1987
Levittown celebrated its 40th anniversary
In order to adjust it to the Gregorian calendar, 1987 was shortened by one second
Cartoon and movie character "Superman" celebrates 50th anniversary, 1988
George Bush defeats Democrat Michael Dukakis in presidential election, 1988
Salman Rushdie writes *The Satanic Verses*, attacked by Muslims for blasphemy, 1988
Cher wins Academy Award for Best Actress in *Moonstruck*, 1988
Naguib Mahfouz of Egypt becomes the first African writer to win Nobel Prize for Literature, 1988
Toni Morrison wins Pulitzer Prize for *Beloved*, 1988
Lt. Col. Oliver North convicted of crimes in the Iran-Contra scandal, 1989
Czech dissident/playwright Vaclav Havel jailed, then becomes president of Czechoslovakia, 1989
The Dalai Lama wins the Nobel Peace Prize, 1989
The Exxon Valdez runs aground in Alaska, spilling 11 million gallons of oil, 1989
The Berlin Wall torn down, Nov. 10, 1989

1990–Present Higher Technology, "New Age," and the Future

Iraq seizes Kuwait, Aug. 3, 1990
Lech Walesa elected president of Poland, and Mary Robinson elected first woman president of Ireland, 1990
Nelson Mandela freed after 27 years in prison in South Africa, Feb. 11, 1990
West and East Germany reunited, Oct. 3, 1990
The Gulf War (Desert Storm) begins in the Middle East, becomes the first war to be televised by CNN (the 24-hour news channel), then other networks, 1991
Anita Hill hearings on sexual harassment by Clarence Thomas, Oct. 1991 Russian government threatened by reactionary coup, which failed; Mikail Gorbachev resigns Dec. 26, and Boris Yeltsin takes over, 1991
Los Angeles race riots after acquittal of police officers for the beating of Rodney King, April 30, 1992
Bill Clinton elected president, Nov. 1992
World Trade Center bombed by terrorists, Feb. 26, 1993
Mass suicide in Waco, Texas, by Davidian cult members, April 19, 1993

William Levitt dies of kidney failure, Jan. 28, 1994
Nelson Mandela becomes the first black president of South Africa, May 11, 1994
O.J. Simpson jailed on double murder charges, 1994, acquitted in 1995 after a lengthy trial
Death toll of 600 follows earthquake in Kobe, Japan, Jan. 17, 1995
Federal building in Oklahoma City bombed by American terrorists Timothy McVeigh and Terry Lynn Nichols, 169 dead, 400 injured, April 19, 1995
Diana, Princess of Wales, and her Egyptian boyfriend, Dodi al Fayed, killed in Paris car crash, Aug. 30, 1997
Mother Teresa dies in India a week later, 1997
The 50th anniversary of Levittown celebrated, 1997
Pacific El Nino storms cause tragic mudslides and flooding in Peru, Ecuador, and other locations, 1998
Tension mounts between the U.S. and Iraq, talk of attack on Iraqi leader Saddam Hussein; UN Secretary intervenes and averts the attack, at least temporarily, 1998
The Olympic games held in Nagano, Japan, where first women's U.S. hockey team and 15-year-old figure skater Tara Lipinski wins gold medals, February 1998
Alleged scandal—called "The White House Under Fire"—steals headlines for months in 1998, with stories that President Bill Clinton had sexual relations with White House intern Monica Lewinsky and several other women; Clinton denies the charges as independent counsel Kenneth Starr leads the investigation, resulting in impeachment hearing not yet completed at the printing of this book

BIBLIOGRAPHY

Conrad, Pam. *Our House: The Stories of Levittown*. New York: Scholastic Inc., 1995.
Dexter, Betsy. *You Must Remember This: 1947*. New York: Warner Books, 1995.
Ferrer, Margaret Lundrigan, and Tara Navarra. *Levittown: The First 50 Years*. Dover, NH: Arcadia Publishing, 1997.
Gans, Herbert J. *The Levittowners: Ways of Life and Politics in a New Suburban Community*. New York: Pantheon Books, 1967.
Gordon, Albert J. *Jews in Suburbia*. Boston: Beacon Press, 1969.
Halberstam, David. *The Fifties*. New York: Villard Books, 1993.
Kaufman, Michael T. "Tough Times for Mr. Levittown." *The New York Times*. 24 September 1989.
Kelly, Barbara M. *Suburbia Re-examined*. New York: Greenwood Press, 1989.
Kelly, Barbara M. *Expanding The American Dream:Building and Rebuilding Levittown*. New York: State University of New York Press, 1993.
Kelly, Barbara M. *Long Island: The Suburban Experience*. Interlaken, New York: Heart of the Lakes Publishing, 1990.
Kleinfelder, Rita Lang. *When We Were Young: A Baby-Boomer Handbook*. New York: Prentice Hall General Reference, 1993.
Lewis, Jeanne. "Jerusalem Remembered." *Levittown Tribune*. 31 January 1980.
Miasotti, Louis H. and Jeffrey K. Haddon, eds. *Suburbia in Transition: A New York Times Book*. New York: Franklin Watts, Inc., 1974.
Mattarese, Lynne. "Levittown's Historic Raceway Site." *Long Island Forum*, 1994.
Mattarese, Lynne. *Levittown*. Long Island: Levittown Historical Society, 1997.
Mumford, Lewis. *The City in History: Its Origins, Its Transformations, and Its Prospects*. New York: Harcourt, Brace and World Inc., 1961.
Smits, Edward J. "Nassau Suburbia, U.S.A." Syosset, New York: Friends of the Museum, 1974 p. 74.
Spagnoli, Joseph E. *Levittown, New York: An Annotated Bibliography 1947 to 1972*. Prepared for the Levittown Public Library.